Bitter Is the New Black

Bitter Is the New Black

Confessions of a condescending,
egomaniacal, self-centered
Smart-ass, or why you
should never carry a Prada Bag
to the unemployment office

A MEMOIR

Jen Lancaster

NEW AMERICAN LIBRARY

New American Library
Published by New American Library, a division of Penguin Group (USA) Inc., 375 Hudson Street, New York, New York 10014, USA
Penguin Group (Canada), 90 Eglinton Avenue East, Suite 700, Toronto, Ontario M4P 2Y3, Canada (a division of Pearson Penguin Canada Inc.)
Penguin Books Ltd., 80 Strand, London WC2R 0RL, England
Penguin Ireland, 25 St. Stephen's Green, Dublin 2, Ireland (a division of Penguin Books Ltd.)
Penguin Group (Australia), 250 Camberwell Road, Camberwell, Victoria 3124, Australia (a division of Pearson Australia Group Pty. Ltd.)
Penguin Books India Pvt. Ltd., 11 Community Centre, Panchsheel Park, New Delhi – 110 017, India
Penguin Group (NZ), cnr Airborne and Rosedale Roads, Albany, Auckland 1310, New Zealand (a division of Pearson New Zealand Ltd.)
Penguin Books (South Africa) (Pty.) Ltd., 24 Sturdee Avenue, Rosebank, Johannesburg 2196, South Africa

Penguin Books Ltd., Registered Offices:
80 Strand, London WC2R 0RL, England

First published by New American Library,
a division of Penguin Group (USA) Inc.

First Printing, March 2006
20 19 18 17 16 15 14 13 12

REGISTERED TRADEMARK—MARCA REGISTRADA

LIBRARY OF CONGRESS CATALOGING-IN-PUBLICATION DATA

Lancaster, Jen, 1967–
    Bitter is the new black / Jen Lancaster.
        p.   cm.
    ISBN 0-451-21760-8 (trade pbk.)
    1. Unemployed women workers—Nonfiction.   2. Job hunting—Nonfiction.   I. Title.
PS3612.A54748B58   2006
813'.6—dc22   2005018193

Set in Bulmer MT
Designed by Jennifer Ann Daddio

Printed in the United States of America

PUBLISHER'S NOTE
While the author has made every effort to provide accurate telephone numbers and Internet addresses at the time of publication, neither the publisher nor the author assumes any responsibility for errors, or for changes that occur after publication. Further, publisher does not have any control over and does not assume any responsibility for author or third-party Web sites or their content.

The scanning, uploading, and distribution of this book via the Internet or via any other means without the permission of the publisher is illegal and punishable by law. Please purchase only authorized electronic editions, and do not participate in or encourage electronic piracy of copyrighted materials. Your support of the author's rights is appreciated.

for my mom despite and because (but mostly because)

for kate who makes the impossible anything but

for auntie virginia and cousin stephen,
my style icon and the man who invented fun

and for fletch — thanks for doing all the
heavy lifting (with love and squalor)

· CONTENTS ·

Part Two: Pandora

This boutique-to-barrio tale is a modern Greek tragedy, as defined by Roger Dunkle in *The Classical Origins of Western Culture*: a story in which "the central character, called a tragic protagonist or hero, suffers some serious misfortune which is not accidental, and therefore meaningless, but is significant in that the misfortune is logically connected."

In other words? The bitch had it coming.

And I am that bitch.

Bitter Is the New Black is my story.

Although this memoir is based on real events in my life, I've taken a few liberties for the purpose of moving the story forward. In some cases names and places have been altered, characters combined, time compressed, and events taken out of sequence.

Regardless of these changes, I assure you, yes, I really *was* that bad.

First she was a seed,
and then she was trouble.

—TODD LANCASTER, DECEMBER 25, 1970

I do much better as a goddess,
she said, since my secretarial skills
have always been limited.

—BRIAN ANDREAS, IN *TRUSTING SOUL*

LINCOLN ELEMENTARY SCHOOL

April 7, 1977

Dear Mrs. Lancaster:

Jennifer is one of the brightest and most articulate students in the fourth grade and a pleasure to have in my class. However, an incident today concerns me. During recess, I heard her remark to another student, "I can make Stacey Coopersmith do anything I want."

I wanted to tell you, as I am sure you want to keep that kind of behavior in check.

Sincerely,

Mrs. C---

THE CAMPUS

Student Newspaper

3/15/84

Jeni—

Pls. see me re. Page One's budget for next week's issue. Although your proposed layout looks great, I'm not sure the headline for the Spring Break story should be **Jeni to Vacation in Europe.** As well, the story may be more interesting if you actually include a broad range of other students' plans, and not just your own.

Thx,

C. H---

VIKINGS RADIO

2/10/85

Jennifer,

Broadcasting on the school radio is an awesome responsibility. If I did not think you were up to the challenge, I would not have awarded you your own show. However, I want to make it clear that you will *lose this slot* if we have a repeat of last night's incident.

I spent my morning fielding calls from parents angry about your commentary. Regardless of your opinion, it is never "OK" to report that the Pep Step Dance Squad members "look fat in their new outfits" nor are you allowed to call them "boyfriend-stealing skanks."

There are plenty of other students anxious to claim your spot if the editorializing continues. Do not let this happen again.

Mr. W---

University English Department

10/05/88

Miss Lancaster,

Congratulations on the commendable job on your essay exam. However, I regret to inform you that I must award you a B+, and not the A- you'd earned. Quite simply, I cannot tolerate your shouting at your neighbor to "stop chewing your gum like a damn cow" during the test.

The reverberation of giggles after your profane outburst was disruptive and inappropriate, and I had no choice but to dock your grade.

Prof. D---

"Lord, what fools these mortals be!"
William Shakespeare (1564–1616),
"A Midsummer Night's Dream,"
Act 2, Scene 2

january 21, 1991

jen,

congrats on the most faboo party!! it was our best ever, thanks to you! you rule as rush chairwoman . . . major snaps!!

however, the exec board has overturned the $100 fines you slapped on sisters not wearing green at the emerald city event. we think your attention to detail is totally awesome, but those fines were way harsh.

pi love and mine,

pres. r---

p.s. we've also turned down your request to fine anyone who called you "hitler" during the party—we were totally joking!!

The Village Idiot
BAR AND GRILLE

5/25/95

Jen,

Thanks for volunteering to be in charge when I took Chris to the emergency room. His burn is healing well, and he will be back in the kitchen on Tuesday. You did an excellent job running things with a couple of small exceptions.

First, Brian will *NOT* be required to provide you with a detailed essay on the virtues of a properly cooked steak.

Second, I know you think the hostess wasn't seating people in an orderly manner, but I DID NOT give you the authority to fire her. She will also be back on Tuesday and expects an apology.

In the future, leave personnel decisions to me.

Thanks,

B---

March 1, 1999

Dear Human Resources,

It is with regret that I'm tendering my resignation as a contract negotiator for Great Plaines HMO, effective two weeks from the date of this letter.

I appreciate the learning experience and I wish your organization tremendous success in the future.

Best,

Jennifer A. Lancaster

P.S. Perhaps the *next* time an angry physician locks a contract negotiator in a storage room as a bargaining ploy, you'll actually admonish the doctor in question. What *you* consider "a blip in the negotiation process with a crucial member of our provider network," *I* consider felony kidnapping.

P.P.S. I lied. It is with NO regret that I tender my resignation. I'm off to the dot-com sector to get rich. And the next time I'm locked in a closet? I'm pressing charges.

PART ONE

Icarus

1

Flying Too Close to the Sun

Camille said you stole a bag from a homeless guy."

"Well, I guess that depends on your definition of 'steal.' I didn't *swipe* the briefcase, but I didn't pay for it either," I reply to my rapt audience with a shrug. They gape at me with open mouths. Apparently this is not a satisfactory explanation.

"OK, I'll tell you the story, but I'm going to need a little lubrication first." I whistle for the waitress' attention and when she looks my way, I shake my highball glass and flash my freshly veneered multiple-thousand-dollar smile. She approaches with trepidation.

"You, bring me one of these every twenty minutes until we dock or I fall overboard," I instruct her while swirling the ice in my jewel-colored cocktail.

Hearing this, my cohorts break into the kind of congratulatory laughter exclusive to drunken salespeople. The waitress emits a fake chuckle, too, although I sense she's almost had it with me. What-*ever*. Have I NOT stuffed her apron full of twenties all afternoon? How about a little gratitude? When I was a waitress, I would have KILLED to work on a boat like this. Instead, I slaved away in a shitty campus bar serving college athletes who considered a good tip a quarter and a grope worthy of a sexual harassment suit.[1] And *I* was thankful for the opportunity. This girl is lucky to have caught me at the beginning of a story, or I would totally give her the news . . . even if it meant my next cocktail came with a spit chaser.

"So, all my assistants are in some meeting and I'm forced to pick up my *own* lunch, if you can imagine. I'm walking along Wacker Drive with my wasabi peas and cup of corn chowder—"

"What are wasabi peas?" interrupts some philistine from the Tucson office.[2]

"For those of you who live under a rock and have never heard of wasabi peas"—I shoot the Tucson rep a withering glance before continuing—"they are dried green peas coated with a hardened horseradish paste, and they're totally low fat and fabulous. AS I WAS SAYING, I'm cruising down Wacker and I pass this filthy street Arab—"

"Jen, please!" Camille interjects. "The politically correct term is *member of the transient community.*"

"Camille, go hug a dolphin or something, OK?" I snap. God, I'm so sick of Camille's PC bullshit. What a pathetic little do-gooder she is. She's always picking my Diet Dr Pepper cans out of the trash

---

[1] Seriously, if the basketball team kept their hands on the ball half as often as they tried on my ass, we'd have totally won the Big Ten Conference that year.
[2] OK, exactly how did *this* idiot get hired here? We're *supposed* to be the best and brightest in our industry (which is media and communications).

to recycle. And she rides her bike to our office when she has a perfectly good car and a parking pass. Once she tried to turn me on to her meat-free lifestyle and I told her to let me know when tofu started to taste like prime rib, because until then, I was *all* about the food chain.[3]

"ANYWAY, normally when I see the, um, *residentially challenged*"—I cock a perfectly arched eyebrow at Camille, daring her to chime in again—"I hold my breath so I don't have to smell them. Also, I traipse past quick as possible, because, really, their begging embarrasses us both. And I was about to do that again when I noticed that this guy was holding a gorgeous new briefcase. Correction, a gorgeous new COACH briefcase."

Pausing for effect, I squeeze a lime wedge into my fresh drink before continuing.

"I thought to myself, if he doesn't have a home, chances are he doesn't have an office, so why does he need a briefcase, especially one that perfectly matches my Coach Station bag? Besides, I was sure it was hot. And I knew if I *my* bag were stolen and I had no chance of getting it back, I'd want its new owner to cherish it, NOT use it as a pillow. I needed to rescue that buttery leather piece of magnificence and give it a loving home."

I take a delicate sip, noticing that everyone on the boat is listening to me. God, I am *so* meant to be in front of an audience.

"I marched up to the guy and honestly? I could actually see the stink coming off him. He radiated like a tar road on a hot day. And, oh sweet Jesus, he was completely whacked out of his mind on malt liquor and meth! So I was easily able to convince him that my lunch was an even trade for his briefcase. And we all lived happily ever after, the end. See? It's really not the big deal that Camille says it was."

---

[3]And why the hell is a VEGAN on a fishing trip in the first place?

"You forgot one significant detail," Camille admonishes with a shake of her head.

Sighing, I turn to her. "Are you my Greek chorus or something?" Rolling my eyes heavenward, I come clean. "OK, maybe the trade wasn't quite so fair. Because I . . . uh . . . uh . . . I told him the wasabi peas were crack rocks."[4]

Everyone on the boat—except Camille and the waitress—explodes into laughter. While they compose themselves, I sip my Stoli Cape Cod and survey the scene. After a frigid Midwestern winter, a day in the Florida sun is pure bliss. Golden rays dapple the Atlantic and a light wind gently buffers our boat. Although the charter seems a bit plush for a day of deep-sea fishing, I'm not complaining. Besides, with all the business I brought in this quarter, I deserve this luxury.

Twenty-five people from various regional branches of Corporate Communications Conglomerate (Corp. Com.) are on this trip . . . and I can't be bothered with most of them. Just look at how some chose to present themselves today. Technically, this is a *company function*. I don't care if we are fishing; tatty jean shorts, stained and wrinkled logo Ts, and—excuse me while I throw up in my mouth a bit—belly-baring shirts are wholly inappropriate.[5] Fashion Police, report to the scene of the crime, please.

Let's look at me now—I'm casual but fabulous. My linen Ralph Lauren Capri pants are pressed to perfection, and my simple Egyptian cotton V-neck is from Saks. My resplendent gold-and-silver twisted cable David Yurman bracelets are stacked up each of my arms, and their tourmaline, citrine, and amethyst stones glint in the sunlight, thus blinding those not clever enough to wear Oliver Peo-

---

[4]Oh, relax. I gave a totally big donation to the local food bank as soon as I started making big commissions.
[5]Your boss does NOT need to know if you possess an *innie* or an *outie*.

ples sunglasses. You know, being on the water should not preclude one from wearing expensive accessories.[6] Of course, my matching Kate Spade bag nicely ties the ensemble together. Yes, it's called STYLE, people. You might want to acquaint yourselves with the concept.

Anyway, what a lousy bunch of suck-ups most of the folks here are. All those losers were hanging on my every word! Now I'm trying to head to the ladies' room and even that's a task. Feels like I can't take a step without being accosted by enthusiastic crowds of parasitic second-tier sales weasels. And all the kudos? Getting a wee bit old.

"Oh, Jen, congratulations! You rock!"

Uh-huh. And your point is?

"Wow, Jennifer, your presentation was, like, amazing. . . . You are, like, so gifted at public speaking."

Yeah, I'm gifted. My smooth, confident delivery had nothing to do with the fact that I practiced my presentation in my hotel room's mirror for ten hours the day before I gave it while everyone else was at a poolside luau. Isn't it, like, a total shock that the most prepared person, like, won?

"Jenny, hey, um, hi. Do you think you could forward me that awesome PowerPoint you created?"

Oh, hey, um, you mean the PowerPoint that I worked on at home every single day for a month? The creation of which forced me to give up four entire weekends of my life? Is that the one you mean? Don't hold your breath. And don't call me Jenny.

"Excuse me, but aren't you the girl who won?"

How ever did you guess, Nancy Drew? Other than hearing the cavalcade of your colleagues congratulating me, I mean.

"What will you do with that big cash prize?"

Funny, but you don't look like my mother. I wasn't kidding when I

---

[6]Seriously, look at all the jewelry pirates wear.

announced at the awards ceremony, "Screw Disneyland. I'm going to
Prada."

In reality, I smile, nod at all the well-wishers, and keep my acid
tongue to myself. It's tough, but I am nothing if not professional.

I head to the washroom in the bowels of the vessel. For such a
nice boat, the bathroom is small, dark, cramped, and . . . is that pot
smoke? Is Captain Hazelwood our skipper? And, eeww! . . . they
have one of those creepy pump toilets. I think I can hold it until we
dock. I'll just fix myself up instead.

There's barely enough room to do a quick twirl, but I manage.[7] I
lean in for a closer look at my reflection and Angelina Jolie gazes
back at me. Well, that may be a slight exaggeration, but my features
are nicely placed, my eyes are a stunning emerald (contacts, but who
cares?), and my skin is clear and golden brown from the sun. I finally
stopped breaking out when I hit thirty, and no wrinkles yet, either.
Huzzah!

Coif? A bit wavy today because we're on the water, but my artfully applied caramel highlights contrast sublimely with my bronzed
visage. Rory, my colorist, does EVERYONE who's anyone in
Chicago and she's well worth the $300.

Cosmetics? All by Christian Dior, so my face is holding up
nicely in the heat. When you're out in the sun, the trick is to use a
light hand with the shimmer powder lest you *want* to look like a
truck stop waitress. One girl on deck now is so sparkly that I'm
tempted to ask her for a pork chop and a side of grits, and a warm-up
when you get the chance, hon.

Body? Tall and strong and lean, of course.

Or, tall anyway. And I'm confident that the rest will be true as
soon as I find time to drag my untoned ass to the gym. But it's hard
given all the hours I work. There's only so much time, and right now,

---

[7]Mmm-hmm, work it, girl.

the bulk is spent advancing my career. Despite my best efforts, I'm not *quite* perfect. Let's just say I'm like one of those Hopi blankets where they leave a tiny flaw so as to not affront the Lord. (Don't want to offend the Big Guy, right?) Besides, after even the most intense grilling, Fletch swears that I'm wonderful just the way I am.[8]

Final assessment: If I were a lesbian and had a thing for narcissistic ex-sorority girls? I'd *totally* do me.

I take one more peek in the mirror. My trademark marble-sized if-I'm-awake-I'm-wearing-pearls are particularly glossy in the diffused light of the bathroom . . . sooo pretty! With a steady hand, I apply Dior Brun Swing lipstick (matte, naturally—don't want to look like I've been licking an oily dinner plate), wash my hands, and mist J'Adore Dior perfume on my neck and wrists before working my way through the smiling crowd. More congratulations and slaps on the back. Ah, the price of fame . . .

I don't blame my colleagues for wanting to bask in my reflected glory. Beating more than five hundred other salespeople in the company by winning the national market leadership award yesterday catapulted me to "legend" status. And, fortunately, this should neatly shut down any lingering doubts about my salary. (Like it's my fault some stupid temp in the New York office left my offer letter in a copy machine? I'm to blame because I talked my way into a fat paycheck? It's called *negotiation*. Try it; it works.)

Thankfully Camille's found someone else to annoy, so now it's just my crowd at the back of the boat. These guys were my pals *before* I became the company rock star, not like the rest of the sycophants buzzing around me for the past few days. The fish aren't biting, so we've set aside our poles in favor of drinks and dish.

Ryan gossips better than any of my sorority sisters, so I sit next

---

[8]Smart boy, and precisely the reason I've never stabbed him with a wayward dessert fork.

to him. I love Ryan. . . . He is SO my style icon. He's always Dolce & Gabbana'd from head to toe and his grooming regime puts mine to shame. His eyelashes are a mile long[9] and he appears to have no pores whatsoever. With his exquisitely maintained stubble, I swear he looks just like George Michael back in his Wham! days. I aspire to be as pretty as Ryan. As he works in the Manhattan office and lives in the city, he's my arbiter of everything trendy.

"Hey, Ryan, what's the hot drink in New York these days?" I ask.

"This week, it's all about the mojito," Ryan says.

"Ooh, fun name! What is it, exactly? Is it good?"

"Absolutely delish. It's made from Puerto Rican white rum, the premium stuff, of course, but I don't need to tell you, now, do I?" He snorts. He knows I don't *do* well drinks. Life is too short not to top-shelf. He places a hand on his chin and the other on his hip with his head cocked to the side in an exaggerated thinking pose. "Anyway, um, there's muddled mint leaves, superfine sugar, club soda, and a lime garnish." He leans in to emphasize his point. "Oh, and, sweetie, this is key. It *must* be served in a highball glass with a raw sugarcane swizzle stick."

"But what if the bar doesn't stock raw sugarcane swizzle sticks?" I ask because I've been here before with Ryan. The last time he suggested a cocktail, I ran all over the city looking for a bar that carried cane-fermented cachaca because I "wouldn't *possibly* know the meaning of life without having sipped a proper Woody Woodpecker." Apparently light rum would have been an acceptable substitute, but the point turned out to be moot because I couldn't locate the shaved navel of a buff young Cuban boy out of which to quaff this particular libation.

Exasperated, Ryan says, "What kinds of savages don't carry sugarcane?"

---

[9]Shhh—it's clear mascara.

Patiently, I explain, "Ryan, although Chicago is a really progressive place, the possibility *does exist* that sugarcane has not yet come to every single Windy City watering hole."

"Then you should move out of that cow town."

"Humor me, Ryan. Let's say I've been dragged to a bachelorette party in some god-awful suburb at the one bar in the metro area not hip enough to carry sugarcane. What do I tell the bartender when he says he's sorry, they don't have it, and is that OK?"

"Then you are obligated to roll your eyes, sigh deeply, and tell him, 'I guess it will *have* to be OK, won't it?' "

"Unless he's cute, of course."

"Naturally."

"Ryan, you are SO my gay boyfriend."

"I know, honey. I know."

I cannot wait to order a mojito at the Hudson Club when I get home. I just love being more cutting edge than the arrogant dot-commers who still hang out there. Yeah, guys, the Internet boom? It's over. And your team? Lost. Why don't you get jobs at a *real* company? You know, the kind that actually makes things and turns a profit.

OK, so selling to those hateful dot-coms in my last job made me kind of rich. And because they threw so much of their venture capital at me, I earned sweet perks at my company, like a great title, my own office, and a pack of assistants to fetch me vanilla lattes[10] on demand. But I left those things to join this organization with its super-stable client base. And I manage a new product line, so it's as exciting as a start-up, only without the threat of bounced paychecks. And it's not like I don't have the opportunity to remind others that I used to be a vice president at Midwest Investor Relations Company.[11] Prediction? I will spend the rest of my career here.

---

[10]Extra foamy, one NutraSweet, and make it snappy.
[11]Which I may have done once. Or possibly twice.

I earn now in a day what I used to make in a week when I started my professional life doing data entry at a health insurance company. And my first shitty studio apartment in the city? Long gone. Fletch and I live in THE hot Chicago neighborhood of Bucktown—known for its trendy coffee shops, chichi boutiques, and the *most* fashionable clubs, in a twenty-five-hundred-square-foot timber loft with tons of space for my burgeoning shoe collection! With exposed-brick walls, fifteen-foot-high ceilings, spiral staircases, marble and granite finishes, etc., we've got the world's coolest pad. Best of all, since we're in the penthouse, I've got an uninterrupted skyline view from my private roof deck.[12] My brother, Todd, tells me we're insane for spending what amounts to five of his mortgage payments on our monthly rent, but I'm not worried about it. He's just jealous, and besides, *my* bills? Are paid.

Ryan gets up to scope out cute shirtless boys and their pale pectorals, so I turn my attention to Jeff. He's a product manager on the West Coast and dresses like an extra from *Up in Smoke*. Don't get me started on his disgustingly crusty feet. . . . He could climb trees with those toenails. Does this man even *own* shoes? I notice he's just dribbled beer on his tie-dyed top. Again. This annoys me.

"Jeff," I ask, as he blots himself with a towel, "do you know what year it is?"

"Huh?" Jeff is puzzled. He's been zoning out of conversations all afternoon and taking inordinately long pauses between thoughts. From his bloodshot eyes and the way he inhaled the crudités tray, I'd wager that he's stoned. Again.

"I'm asking because I thought it was 2001, but judging from your shirt and your patchouli-scented cologne, I'd say it was more like, what? 1969?"

Like the swordfish today, Jeff doesn't take the bait. He languidly

[12]Share my roof deck? Never!

exhales a stream of Marlboro smoke, slightly jarring his tarnished nose ring. "Wardrobe pointers from a chick who brought a"—he lifts my bag and reads the label—"*Kate Spade* purse on a deep-sea fishing trip? Yeah." Then he goes to take another drag on his cigarette and entirely misses his mouth. He giggles.

I lean in and exclaim in a hushed voice, "Ohmigod, YOU'RE the one who got lit in the bathroom!"

No response except for more giggling. Houston, we have a stoner.

"I can't believe you'd do THAT *at a company function*! What could you possibly be thinking?"

Jeff does a full-body stretch and says, "Guess someone's still bitter that my sales were higher than hers last month. Again." Ouch. He's right. It makes me crazy that Cheech-freaking-Marin's team sold more than mine.

And what a bang-up team I have. Out of the twenty people in my group, my "shining stars" are: Courtney, the *only* one who's normal; Camille, who's decent in front of clients but unbearable otherwise; and a few gals from Texas who might be good if they didn't consider their sales calls to be husband hunts. The rest of my account executives are wholly incompetent. When I first complained about them, Fletch was skeptical. He doubts my credibility because I tend to throw that word around *a lot* . . . about cab drivers, sales clerks, bartenders, etc. But A) my driver got lost on the way to Wrigley Field, B) it took the cashier twenty minutes to ring up one shirt, and C) how could a bartender *not* know what's in a dirty martini? So he didn't quite believe my bitching.

Until he met Arthur.

Arthur, the BB gun in my arsenal, ran into Fletch at my office one day when he was picking me up for lunch at our private dining club. While we enjoyed miso-glazed sea bass and crystal goblets of Chalk Hill chardonnay, Fletch remarked, "It's nice to see Corp. Com. mainstreaming people."

Huh? I looked at him quizzically with a mouthful of julienne carrots. Finally swallowing, I asked, "What are you talking about?"

"You know, your company. Mainstreaming. They hired that nice kid with Down syndrome," he replied.

I shook my head and dabbed at my mouth with a linen napkin. "Fletcher, I have no clue who you're talking about."

"The tall kid. He was blond with a striped shirt and gapped teeth."

"In MY office?"

"*Yes*. He was walking by the reception desk when I came in. When I asked for you, he got nervous and started to pace back and forth. I felt bad because I think I confused him."

"Today?"

"YES."

"How much wine have you had?" I picked up his goblet and inspected it. Honestly, I always have to monitor that boy's intake. He gets into his cups a little too easily sometimes.

"Whatever was in the glass you're holding."

"Well, if you're not drunk, then you're hallucinating. The Chicago office only has salespeople in it. Maybe you're thinking of one of the suburban offices."

Fletch insisted, "Jen, *you saw him*. He took me to your desk."

"Noooo," I said slowly, the puzzle beginning to piece itself together. "Arthur brought you over to me."

"Yes! Arthur. That was his name. Striped shirt. Eager to please. Nice kid."

"Fletch," I said, shaking my head, "he's one of my salespeople."

"But I've never heard you mention him."

"Yes, honey, you have."

Fletch sat quietly for about thirty seconds, until he finally understood.

"Holy shit . . . was that . . . was that . . . was that *Retard-y Arty?*"

I know it's a mean nickname, but before you judge me, I challenge you to look at Arthur's empty sales funnel. I've taken my valuable time to coach him in the field for six whole months, but he's just hopeless. He hems and haws and stammers in all our practice sessions, and despite the fact that I've yelled at him a million times, he never seems to improve.

I'd fire him, but I don't have that authority. Technically, although I'm responsible for getting my people to push my products, they report to Will, the totally feckless sales manager. I secretly refer to Will as *Won't*, as in "I *won't* force the account executives to meet their numbers because I'm more interested in having them like me." Or "Jen, you *won't* ever make the cover of *Fortune* magazine as one of the fifty most powerful women in American business leading this uninspired team." And one time? He asked Camille if any of her granola friends sold pot because he needed a new dealer.[13] The bottom line is if I want sales, I have to make them all myself, and this is precisely why Jeff's team beats mine.

"That's right, Jeff. . . . No one's *ever* higher than you," I scoff.

He takes another indolent pull off his cigarette and shrugs philosophically. "Hey, it's relaxing. You can't argue relaxing. You ought to try it. Maybe help you sell more." He smiles beatifically and gives his scraggly goatee a good scratch. Random bits of crud fall out when he does this. Gack!

"Honestly, thanks for the offer, but if I need to relieve stress, I'll call on my old friends Little Debbie, Dolly Madison, and Johnnie Walker."

"OK, whatever, Nancy Reagan. Just say no." This cracks me up, so I raise my glass in a toast to him.

"Here's to you, Potty O'Tokes-a-lot," I say.

"Back at you, you ball-breaking hag." We clink beverages.

---

[13]Fucking loser.

"Waaaaait, what ah all y'all talking 'bout?" Laurel chirps from her perch on the end of the boat.

"Laurel, take some of that shit off your head and maybe you'll be able to hear us," I yell back at her.

Laurel, from Charlotte and in charge of the South, is swaddled in a straw hat, a scarf, and huge Jackie O sunglasses. Her nose is coated with an inch of zinc oxide, and she's wearing a Windbreaker with a towel wrapped on top of it while holding an umbrella.

"You *are* aware that it is almost eighty degrees out here, right, Laurel?" Ryan asks. He's back from cruising. Apparently no one was hairless enough for him.

Jeff inquires, "Are you, like, allergic to UVA rays? That would be a bummer."

"Or has a recent bat bite made you an unholy creature of the night?" I query.

"Y'aaaaalllll," she whines in a honeyed North Carolina drawl. I wish I had an accent like that. The Texan girls on my team can tell you to go to hell with such a lovely magnolia-and-molasses twang that you look forward to the trip.[14] "Don't make fun of me. Y'all know my weddin' dress is strapless and ah'm trying to avoid unflatterin' tan lines."

Ah, yes. Her weddin'. How could we forget Laurel's upcoming nuptials? She's not only discussed this topic TO DEATH for the past three days, but also weekly on our group's conference call, and monthly in our New York meetings. I enjoy Laurel's company, but if I hear another word about bridesmaids, tulle, or "the most gorgeous little petite filet mignons y'all ever did lay eyes on," I'm pushing her over the back of the boat and I am not kidding.

"Laurel, I was asking Jeff if that was St. Augustine over there," I

---

[14]Somehow, my flat, slightly nasal, dandelion-and-Bud-Light Chicago accent is less inspiring.

say, pointing at the distant shore. Oh, please. Like I'm going to share Jeff's recreational drug use with the rest of the class?[15] Besides, I *am* curious to know more about St. Augustine. Meri says they have great shops, so I make a mental note to check out the stores when our conference ends tomorrow. I haven't shopped *at all* while we've been down here. When I get back to the resort, maybe I'll do a bit of eBaying before dinner. I considered buying a few items in the Sawgrass gift shop yesterday, but it's mostly golf-related, and I do hate me some golf. Any "sport" where you can smoke and drink while playing is not exercise.[16] Why not just go to a bar and save the greens fee?

Speaking of Meri, she's a shoo-in to be named manager of the year at the final banquet tonight. She runs the Houston office and helped her team raise sales almost 400 percent last year, so the fact she's sleeping with her director is totally irrelevant. (Although don't think for one second it's not what we talk about every time she leaves her seat.) And who starts sleeping with their boss AFTER they get promoted, anyway? However, I'll cut them some slack because they're both single.

My account executive Courtney, however, is NOT single. She recently became very much engaged, which is why I'm aghast to notice her foot disappearing in the direction of Chad-from-California's lap. (When we met, he told me I could call him *Chadifornia* or *CaliChad*, but I told him that stupid nicknames render me mute, what with all the bile rising in my throat. He laughed because he thought I was joking; I wasn't.)

Courtney and I sit next to each other in the primo cubicles with the lake view in the Chicago office. Since I joined the company, Courtney's become one of my confidantes, and within the confines of our

---

[15] I'm a bitch, not a tattletale.
[16] Bowling, I'm also looking at you.

jobs, we hit every networking event together. Lately, we've socialized outside the office, too, which is part of the reason I'm so appalled. I don't mean to sound self-righteous, but in the seven years I've been with Fletch, I've never even flirted with another guy,[17] let alone stick my foot up his shorts *at a company function!*[18]

I learned about Court and Chad's little tryst last night. I stopped by her room before heading to dinner, and it took her a long time to come to the door. I knew she was there because I'd just talked to her from the house phone. It's not like our hotel rooms were huge and she couldn't hear me. *Must be in the bathroom,* I thought. I knocked harder and waited.

When she finally opened the door, I saw that she was dressed for the banquet . . . sort of. The buttons on her summery cotton cardigan were askew; her floaty chiffon skirt was inside out and the pleats were mashed. Her normally impeccably smooth blond bob was completely bed-headed. Did she get dressed in a hurry?

"Hey, Court." I invited myself into her room. "What happened to you? Looks like somebody rode you hard and put you away wet." HA! I *so* crack myself up sometimes. "Have you been napping or something?" At that point, I noticed Chad, also in a state of disrepair looking sheepish on her mussed bed. A lightbulb went on in my head as I worked my way through the equation.

Ohhh . . . yes, there were *napping.*

Together.

Napping together?

Napping together.

Napping together . . . Chadifornicators!

Then I remembered that she was engaged to Brad and got mo-

---

[17]I mean another straight guy.
[18]Being a bitch is fine. Being a cheater is not.

mentarily flustered. I don't know how to handle it when normally good people go all untoward.

"Welllllllll, hiiiii there, Chaaaaad. It's nice to seeeee you again." I drew out my words because I had no idea what to say next. I started to stammer. "So, um, what have you guys been doing? Been sleeping together? Wait! No! Not like that, I mean, not together, like, you know, nap time? In kindergarten? And, um, no, no—I mean—so, are you going down on each other? Gah! With! With each other! To dinner," I finally spit out. Subtlety has never been one of my finer qualities.

Chad turned beet red and busied himself with his shoes. I caught Courtney's eye in the mirror and raised an eyebrow at her. Her flush confirmed the most indelicate of my suspicions. So busted.

Witnessing their guilt helped me recover my composure. "Oh, gr-gr-grow up," I finally sputtered. "What I meant to ask is if you're going down for cocktail hour?" They nodded in sheepish silence. We stood around looking at one another for a minute, and I realized I needed to take command of the situation lest they fall back into bed. I snapped into drill sergeant mode, determined not to let Courtney's indiscretion in any way mar *my* big night. Dammit, I was about to win the market leadership award, and this victory would not be overshadowed by tawdry gossip about my team.

"OK, you need to fix yourself up, pronto. Take a quick shower because you REEK of Chad's cologne. And, Chad, really? Drakkar Noir? No." They stood mute in front of me, not moving.

"Courtney, when you're done in the shower, be sure to go heavy on the foundation to cover up the whisker burn," I said pointedly in Chad's direction yet again, "and I'll find you an outfit to mask your— ahem—*hickey*." I directed her toward the bathroom with a gentle shove. "GO! Don't worry. I'll entertain your gentleman caller." Reluctantly, she entered the bathroom and closed the door.

"Well, Chad, we're faced with the dilemma of covering a hickey because apparently you make out like a high school sophomore. Let's see . . . scarves, scarves, does she have any scarves in here? Oh, I see some attached to the headboard, so, yeah, scarves are probably out. My, my, aren't *you* an interesting first date?"

I headed over to her closet to paw through the hanging garments, lingering over each item I inspected. "Let's see, no . . . no . . . cute but V-neck, so no . . . Ew, this one's atrocious, don't you think?" I asked, waving the hideous embroidered tunic in front of me like it was made of kryptonite. "Chad, could you fuck a girl wearing a shirt this ugly? Wait, don't answer that. OK, no . . . no . . . Ooh, this one would look good on me," I said, holding a blouse up while admiring myself in the mirror, "but, no, it won't work for tonight. Almost out of options here. No, no, hey . . . wait, we're in luck! This will nicely do the trick."

I banged on the bathroom door, yelling over the sound of rushing water. "Yo! You're going to wear your cream sleeveless Ann Taylor turtleneck. Pair it with those cute Stuart Weitzman snakeskin slides, your khaki Gap Capris, and a wide black belt, and no one will know you've been whoring around this afternoon. And you know what would totally enhance the outfit? *Your engagement ring.*"

Task complete, I examined the contents of Courtney's minibar. "Can I fix you a drink?" Chad appeared to be mortified beyond belief. Good. I'd heard through the corporate grapevine he was trouble, and I didn't want him corrupting *my* top producer.

"Yes, please," Chad croaked.

I tossed ice in glasses, poured a couple of strong gin and tonics, and grabbed a can of macadamia nuts. I settled on the couch across from him. He clung to his drink like a drowning man to a life preserver. "Oh, Chad, I'm making you nervous, aren't I? Forgive me. I'm just really protective of my friend. I guess I let the rumors about your lack of ethics affect how I treated you, and I'm sorry. I bet you're a really nice guy and not nearly as slimy as everyone says. Why don't we start over, maybe get to know one another?"

Exhaling for the first time since I'd entered the room, Chad said, "I'd like that."

I gave him an angelic smile and said, "Tell me, Chad, what do you like to do for fun when you're not nailing other people's fiancées in a sadomasochistic manner?"

Anyway, I'd thought I'd nipped yesterday's infidelity in the bud, but Courtney and Chad have been pounding beer today and have completely lost their inhibitions. Right now they're snuggled up in a sheltered corner of the boat and—*are they heavy petting*? Fortunately, the way we're all sitting, I'm the only one who can see them.

Though it's probably none of my business, I'm pissed because Courtney's fiancé, Brad, is such a nice guy. He worships her. Sometimes we do couple stuff together and that obligates me to protect him. Hell, he took her to Hawaii two weeks ago, and she didn't get back until right before we left for Florida. I doubt his credit card statements have come yet. Besides, her slutty behavior makes the whole Chicago office look bad.[19] Their mashing gets more heated. I see tongue. Ugh. I stand on my chair and shout, "*WAITRESS! DRINKS! NOW!*"

Oh, Court, just because you look like Sharon Stone in *Basic Instinct* doesn't give you license to act like her. C'mon, guys, these are your coworkers and this graphic public display of affection is both embarrassing and unprofessional, and . . . wait a second—*Courtney,* WHERE DID YOUR HAND JUST GO?

GAH! This is a *company function* and in broad daylight, you are giving Chad a—

The waitress returns with beverages at this exact moment. I can

[19]And I am all about looking good.

tell from the look on her face that A) she also witnessed Courtney's *busy* hands and B) she's utterly mortified. Bad touch! The rest of our group notices the waitress' discomfort and cranes to see what she's gawping at.

For God's sake, now I'm going to have to something noble to distract everyone from Courtney and Chad and what looks like the beginning of a porno movie. And chivalry is SO not my style.

"Hey!" I bark so abruptly that the server almost drops all the drinks she's carrying. It's also loud enough to bring Ron Jeremy and Jenna Jameson to their senses. Everyone looks at me while the horn dogs pull themselves apart.

I yank a crisp hundred-dollar bill out of my coordinating floral Kate Spade wallet and smack it on the waitress' tray. "Next time, could you please serve our drinks a little faster?" I tap the face of my TAG Heuer watch while my enormous Lagos Caviar jeweled ring catches the light. "The clock is ticking, you know."

Her eyes narrow, but she accepts the tip. White lipped, she tucks my Benjamin into her cargo shorts while glaring hot-red death at me. But I had to divert everyone's attention somehow, right? Had I been thinking, I would have yelled, "Shark!"

I arrange a smirk on my face for the benefit of my companions and shrug. "I just don't like to wait," I explain as the waitress retreats. Everyone hoots in appreciation, except for Courtney, who silently mouths *thanks* at me.

Yeah, you're welcome. Because that waitress is *SO* spitting in my next cocktail.

Our conference ends without incident and we head home to Chicago. Fletch will pick Courtney and me up from O'Hare. Even though we've been together forever, he still voluntarily does the airport run, and if that's not a true sign of love, I don't know what is. Except maybe a princess-cut Tiffany engagement ring . . .

Actually, our not being engaged is my fault. I keep upping the ante on the cut, color, clarity, and carat that I require, and I think he's afraid to price rings. Yes, he's successful, but I doubt that Bill Gates could keep me in the kind of jewelry that I want. Besides, a ceremony isn't necessary for him to prove his feelings to me, especially since we have a very expensive apartment to support.

OK, I will admit the idea of a big Michigan Avenue production, complete with all my sorority sisters in hideous matching satin dresses,[20] a scrillion yellow tulips tied with pink-and-mint-plaid ribbons, and a big catered to-do at the Drake with a top-shelf open bar and peapod-wrapped shrimp trays circulating while a string quartet plays right before your choice of prime rib or lobster tails is served *may have crossed my mind*. But only once or twice.

Courtney and I meet up at the baggage claim to wait for Fletch. Until now, we haven't had a chance to talk. She sat with Chad on the bus from the resort and dawdled with him so long in the Jacksonville airport that we couldn't get seats together on the flight. At one point, I noticed her quietly crying on the plane. Out of guilt, I assumed.

I interrogate her about what happened with the Chadifornicator, and Courtney blurts out that she's in love.

"Of course, you're in love. That's why you're getting married. It's not uncommon," I say.

"No, with Chad. I'm in love with Chad," she sniffs.

"WHAT?!?" I shout, attracting the attention of every single person on flight 973 from Atlanta waiting around carousel five in the baggage claim. "You met him five freaking minutes ago! That's not

---

[20]So I look prettier in comparison, of course.

enough time to fall in love. That's not even enough time to fall in like. Lust? Maybe, but definitely not like. And *what about Brad*? Did you NOT just get engaged?"

"I know," she weeps. "I'd been planning to break up with Brad because things just weren't working anymore between us. But then Hawaii was so romantic and the sun was setting and waves were crashing and we were drinking mai tais and his proposal was so sweet . . . I didn't think. I just let myself get swept up in the moment. I knew it was wrong the minute I said yes. I haven't even told my family about our engagement yet," she says. Her eyes get watery and she begins to sniffle. I root around in my bag to find her a Kleenex. *Ooh, look, I have gum!*

I remember something. "Wait, weren't you drinking mai tais with Chad at the sales conference when you hooked up?"

Courtney blows her nose while nodding yes.

"Essentially, you allowed a fruity rum punch to alter the course of your life TWICE? Oh, my God, you're such a WHORE!" This brings a fresh spate of tears. I know I should be more compassionate, but when you sleep around while wearing someone else's ring, I have trouble mustering sympathetic noises.

"Court . . . Court . . . COURTNEY! Listen to me. You have to be honest with Brad. Not later. Now. You cannot string him along anymore. It's just not right." Courtney begins to cry huge racking sobs.

"People are looking at us. Can you please make them stop?" she begs.

"What do you expect? Acting like a whore attracts attention. They probably think you're here to go on *Jerry Springer*."

"WAH!"

"OK, OK, I'm on it." I look around. Although everyone from the Atlanta flight has collected their luggage, they've yet to leave. A sweaty fat man with an orange flowered vinyl bag has moved right next to us to hear better. I whirl around to face him. "Yo, Marlon Brando, yeah, with the ugly carry-on, move along. Also? Burn that bag when you get home." I see an older woman with stop sign red hair pretending to tie her shoes. Perhaps if they weren't LOAFERS her ruse would be more credible. "And you, Red? Aren't you old enough to know better? FYI, a six-dollar box of hair color is NOT a bargain. Get going. And the rest of you?" I sweep the crowd with an accusatory finger. "Seriously, piss off. This does not concern you." I stomp a pony-skinned mule and make shooing motions.

We attract the attention of airport security. An officer cautiously moves toward us and I see him pat his waist in the direction of his side arm. "Oh, keep your polyester pants on, Rent-a-Cop," I say, waving dismissively in his direction. "Everything is fine. The situation is handled. My friend here is simply dealing with the ramifications of being a whore."

"Please stop calling me that!" she howls.

"Stop making me. If you know in your heart that it's over, then you have to do the right thing. Promise me that you'll end it with Brad before you take up with Chad.[21] You owe him that much."

She whimpers and nods. "I promise."

At this moment, Fletch breaks through the retreating travelers. He looks at their shell-shocked faces and shakes his head. He readily recognizes the victims of Hurricane Jen. "Hey, stranger, welcome home! How was your trip?" he asks while giving me a bear hug. He swoops down to grab my bags. Didn't I say he was a keeper? "Jen, you left with two bags, but now I see four. You do some shopping?"

"I had to buy extra bags for all the treats I bought you."

"I'll bet." His face is wreathed in an ironic smile. Apparently he didn't care for last present I got him . . . a pink Ralph Lauren V-neck tennis sweater that *just happened* to fit me.

---

[21]Or Tad or Vlad or anyone else.

He notices Courtney and says a cautious hello as he takes in her tearstained countenance. I shake my head and whisper, "Don't ask," as we stroll to short-term parking.

On the drive back to the city, Fletch attempts to distract us with boring stories about work. Oh, sweetie, I love you, but do you really think anyone in this car cares about the IP-data-transport-telecom-bandwidth-blah-blah-whatever-it-is-you-do? Your job is to look pretty and keep earning fat commission checks, agreed? Agreed.

We get back to the city and drop Courtney at her high-rise apartment over by the lakefront. In the rearview mirror, I see her whip out her cell phone and one of our company's business cards. She's calling Chad! Stinking liar. I roll down my window and shout, "Get off the phone, whore!" as we pull away. Courtney smiles and give me a wan one-finger wave, phone cradled in her shoulder as her doorman grabs her bags.

"What happened to Courtney?" Fletch asks.

I sigh. "Mai tais."

2

The *What* Street Journal?

Washington Times-Herald Opinion Page, March 6, 2001

$6 HOT DOG BETTER BE GOOD

Rarely do I feel the need to skewer a family member publicly, but recently my younger sister made a comment that deserves some scrutiny.

My sister, a successful high-tech something.com salesperson in her early 30s recently announced that Chicago was "growing a little too small" and she might be ready to move on. Hoping for the best, we thought that she might be ready to move a little closer to home. We were wrong.

She said that she thought the Big Apple was in her future because Chicago was just "too Midwestern."

We decided to dissect this statement over breakfast. Having lived in the New York metropolitan area, I felt I could give my sister some loving advice.

First we looked at housing. We established that her old Lincoln Park apartment (one bedroom) would quadruple in cost to $3600 per month in midtown Manhattan. I assume that this prime location would give her unfettered access to the beautiful East River and $40/day parking spots.

She said she would have better access to Broadway shows. When I asked her how her life has been short-changed by having to wait six months for the three Broadway shows she has actually seen, she quickly moved on.

On to restaurants. She said that New York has the best restaurants in the world and one can get whatever they want around the clock. I reminded her that no one actually goes to those places, they just talk about how nice it would be if they could. And if the food is so great, then why do all those people stand around eating $6 hot dogs?

I guess "too Midwestern" would also mean she would get four extra ounces of steak for the same price in Chicago, but she wouldn't have access to goat tripe at 4:00 AM.

Books, music, shopping—all were bantered about at the kitchen and I felt like I made a pretty good argument for man's ability to survive if one had to shop at Marshall Field on Michigan Ave instead of Bloomingdale's on Fifth Ave.

The final straw was coffee. She said the Big Apple had better coffee than Chicago and that was an important part of her daily routine.

So we added up the totals for the environmental bliss of life in Gotham, $3600 in rent, $1200 a month in parking, $12 a day in coffee, $200 a week in Broadway tickets, and $96 a month in hot dogs.

After explaining that the rest of America goes to about one movie a month, pays an average of $600 a month for a mortgage, and could make four car payments on the $1200 a month parking fee, I knew I had made an impact.

My sister turned to me and said, "I suppose I could do without the hot dogs."

—Todd Lancaster

Ah, home sweet home. Fletch hauls my bags up the fifty steps to our apartment . . . the one drawback to living in the penthouse. You'd think my ass would be smaller from all the climbing.

As I unpack, I shiver with delight over all the designer labels . . . Tomatsu, Karen Kane, Dana Buchman, Ralph Lauren, a few prized pieces of Chanel and Versace, etc. I really ought to thank Shelly Decker for my fabulous wardrobe. No, Shelly isn't my personal shopper. She's the hateful little troll who drew the thinly disguised comic strip about me (*Muffy the Preppy,* my ass) and abused her position as features editor to place it smack on page two of our high school newspaper. If it hadn't been for her public goading, I'd never have become the fashionista I am today. Even almost eighteen years later, my blood boils about the day I saw that stupid cartoon. . . .

"Look at this," I shrieked while throwing open the front door and tossing my book bag in the corner. "Look! LOOK! I have been *wronged!*"

"S'matter with you, Peeg?" Todd asked from the couch in the family room off the kitchen. My brother had stationed himself there before I left for school hours earlier, apparently still recuperating from his freshman year of college. He'd indulged in a steady diet of ginger ale and *Gomer Pyle* reruns for the past three days. The nine months without him in the house had been heavenly, as his sole purpose in life was to make mine miserable. Normally I'd attack him for the "peeg" comment (really, how can you be a pig when you can squeeze into size five Jordache jeans?) but I had other priorities.

"I'm not talking to you, TOAD. Mom, look at this. . . . It's awful! I'm ruined! I have been personally attacked!" I wailed while wildly waving a copy of my high school newspaper.

"Oh, Jen, I'm sure you're overreacting again. Let me see." Mom put down her load of clean laundry and perused the offered page, eyes scanning back and forth. She wrinkled her brow. "You're ruined because the drama club chose *Little Mary Sunshine* for the fall play?"

"No, it's this right here!" I stabbed the offending section with a pointed finger.

"The *Muffy the Preppy* comic strip?"

"Yes! Read it!"

"Muffy the Preppy says . . . hmm, hmm, hmm . . . *real* pearls from Hudsons . . . hmm, hmm . . . shut up, you animals . . . hmm, hmm . . . and I'm done. It's cute. Did you draw this?"

"MOTHER! How could you think it's cute? That bitch Shelly Decker drew this about ME! See? She's got the pearls and the Shetland sweater tied around the shoulders and everything. And it's the last day of school, and this insult is all anyone will think about the whole summer."

"I know you feel you're an adult, but you may not swear in this house." Over my mother's shoulder, I could see Todd making faces and flipping me off. I'd deal with him later. "I think you're being melodramatic. What's the big deal?"

"Do you not understand that I have a reputation to uphold in that school? I cannot just have my character assassinated by the media."

"Sorry, *Zsa Zsa*, I forgot that you were so averse to negative publicity." My mother resumed folding the load of whites she'd been holding.

"Mother! You're not taking this seriously! Don't mock me! I had to work really hard to fit in here after we moved from New Jersey. It took YEARS for me to work my way up to the semicool crowd, and I had to lose the atrocious Jersey accent to do it. The last thing I need is some asshole pointing out how I'm different from the rest of them. Don't you realize that the animals separated from the herd die? DO YOU WANT ME TO DIE??"

"WATCH THE MOUTH, missy. I understand you're upset. What I don't understand is why Shelly would draw a cartoon about you. She's your best friend."

"Well, yes, she was, but not anymore."

"Since when?"

"A while, OK?"

Todd interjected, "Hey, Mom, better get Dad's attorney on the phone to talk about suing the school paper for libel."

"MOM!"

"Now you're both being ridiculous. Todd, pipe down. What happened with Shelly?"

"It was all her fault."

"Jennifer, what did you do?" Why did she always assume it was my fault?[22]

---

[22]Granted, it generally *was* my fault, but it would have been nice to get the benefit of the doubt once in a while.

"She was jealous."

"Of what?"

"Nothing."

"I think there's more to the story," Todd volunteered helpfully from the other room.

"Shut UP, Toad. OK, remember when you had to go back to Boston to help Grampa after his surgery? Well, I kind of wore your pearls while you were out of town."

"I do not recall giving you permission to wear them."

"I was allowed to because Dad saw them on me and didn't say I couldn't."

"Not an excuse. Your father is oblivious. He didn't notice for three weeks when we painted the den. But why would my necklace upset Shelly?"

"I might have mentioned they were *real* pearls. From Hudsons."

"So?"

"About fifteen times."

My mother sighed deeply. "Where did we go wrong with you? You didn't learn this behavior from me. When I was your age, I never had new clothes. All I had were the items my sisters handed down to me. The only reason I dressed as nicely as I did was because I taught myself to sew and—"

"Is this where you tell us how you only had one pair of wool socks when you were a girl and you had to hand wash them every night?" I whined.[23]

"I can't believe she has *any* friends the way she acts," my brother added. Why couldn't I have been born an only child?

"Shove it, frat boy. Mom, do you see the problem I have? Shelly just threw down the gauntlet, OK? She issued a challenge. If she's

---

[23]Seriously, you'd have thought she grew up on a dirt farm in Appalachia instead of a working-class duplex in Boston.

going to label me in a public forum, then I have to be the preppiest preppy to ever walk the halls of my high school. Now that I've been singled out, I'm obligated to deliver. People are going to expect it. I didn't start this feud, but I'll be damned if I don't finish it. So, I'm going to need a LOT of new stuff for back to school. Why don't you get Dad's credit card and we can start shopping now. You know, beat the rush and all."

"Ha! Good one, Jen."

"You're not going to help me? Why? Because of your boring sock story?"

"You get $100 for back-to-school clothes, and you know it, and that amount will decrease if you don't watch it with the cusses. If you want more than I plan to pay for, then I suggest you get a job."

"How am I supposed to do that? I can't drive yet, and there's no place to work in this stupid subdivision."

"When I was your age, I made money for fabric by watching my sister's children. This neighborhood is full of kids—why don't you give babysitting a try?"

"But I hate kids."

"Yet you love money."

"You make an excellent point."

Why had I never considered babysitting before? Our neighborhood was crawling with little kids. . . . It was a veritable gold mine! I quickly ran figures in my head—if I could earn fifty dollars a week for the next ten weeks of summer, then—holy cats!—I'd be the best-dressed girl in the whole TOWN. Visions of pink oxford cloth and tartan plaid danced in my head. With five hundred dollars, I'd get tassel AND penny loafers, puffy velvet headbands, whale-print miniskirts, and a Bermuda bag to match every outfit!

"Do you think if I typed up a flyer Dad's secretary could make copies? That way I could pass them out to neighbors."

"I'm sure she would if you asked nicely."

"I'm going to work on it now!" I grabbed my book bag and headed for the stairs. Remembering something I'd left undone, I returned to the kitchen. "I forgot to tell you guys . . . hey, Toad?" I pulled an envelope from my bag and handed it to my mother. "Your grades came today!" I dashed to my room as the blood drained from my brother's face.

That's how in the summer of 1983 I became known as Babysitter Über Alles. I was in demand, but not because of my tremendous prowess with children. I've never been great with kids—they are self-centered, attention-grabbing, illogical, sticky little beasts with terrible taste in TV shows.[24]

I was nice to my charges for the most part, but any maternal stirrings I might have had were squelched by their shrill voices and garbled English, which I found annoying, not endearing. Don't get me started on their rambling stories and barrages of precocious questions. "Jen, why do the birds sing? Jen, why does the grass grow? Jen, how do sharks sleep? Jen, why is the sky blue?" *The sky is blue because God hates you, OK?* Worst of all, kids always seemed to think it was *all about them.*

And everyone knows it's really all about me.

The sole reason I was popular was because I tackled housework without being asked. My clients knew that upon their return, they'd find gleaming appliances, empty sinks, and pristine carpets. I quickly learned that elbow grease equaled more penny loafers and oxford cloth shirts, and the more I had, the more Shelly would turn pink and green with envy. Heh.

Much as children annoyed me, dealing with them was a necessary evil. Once one young insurgent, Daniel Bedlamski, wouldn't get out of the pool, forcing me to enact Jen's Babysitting Axiom #95: *First Ask Nicely and Precisely.* I crafted these rules of engagement to

---

[24]A lot like most of the guys I dated before I met Fletch.

better deal with Danny, as arguing with him instead of scrubbing had cost me more than one tip.

Prior to his refusal, I'd been perusing for the umpteenth time my new personal bible and style guide, *The Official Preppy Handbook*. I flipped through it while keeping one eye on Danny, as I figured his drowning might negatively affect my compensation. But then he wouldn't get out of the pool, so I closed the book and headed toward the water.

I swiftly removed my Bass Weejuns and argyle socks. I cuffed my khaki walking shorts, climbed down the first two steps in the shallow end, and met Danny's gaze. I smiled and adjusted my strand of pearls.[25] He splashed a bit and grinned back at me, his white-blond hair slick with water, cheeks pink and freckled, and cerulean blue eyes dancing. Jen's Babysitting Axiom #37: *The More Angelic They Look, the More Evil They Are.* With Danny's cherubic features, he was the devil incarnate.

Sweetly, I said, "Danny, honey, I asked you to please get out of the pool." I'd taken to calling the kids endearing pet names instead of swearing since I'd been fired for calling Markie Everhart a "fuck-tard."[26]

Danny shook his head wildly and droplets of water made patterns on my linen shorts. He squealed and shrieked while I smiled more widely through gritted teeth. (Jen's Babysitting Axiom #421: *Assume a Healthy Glow, Agitation Never Show.*) I flipped up the collars on my layered polo shirts and tilted my head in the trademark flirty manner Britney Spears would eventually steal from me.

I said, "I bet you're having so much fun right now that you don't want to stop." He laughed and splashed some more, this time

[25]Faux.
[26]If you have a better term for a ten-year-old who insists on shoving crayons up his nose, I'd certainly like to hear it.

speckling the natty tortoiseshell Ray•Bans that I'd swiped off Todd's dresser earlier that day.

I glanced at my cheap Timex fitted with a grosgrain watchband. I needed to get that brat out of the pool tout de suite if I was going to tackle the sink full of dishes. I was counting on Mrs. Bedlamski's tip. The club pro at the local golf course was holding a particular Izod for me, but only until the end of the afternoon.

And this was no ordinary polo. It was bubble gum pink and Kelly green striped, and instead of a boring old knit collar, this one was constructed of crisp and immaculate white cotton. This shirt spoke of prep schools and old money and summers on the Vineyard and the kind of old-boy networks that don't exist on the plains of northeast Indiana. I knew the minute I put that shirt on, I'd immediately be catapulted away from my painfully average Midwestern roots. To this day it is singularly the greatest shirt I've ever seen in my life. Also? I knew that Shelly Decker would shit itty-bitty alligators the minute she saw it on me.

"Danny, sweetie"—really meaning *fucktard*—"I have to go in the house and you can't swim alone. You need to get out of the pool right this second." He giggled and screeched and ducked his head under water. This time his splashing hit my book.

OH. NO. HE. DIDN'T.

When he came up for air, I brushed the pageboy out of my eyes and retied my tartan hair bow, careful to do something with my hands to keep them from making choking motions around the hell spawn's neck. It was time to break out the big guns . . . Jen's Babysitting Axiom #578: *Don't Get Mad, Get Medieval.*

I leaned in close and whispered, "Danny boy, you are coming out right now. Or else I'm going to take that radio from the table, throw it in this pool, and electrocute you."

Tell me that little bastard didn't fly out of the water.

Harsh? Perhaps. But I finished the dishes, got the extra tip, bought the shirt, and wore it on my first day of eleventh grade. Shelly *was* beside herself when she saw me. In a deliciously ironic twist, my best friend, Carol, had been named editor in chief and she appointed me to be the new features editor. My first order of business? Scrapping the *Muffy* strip, of course.

As for Danny, he's all grown-up now. But I have to wonder if any time he sees madras plaid, he doesn't die just a tiny bit inside.

· ·

You know, the corporate world really isn't that different from babysitting. It's all a matter of understanding when to kick off your loafers and take charge.[27] Plus, most of the people I work with act like children, so the transition to the professional world was practically seamless. No wonder I rock it so hard.

However, I will concede that working for a nice company makes things a lot easier. I am *so* much happier at Corp. Com. than I ever was at my last job at Midwest IR. The work environment is really positive and the pressure is way less intense, even though I have to put up with Will's antics. What a colossal washout he is. Although I report to the head of my product line in New York, I had to interview with Will because he runs Chicago. And what do you think his selling point was in my interview? Room for advancement? Stock options? A generous 401(k) match? No. Will loved Corp. Com. because they gave employees *free sodas*. Yes, and so does McDonald's but you don't see people lining up to work there.

My problem with Will began on day one of my employment. I arrived sporting a smashing tweed Tahari suit trimmed in striking black fringe, ready to get down to business.

[27]And threaten bodily harm (when necessary).

"Hi, Jen Lancaster, pleasure to see you again," I said, extending my hand.

"Yeah, um, hey, Jenny, I, uh," he started.

"It's *Jen*," I interrupt.[28]

"What? Oh, yeah. Sorry. Um, yeah. So, um, welcome. Yeah. You want a soda or something? They're free!" he reminded me.

"Thanks, no. I'd just like to get started. I've got a lot of ideas to flesh out, so if you'll be so kind to show me the way to my office, I can do just that."

Will nervously looked around, pulling his collar open with one finger. "Um, yeah. There's a slight problem. I, um, kind of turned your office into a storage room."

"What?" No. No, no, no! Part of the reason I agreed to join the organization was because they promised me my own office. I was NOT about to rejoin the land of the cubicle dwellers.

"Yeah, I accidentally ordered too much marketing material and I needed a place to keep it and corporate won't let me send it back. So, um, yeah, sorry 'bout that."

"OK." I wasn't thrilled, but they were still paying me an outrageous sum, so I guessed I could make do. "Where will I be sitting?"

"Um, we don't have a receptionist anymore, so her desk is open. Would that be cool? It's, like, a really big work space."

I glanced at the desk. "Don't people enter through these doors, and won't they naturally come to me—the person sitting at the reception desk—for assistance?"

"Um, well, not that much, and you could page people if they had a visitor and delivering stuff won't take you too long and—"

---

[28] I was *Jeni* for about five minutes back in high school because I liked to dot my *i*'s with a sunflower. But I'm a big-time professional and those days are long over, OK?

I interrupted again. "Will, would distributing UPS packages really be what you consider the best use of my time and salary?"

"Um, um . . ." he stammered.

"No? Then get me a different work space."

"OK, follow me." He took off down a long hallway as I trailed behind him a few paces.

"And, seriously? Consider Ritalin. They're doing amazing things with adult ADD lately."

"What'd you say?" Will turned with an accusatory look on his face.

"I said I was seriously G-L-A-D to be on board. Now let's find me that desk."

So I'm back in a cube again. It's not as bad as I thought since it's relatively private and I've got a great lake view. Still, there's nothing more satisfying than righteously slamming your office door when the hoi polloi gets too loud. Speaking of loud, the salesmen at Midwest IR were incredibly noisy. Someone thought our team would produce more if we had a creative outlet. Were we supplied with piped-in music or theater tickets or thought-provoking team-building exercises? No. We got an air hockey table. I can't tell you how annoyed I was by the testosterone-charged cheers that ricocheted off the walls all day. Most days I'd swear I worked in a sports bar.

My old coworkers used to bitch when I'd scoot out of the office after eight hours. They didn't understand how I managed to meet my goals, especially since *they* claimed to work twelve-hour days. Yeah, you know what, guys? I actually *have* worked twelve-hour days. Those four hours you played air hockey? Don't count.

I suspected my old job would be a challenge because it was an investor relations firm and I knew *nothing* about the financial world. I thought PE ratios had to do with gym class statistics and mutual funds were the bills in Fletch's wallet.

Stan, Midwest IR's chief operating officer, promised to teach me everything I needed to know about the business. I jumped at the chance to learn from him. He may have been clad in a $1200 suit and Ferragamo loafers, but he was still "straight outta Jersey." I was enamored by his Newark-tinged plain talk. Such a refreshing change from the mild-mannered, mealymouthed Midwesterners at the HMO! Sure, my old bosses were pleasant and polite, but they tried to steal credit for my deals and ideas more times than I care to mention.

The last thing Stan said in my final interview was "This is a male-dominated company in a male-dominated industry. I'm talking total boys' club heah. I never hired a woman to do sales befoah because I don't wanna deal with complaints. Ya wanna run with the boys, ya gotta let 'em be boys. I need to know, Jen, what would ya do when ya heah the guy sitting next to ya say, 'I banged my girlfriend in the ayse last night'?"[29]

Momentarily stunned, I answered truthfully, "I'd probably laugh."

"Good ansah. 'Cause I don' like bein' sued. Ya hired."

What's funny is that I was usually responsible for the embarrassing. The other salesmen had graduated from various Ivy League universities and many had been brokers. Although competitive air hockey players, they were as dull as dry toast and spoke endlessly about their portfolios. I'd have welcomed a sodomy story just to break up the monotone ejaculations about market capitalization. Even after I'd been there a few months, I called them all Josh because I couldn't tell them apart. Franco, everyone's favorite Lincoln Park barber, gave them all the same haircut, and every day they showed up to work in tan pants and French blue dress shirts. I'm not sure Stan could ever differentiate between them, either.

Fortunately, cohesion was Stan's goal. As part of his plan, we

---

[29]Honest to God, this is a direct quote.

were required to take business trips en masse. He liked the idea of all his salespeople out together at trendy eateries, sporting our logo shirts for branding purposes. However, being with these guys every day and most evenings began to wear on me. One can only hear about Cornell's winning football program so many times, you know?

On my first joint venture to New York, I got stuck with one of the Joshes for the day. Josh had *trained* me, and I use that term loosely. His sales pitch entailed boring the customer into submission. The only thing I'd learned from him was how *not* to sell.

"Explain to me again why I have to come with you today," I said during our mandatory group breakfast. I'd already closed three deals on this trip, and dammit, I'd EARNED an afternoon of shopping by myself. The closest I'd come to Fifth Avenue so far was an airport candy bar.

Josh sighed and paused before answering. He took a handkerchief out of his pocket and used it to wipe his glasses. "Jennifer, I've been tasked with training you and I take my responsibilities seriously."

No shit, you giant handkerchief-carrying dork. You take everything seriously. You wouldn't know a good time if it bit you on the ass.

"I've retired my sales goal for the entire year and it's only March," I replied. "Shouldn't that prove I'm already trained?"

I should be giving YOU lessons on how to work a customer, pal.

"All it proves is that I've done a first-rate job in your sales education. Imagine how much more effective you will be when we reach the conclusion of our sessions together."

Imagine how effective I could be at removing your pancreas with my grapefruit knife when we reach the conclusion of this conversation.

That afternoon, I sulked all the way from our midtown hotel to lower Manhattan. After passing what seemed like a million cool shoe stores and indie coffee shops that I *could have been patronizing*, we arrived at our destination.

We were to meet with Lawrence. Lawrence was a vice president at, um, let's call it an *influential* business publication. I was, of course, stoked because there's nobody more interesting than a financial journalist, especially once he's become management.

Oh, wait, except *everyone*.

It was going to be a long afternoon.

We gave our names at the security desk and were guided to a bank of elevators. I punched the UP button and waited. Josh pressed right after me. Apparently I hadn't pushed it to his satisfaction, but I bit my tongue.

As we entered the elevator, Josh turned to me and said, "Since you're still learning the sales process, I'd prefer that you not speak in this meeting."

"Come again?" Did I hear him correctly?

"In the meeting, please don't say anything unless you've been addressed. I don't want the client to get confused. You are not yet up to speed on the way I pitch, and I want to present a consistent message."

I had to give up shopping for this?

"Shall I also walk three paces behind you, Josh-*san*?" I asked, bowing slightly.

"Oh, I don't think that will be necessary," he replied. Apparently Harvard didn't teach him to detect sarcasm.

We got to reception and a secretary guided us to a lush conference room on the fortieth floor and brought us espresso in beautiful enameled cups. The chairs were elaborately hand-tooled leather jobs and the giant round table had cherrywood inlays. The mahogany paneled walls were covered with Asian-influenced oil paintings, and a variety of interesting vases were scattered artfully about the polished sideboards.[30] I took a deep breath and realized that all I

---

[30]OK, I honestly wondered if one would fit in my bag, but only for a second.

could smell was money. The windows of the room ran floor to ceiling, and there was nothing but glass between us and a sun-dazzled Manhattan skyline. Wow, just wow.

Lawrence joined us momentarily. He was immaculately appointed in Brooks Brothers, and his powerful handshake crushed one of my metacarpals. We exchanged business cards, and I'd barely gotten my name out before Josh gave me the stink eye. Oh, yeah. No noise from the peanut gallery.

Josh launched into his tedious pitch immediately, and I zoned out. He blathered on about our products and services for a while, and I'd occasionally smile and nod. I didn't care to listen, and I might not be allowed to participate, but at least I could *look* like my presence served a purpose. I pretended to take notes in my leatherbound Filofax but was actually penning flattering assessments about myself. *Jen is smarter than Josh. Jen is a better salesperson than Josh. Jen is more interesting than Josh.*

Eventually, their conversation turned to Harvard. This was not surprising. Because he was an alumnus, ALL of Josh's conversations eventually led to Harvard. Frankly, I was shocked he'd kept quiet about it that long. Usually he introduced himself as Joshua, and would add, "But my friends from Harvard call me Josh." Luckily, he also wore a Harvard ring and rep tie in case the introduction was too subtle. And what a lucky day! Lawrence had gone to Harvard, too. Yay, or boola, boola, or rah, rah, or what*ever*!

Josh and Lawrence prattled on about Crimson, Cream, the Boat House, Steve's mix-ins, the Coop, and Beat Yale! as I stared out the window. At some point, they realized that I was still in the room and Lawrence finally decided to include me in their nonversation.

He began, "Tell me, Jenny . . ."

Whoa, hold it right there. Does it say Jenny on my business card? Did I introduce myself as Jenny? Do I look like a Jenny? No. Strike One, pal.

". . . did you also attend Harvard?" he finished.

If I had, wouldn't I have mentioned it at some point in the last half hour?? Stee-rike Two.

With a sneer, Josh interrupted. "No, she went to some Big Ten school."

I tried to smile through my aggravation. I may not have gone to Harvard, but I was proud of my education, especially since I paid for a lot of it myself. "That's right. I graduated from—" I began.

But the damage was done. Lawrence and Josh were already exchanging barely perceptible smirks at the idea of a *state school.* Armed with that little nugget of information, Lawrence deemed that I wasn't good enough to be included in their conversation and I became invisible again. *Strike Three. Thanks for playing.* I returned my attention to my notebook. *Jen is not a condescending jackass like Josh. Josh sniffs his own farts. Josh has dirty fantasies about Alan Greenspan.*

Eventually, Lawrence gave us a tour of their operations. When we passed by the team of Web developers Lawrence oversaw, I noticed that all of them were busy trolling sex Web sites. And none of this arty, I'm-only-modeling-to-pay-my-tuition stuff, either. I'm talking hard-core with money shots and everything.[31]

Curious, I thought. *Shouldn't those developers look guilty having been caught ogling beavercentral.com?*

When we returned to the conference room I still smarted from being silenced and having my college slighted. Who could blame me? I decided it was time to have some fun.

As we arranged ourselves in the posh softness of the leather chairs, I asked, "Hey, *Larry*, what's the deal with the nudie sites?"

Call me *Jenny*, indeed.

---

[31]Not that I've ever seen a money shot. Or am familiar with the concept. Because I am a nice girl who is saving herself for marriage despite seven years of cohabitation. Hi, Mom!

Josh gave me that *look*, but I ignored it.

"How observant of you. Our developers are attempting to add more subscribers to our online venture. They have been studying how pornographic sites use interstitial windows to capture registrants' information. They have been working day and night on that technology," Lawrence replied while nodding his head, agreeing with himself. What an ass.

"Let me see if I understand this, Larry," I proceeded. "Your team spends all day looking at pornography."

"That is correct." More nods.

"You sanction this?"

"Absolutely." Bobble, bobble, bobble.

"Because they tell you it's for business?" I continue.

"Affirmative." Josh started to shake his head, too. They both appeared to have contracted Parkinson's disease.

"And you BELIEVE them? HA!" My laughter bounced off the urban canyons of lower Manhattan while Lawrence and Josh blanched, realizing that the emperor was as pants-free as all the girlies on those Web sites. Our meeting ended shortly after that, as did my formal training sessions with Josh.

Diss my alma mater, indeed.

I'm thankful for my time at Midwest IR. Working with all those boys taught me to compete like a man.[32] I gained the confidence to look my present employers in the eye during salary negotiations and ask for a sum so outrageous that they should have laughed me out of the interview.

---

[32]The Ivy League–caliber ego and smug sense of superiority I developed are unfortunate side effects, but what are you going to do?

Should have.

But didn't. I refer you again to the careless temp.

Suckers.

My work ethic being what it is, I'm always the first person here in the morning and the last one out at night. Since we returned from Florida, I've been especially buried. I've done three appointments today and can't count how many calls I've taken. Which is why it's four o'clock and I have yet to eat lunch.

I catch a glimpse of myself in the mini mirror hanging on my cubicle wall. Yikes. My lipstick is a distant memory and my mascara is everywhere. And, ugh . . . the chlorine in the resort's pool completely bleached out my highlights and my roots are overgrown. I look like one of the easy girls at my high school who'd sit on the hoods of their boyfriends' Monte Carlos wearing roach clip earrings and eyeliner heated with a lighter for maximum smudge-ability. All I'm missing is a Billy Squier tape, a Virginia Slims cigarette, and the desire to cruise Dairy Queen's parking lot.

I glance over at Courtney's desk. Earlier she was weeping, but now she's whispering into the receiver and giggling flirtatiously. She's still wearing her engagement ring, yet I get the sense she's not speaking with Brad. Courtney has tried to catch my eye numerous times, but I've been on conference calls. I contemplate slipping some lithium into her frappuccino because I don't have the time to ride her emotional roller coaster; I have sales to close, proposals to draft, and hair to fix.

I look in the mirror again. Sales and Courtney's mental health can wait; my hair takes precedence.

I pick up the phone.

"Good afternoon and thank you for calling the Molto Bene Salon on North Michigan Avenue. How can I help you?" a pleasant voice asks.

"Hi, this is Jen Lancaster. I need to make an appointment with

Rory for highlights. If you have something sooner rather than later, I'd really appreciate it," I say.

"Let's see . . ." As I wait, I hear a keyboard clicking efficiently in the background. "You're in luck! Rory just had a cancellation and can take you at three thirty tomorrow if that works for you," the voice asks. Ding, ding, ding, score! You can never get an appointment on Saturday this late in the week.

"That would be so great. Thanks very much," I gush.

"All right, that's three thirty p.m. tomorrow for full highlights with Rory. Thanks, and we'll see you then, Jenny."

I'm going to let that one go.

· ·

I arrive at the salon early so that I can commit a little commerce in the shops located next to it. Spring has finally sprung and I've got a hankering for some mules. I kill about an hour in an upscale shoe store ogling the newest kicks from BCBG and Via Spiga. I can't decide if I want the strappy black alligator sandals or the glossy brown kitten heels, so I buy both. I tell myself that I will return one pair, but even the crazy homeless guy I saw earlier today wearing a burlap sack and a garbage can lid knows that's a lie.

Laden with packages and a white chocolate mocha, I make my way down the escalator at three twenty-five. I may be late on occasion for other events in my life, but *never* a hair appointment. Having good hair is too important to my mental state, and if it costs me the GNP of Guam, so be it. That's why I work hard.

I was born with the kind of tresses that would frizz on a bet. I had fourteen years of bad hair days until I discovered vent brushes and styling mousse my freshman year of high school. Thank God, I figured it out before class pictures were taken.

In college, I had a great big eighties mane. When I graduated, I decided I needed professional hair, and that meant short. I cut almost sixteen inches off when I started at the insurance company and it's the only time I've ever seen Fletch close to tears. Biggest mistake ever. It took FOREVER to grow it shoulder-length and the next fall when my Brazilian ex-stylist accidentally cut layers in it because he was high on Sudafed, I tried to have him deported.

Prior to this job, I wore my curls bobbed and dyed them black. I made a point to wear nerdy, Italian cat's-eye glasses so I'd blend in when meeting with dot-com chicks.

Now that I have to deal with media people, I'm practically blond and do a full blowout every morning. I like it, but it takes an awful lot of maintenance to look good. I get it cut and colored every month, and every two weeks I do a deep conditioner. And since I'm already at the salon on those days, I indulge in spa services. Although I get a lot of specialty services like wraps, scrubs, and mustache removal[33] my favorite is the simple manicure/pedicure. They work on your hands and feet at the same time while you sit in a vibrating chair. I call it the sorority girl's version of a threesome.

I walk up to the check-in area. Half a dozen anorexic twenty year olds, clad entirely in black, chat and pose behind the chrome-and-frosted-glass desk. I look at them expectantly and smile. I'm a regular here and a legendary tipper, so I expect them to snap to attention. They gaze back at me with their dead-doll eyes and my presence doesn't register. My mistake: I forgot that a lot of wannabe models work the desk on the weekend. I'll need to use small words.

"Hello, how are you? I'm here for a three thirty with Rory. The name is Lancaster." I grin again. A couple of them blink lazily back at me and continue their scintillating conversation about the do-ability of Justin Timberlake. Such pretty faces, such empty heads.

[33]Shut up.

"I'm getting my color done," I say.

No response.

"With Rory," I clarify. I can almost hear the wind rush through their ears.

"At three thirty." Maybe if I break the information down into bits, it will be easier for them to digest.

Nothing.

"My name is Lancaster." I wait. That should do the trick.

It doesn't.

"Hello!" I exclaim while banging on the glass counter with one of my rings.

"Oh, what? OK," finally replies a tall girl with orange bangs and almond-shaped eyes. She's stunning but vapid. She starts to tap at the desktop computer. "Are you checking in?"

"No, I'm here to discuss quantum physics with you. Tell me, what are your thoughts on the Heisenberg uncertainty principle?" I ask.

"Huh?"

"Yes. Yes, I'm checking in."

"What's your name?"

"Lancaster."

"And who are you here to see?" More tapping.

"Rory."

"For what?"

"Full highlights and a base bump."

"At what time?"

"THREE THIRTY." I start to speak in capital letters. Did I not just cover all of this?

"For what again?"

"COLOR. I'M GETTING MY COLOR DONE WITH RORY AT THREE THIRTY."

"What's the name?"

"LANCASTER. THREE THIRTY. RORY. COLOR." I point

at my head for emphasis and fight the urge to swing a shoe box at her. She pecks away at the computer.

"I'm sorry, Miss Lancaster, but I don't see nothing in the computer for you. Do you wanna reschedule?"

"Are you kidding? I just booked this yesterday. Check again! I'm sure it's there." I begin to panic. I cannot spend one more day looking at these platinum streaks and dark chestnut roots.

"Ooooh. I see the problem. Your appointment was *yesterday* at three thirty. You're mistaken. You gotta reschedule."

OK, deep breath, I tell myself. *Let's not go to jail for punching an aspiring model. They won't let you wear cute shoes in jail and you're already someone's girlfriend. Maintain, maintain, maintain.*

"No, *you're* mistaken," I say as calmly as I can, resisting the urge to get all Sean Penn on her. "You see, I didn't call to schedule until after three thirty yesterday. My appointment, FOR COLOR, WITH RORY, was for today at three thirty."

"You sure?" she asks.

"Positive."

She does some more tapping. She swivels the monitor toward me and points to the time with a French-manicured nail tip. "See? We got you down for three thirty yesterday. So you musta got the day wrong. Care to reschedule?"

Good air in, bad air out. Good air in, bad air out. I force my hands to stop making fists and I mentally talk myself down from the bell tower. She can't help it if she grew up eating lead paint chips, right? I force my pulse to slow as I gulp down air. OK. I'm OK. Crisis averted.

I clear my throat and speak in tones so clipped I could cut my own hair. Very slowly, I say, "It. Would. Have. Been. Impossible. For. Me. To. Have. A. Three thirty. Yesterday. Unless I had a time machine. But, unfortunately, I am not a character in an H. G. Wells novel. So, my appointment is at three thirty TODAY."

She cocks her head and begins to peck away again. I wait while she pulls up another screen on the computer. "Nope, sorry. I don't see no appointment for a Wells either."

AARRRGGGHHH! I'm so tired of dealing with idiots with jobs. People are rude and stupid everywhere I go. At the grocery store, it's like pulling teeth to get the cashier to say thank you. It would take an act of God or Congress to keep her from packing my toilet bowl cleaner and bread in the same bag.

Or how about all the buffoons who drive buses in this city? The few times I've ridden the 56 route, the driver acts like he's doing me a favor if he comes to a complete stop when it's time to exit. Yeah, sorry, Manuel, but it's kind of hard for me to tuck and roll in a Calvin Klein cigarette skirt. No wonder I always take cabs!

How are *any* of these people still employed? And you want to talk about witless wonders? What about the brain trusts I encounter every day on sales calls? I don't know how these people get to work every day without bumping their heads, let alone make the kinds of decisions that keep their respective companies in business.

You know what? We need a recession in this country, because that would finally weed out all the subnormal, underdeveloped, stupefied, puerile people in this workforce.

Before I unleash my secret weapon[34] and hurl myself across the desk to throttle Miss Orange Hair for her crimes against me and the English language, Rory appears.

"Rory! Thank God! I'm about to commit a felony."

"Please don't do that—you'd hate jail. They don't provide conditioner."

"The MENSA members you have working here say I don't have an appointment." The handful of clerks bright enough to realize I'm insulting them glower in my direction.

[34]Yelling.

"Honey, you're going to have to start taking your hair a little less seriously."

"Never."

Rory laughs. "Regardless, I have time and I can take you now. It's the weirdest thing—my afternoon is clear because none of my appointments showed up." We walk back to her color station.

"Yeah? Ten bucks says they come in tomorrow."

3

Crash and Burn

CORP.COM.EMAIL

To: SweetMelissa
From: Jen.Lancaster@Corp.Com.biz
Date: July 10, 2001
Subject: No Lunch For You

Yo, Meliss—

Change of plans—can't meet for lunch today. Apparently I'm needed in Cleveland TOMORROW, so I've got to spend this afternoon getting ready. Sorry for canceling on such short notice.

Let's catch up soon,

Jen

****

Jennifer A. Lancaster

Manager, Interactive Products, Midwest

312-555-2790

CORP.COM.EMAIL

To: SweetMelissa
From: Jen.Lancaster@Corp.Com.biz
Date: July 13, 2001
Subject: FYI

Melissa,

Cleveland DOES NOT ROCK.

How does Thursday, July 19 look for dinner? I'm thinking chopped chicken salad and buckets o' margaritas at Banderas.

Si, si?

El Jen

****

Jennifer A. Lancaster
Manager, Interactive Products, Midwest
312-555-2790

"This communication is for discussion purposes only and does not create any obligation to negotiate or enter into a binding agreement with Corporate Communications Conglomerate, Inc."

CORP.COM.EMAIL

To: SweetMelissa
From: Jen.Lancaster@Corp.Com.biz
Date: July 18, 2001
Subject: Mexican Cuisine

Hola,

First the good news . . . tomorrow I'll be having authentic Mexican food.

And now the bad . . . unless you're going to be in Tucson, too, we won't be eating it together. Dreadfully sorry and all that.

Jen

P.S. 'Have I mentioned how excited I am to go to the hottest place on the face of the earth in the middle of the freaking summer?

****
Jennifer A. Lancaster
Manager, Interactive Products, Midwest
312-555-2790

CORP.COM.EMAIL

To: SweetMelissa
From: Jen.Lancaster@Corp.Com.biz
Date: July 31, 2001
Subject: Scratch That

Howdy,

Correction: Tucson is NOT the hottest place on the face of the earth.

Minneapolis, MN is.

It was 100 degrees there yesterday. I'm pretty sure I saw a bird spontaneously combust.

Who knew?

Jen

****

Jennifer A. Lancaster
Manager, Interactive Products, Midwest
312-555-2790

CORP.COM.EMAIL

To: SweetMelissa
From: Jen.Lancaster@Corp.Com.biz
Date: August 13
Subject: This Is Getting OLD

Greetings and salutations,

Since it's fairly obvious we're never going to catch up in person, I may as well brief you via email. What a miserable couple of days I've had. Left for Dallas on Monday and took a long, HOT cab ride to Midway. The AC worked in the front seat, but not in the back. Unfortunately I wasn't sitting in the front seat and driving—a shame really, as my cabbie was busy eating lunch with a fork while talking on the phone.

After a long, HOT wait in the one un-air-conditioned part of the newly rehabbed airport, I boarded the plane and sat there for 1.5 hours—again with no AC—until we took off. At one point, I think I fainted.

So imagine my pleasure at coming back to the Great Midwest Swamp. It's actually worse here, and it was 98 degrees in Dallas, but not humid. I demanded my cab driver last night crank the air conditioning which he did, but he only left the partition open a crack. I sweated like it was my job the whole way home. I guess what I don't understand is WHY THE HELL COULDN'T HE OPEN THE FREAKING PARTITION? Was he afraid of the well-dressed white woman with luggage going home to her upscale neighborhood? And why does no cab driver help me with my suitcases any more?

Did I mention that I worked/traveled for 18 straight hours on Monday, then worked/traveled for 16 hours yesterday, and spent a solid 10 of those hours giving back-to-back presentations? I am so tired I can't even see straight.

Now I have to grab a cab so that I can sweat on a client during a lunch before I head to New York. Which, of course, means we can't meet today YET AGAIN. Want to cry, but more likely will punch someone. Oh, and how are you?

Jen

****

Jennifer A. Lancaster
Manager, Interactive Products, Midwest
312-555-2790

Perhaps my first mistake was taking financial advice from a book titled *Confessions of a Shopaholic.* But when you're desperate to raise sixty-five hundred dollars, you're willing to embrace even the *craziest* of ideas.

Like spending an entire summer sweating your ass off in the back of a cab.

Or living within a budget.

Following in the divine Miss Becky Bloomwood's Louboutin-clad steps, I decided I, too, would *Spend Less Money.*

"A lot of innocent muppets died for this piece," Fletch says, running a skeptical hand over a hairy lime green ottoman in the too-trendy-for-words Gold Coast furniture store. "Tell me again what's wrong with the couch we have now."

"It's icky," I reply.

"That's not what you thought a year ago when you threw a fit in Pottery Barn. If I recall correctly, you claimed your life wasn't worth living if you didn't own the Charleston model. You even threatened to stab yourself Dracula-style with a wooden slat from the back of the futon if I refused you."

"I never said anything of the sort," I say, attempting to look innocent.[35]

He laughs. "You're a terrible liar. Then you were so excited when it arrived, you tried to shove the deliverymen out of the way to carry it up the stairs yourself."

"Their overalls looked dirty, and I didn't want their grubby paws on my clean new upholstery. Besides, I hated that futon more than pleather shoes and acid-washed jeans combined, so I was just trying

---

[35]Lies! Lies, I tell you!

to speed the process of getting it out of the living room and into storage."

"I was glad to be rid of the futon, too," he concedes. "*That's* why we bought the soft, down-filled couch. I still don't get why we're here looking at furniture we *do not need.*"

"Everyone and their brother owns our stupid sofa now. I'm tired of stepping into every apartment in the city and seeing my generic old furniture. It may as well be white with a black bar code and a label reading *Couch*. Where's the originality? Where's the creativity? I don't want people looking at my furniture and thinking, 'Oh, great, another yuppie lemming who ordered off page forty-three.' I want them to exclaim, 'What an exquisite collection! Jen, as always, your taste is second to none.'"

"Who are the 'they' in this scenario?"

"The stylish people we're bound to meet sooner or later."

"But we don't know them?"

"Not yet. And we won't ever if we don't get some trendy new pieces."

Fletch throws his hands in the air, completely resigned. "I certainly can't argue with your logic."

"See? I knew you'd agree." Actually, he's a lot less disgusted with me than he sounds. The way we bicker, people always think we're on the verge of a breakup, but that's totally untrue. We simply communicate better by arguing. We spend so much time fighting tiny battles, e.g., which was the better Darrin on *Bewitched*,[36] that we never seem to have any steam left over for big ones.

We wander around the store for a few minutes until I spot something that takes my breath away.

"Oh, Fletch, look, isn't it dreamy?" I ask, caressing the side of the loveliest couch in the entire world. This magnificent piece of

[36]It was SO Dick Sargent.

craftsmanship is covered in creamy taupe leather and shaped like a twin mattress standing on glossy cherrywood legs. Dotted with tufted buttons, the ends swirl up into delicate rolled espresso-colored suede armrests. I'm not sure if I want to lie on it or lick it.

"You certainly have the eye," says a salesman, appearing out of nowhere. "The MOMA featured this couch in a minimalist design exhibit."

"Fletch! Did you hear that? The MOMA! A MOMA couch would definitely suit my, er, I mean, *our* needs," I gush.

"Do you even know what the MOMA is?" he asks.

"Shut up! Of course, I do," I snap.[37] "Don't you love it? Don't you want to have it *right this minute*?"

"This is the finest piece in our collection. Each one is hand-crafted by a master carpenter in Italy," notes the salesman.

"Fletch! An Italian master carpenter!" I am practically swooning.

"Do you notice what it's missing?" he asks.

"Nothing! It's perfect!" I exclaim.

"Jen, there's no back. This is a *backless* couch. How do you get comfortable on a backless couch?"

"Oh. I think you lie flat on it." I sit down with a thud for a trial run. Ow! For such a pretty piece, it's surprisingly uncomfortable. When I lie down, each tufted button digs into my back. I sit up, and that's not so nice either. . . . It kind of feels like I'm straddling a bucket of golf balls. But so what? It's still exquisite and I must make it mine. "Or, um, we can put it against the wall and not really sit on it. We could just admire it and use it for company. Maybe once in a while I'd pose on it and eat a peeled grape or something? You really wouldn't want to sit on a couch this beautiful *every* day."

[37]It's a museum, right?

"Let me get this straight. . . . You advocate we trade our like-new and incredibly comfortable down sofa for one we can't use to impress people we don't know?"

"Handcrafted!" I bleat, mesmerized by the thought of me supine, sipping a dirty martini and entertaining my haute couture minions.

The salesman chortles at us. "You married couples are all alike. She wants style, he wants substance."

"We're not married," I reply.

"And we never will be if we spend"—Fletch pauses to pick up the price tag—"almost seven thousand dollars!" He clutches his heart in what I *think* is mock terror. Turning to the salesman he says, "Please excuse us for a moment." He waits while the salesman sails away in a really yummy pair of buckskin Kenneth Cole loafers.

"Jen, seriously, no. Listen to me, N-O. No, no, no, no, no. There is no way in hell I'm paying for a couch I'm *not allowed to sit on.* Absolutely not. I'm putting my foot down. Completely out of the question. Get it out of your mind."

"But why not?" I whine.

"Because we could buy a used car for the same price."

I'll admit he's got me there. But what of my minions? No self-respecting minion is going to kneel at the foot of a khaki canvas chain store divan.

"Fine! Then . . . then . . . then . . . I'll buy it myself! I don't need YOUR money!" I say, a bit louder than intended.

"How? You have no room left on your Visa, you destroyed your credit rating with your 'They don't really expect me to pay in full each month' American Express experiment, and you spend all your cash shopping during your lunch break."

"I'll economize. I'll stop taking cabs to work," I pledge.

"Ha! You were the one who said, 'The thing about mass transportation is it transports the masses.' You won't last five seconds on the el, Your Majesty."

"Then I'll ride the bus. It'll be fine. You'll see." As we retreat from the store, I call over my shoulder to the salesman, "Remember us—we WILL be back."

Public transportation doesn't quite work out as planned. To save a thirty-cent transfer, I walk up Michigan Avenue to catch the express bus to Bucktown just past Neiman Marcus. Inevitably I need change, so I end up stepping inside to buy something little. Like a pair of trouser socks.

Or a wee handbag.

Or a five-carat white topaz ring.

Riding the bus has been a bit of a false economy.

I guess it's time for Plan B: *Make More Money*.

. . . .

Courtney sashays up to my desk with a giant smile on her face, waving what looks like an MNOW contract. MNOW is the abbreviation for one of the products I manage. Once I tried to list all the acronyms we use here and I gave up around seventy-six. Alphabet soup has nothing on us.

"Guess what, guess what, guess what!!" she shrieks, doing a small victory dance.

"You sold an MNOW?" I correctly surmise. "Congratulations, Court! Well done." Woo-hoo! That commission is going straight into the couch kitty.

Courtney is the only account executive who moves my line without major hand-holding. In theory, my AEs should sell to clients, and I support the effort by creating marketing tools, training, strategy, and giving the occasional presentation, but it never shakes out that way. The last time Retard-y Arty sold an MNOW, I uncovered the lead, scheduled the appointment, conducted the meeting, did the follow-up, drafted the contract, and closed the deal. Yet he still paraded around the office exclaiming, "I made a sale!"[38]

Courtney hands me the signed agreement with a flourish and says, "Check it out."

I scan the contract for the project details. "Let's see, client is Wake-Hammond . . . nicely done! Once your other clients hear W-H uses the MNOW, they'll want it, too. OK . . . MNOW needs to be live by August first . . . uh-huh, I'll get the technicians on this immediately. . . . They expect to have around one thousand users . . . a little bigger audience than usual, but certainly within our parameters . . . and we'll bill out at $70,000."

I hold the contract up to my eyes and it still looks like it says "$70,000." Whoa, I'm seeing extra zeroes. Aren't I too young to be going farsighted? Am I going to have to get those ugly half-glasses that hang on a gold chain? And start doing needlepoint? And complaining about my bunions and no-account grandchildren who never call their nana? I hold the paper out at arm's length, and although it's blurry, the number doesn't change. Yes, I definitely see "$70,000," which is totally wrong, but thank God, I don't need bifocals.

"Hey, Courtney? You have a typo here. These cost $7,000."

"No, that's right. They have one thousand users, so I took one thousand times the selling price," she explains.

---

[38] Of course you did, sweetie! Now let's see if you can make squirty in the potty like a big boy!

"Does *no one* listen to me when I do product training? We went over pricing two days ago. MNOWs don't have a per-user cost, remember? We charge a flat $7,000."

"Yes, but if they weren't willing to pay $70,000, then they wouldn't have signed the contract," she argues.

It takes me a moment to process what she's saying. "You knew you overcharged them?"

"You said in our training session there's no margin on this product. W-H said they always paid a per-user fee so that's how I billed them. Now at least we're making a reasonable profit."

I quickly multiply my commission. Holy cats, I could buy my couch TOMORROW with a sale like this! Let's see, it would take a couple of months to build it and maybe a few weeks to ship the piece, so I estimate I could be eating peeled grapes from the comfort and elegance of my prize possession by late August! That would give me enough time to make stylish new friends and buy cool new martini glasses and take tango lessons and—oh, wait. Hold the phone.

I can't do this.

I can't willingly bilk a 900 percent profit from a client. It's wrong. God knows I want the commission, but I just can't do it. All of a sudden, I'm a kid again, and my dad is taking bids to build his company's new warehouse in Indiana. He's back from his business trip, disgusted a shady developer offered him a 10 percent kickback on all construction costs. Although he stands to gain about $400K, he won't even consider it. Dreaming of ponies with braided manes and Barbie dream homes with built-in swimming pools, I tell my father he's crazy for not taking the offer. Big Daddy replies, "Jennifer, at the end of the day, all I have is my integrity."

At ten, I didn't understand what he meant.

But now I do. Dammit.

I have to do the right thing even though I REALLY, REALLY don't want to. I sigh deeply and shake my head. "Courtney, we can't."

"Of course, we can—we'll be heroes!"

"Read my lips: No. We. Can't. We're redoing the contract with the correct price."

"But, but," Courtney begins to protest.

"Believe me, W-H is going to be thrilled to spend so much less. If you need to save face to maintain the relationship, tell them we've done away with a per-user cost. Yes, it's a lie, but it's a $63,000 lie in their favor, so it's OK."

"They already said yes! They agreed to the price—they think it's a fair deal!"

"We both know it isn't."

"But . . ."

I blame Courtney's newly amorphous ethics on her relationship with Chad. Back in the Brad-days,[39] she would have never pulled something like this. "Enough with the buts. This is my decision, it's the right thing to do, and I don't care if you don't like it."

"Kathleen already signed off on the deal. She was really pleased about it and congratulated me for thinking outside the box." Courtney is clearly conflicted.

Ugh, *Kathleen* again. Kathleen took over the Chicago office a few months ago when Will was fired. (The dumb ass left his résumé in the copy machine, and someone put it on the conference table the day all the VPs were here.[40]) Although she was from the Chicago office, I didn't know her very well. She worked for a different division of Corp. Com. and went on an extended maternity leave shortly

[39]Yes, she FINALLY ended it last month. Whore.
[40]No, it wasn't me. But given the opportunity, I would have done the same thing.

after I joined the company. A few times last fall I noticed her napping in her office, but I assumed it was a side effect of a difficult pregnancy.

When she came on board a few months back, I was not disappointed. She was smart, creative, and unlike Will, not allergic to success. Finally, the AEs had a proven leader!

Right out of the gate, she was fantastic . . . totally strategic and motivated. Every Monday in our staff meeting, she had the most revolutionary thoughts about driving sales. She was so sharp I regretted privately questioning the company's decision to hire a new mother; she blew every unflattering stereotype out of the water.

Naturally the salad days never last.

Not long into her tenure, she started going out with some of the account executives after work, getting sloppy drunk and pouring her heart out about the intimate details of her marital problems.

And *then* she started grad school.

Our once worthwhile staff meetings became a chance for her to trot out textbook management theories and ridiculous buzzwords. Suddenly, I had to rearrange my plans on a moment's notice because Kathleen needed to discuss "paradigm shifts" and "synergistic methodologies" with us as a group. After having to cancel my third appointment in a week, I finally figured out the problem. Kathleen was using our team to do her homework assignments. Her statistics projects took precedence over sales forecasts, and her unpredictable emotional outbursts put everyone on edge. *Uncomfortable!* Then due to nanny issues, she started arriving late and leaving early.

Now, when I sit down with her, I get the distinct impression she's out to get me. It feels like she's gunning for me. You wouldn't think she'd plot against her top producer; then again, it makes sense because I'm the only one who's figured out how much she's been slacking.

"I'm sure it was an oversight. Kathleen wouldn't want us to rob our clients, right?" That bitch is SO trying to set me up. "Don't worry. I'll take care of it with her. Now give me the old contract so I can shred it while you generate a new one."

I watch as my new couch turns to shards in the shredder, and I want to cry.

Shouldn't doing the right thing feel *good?*

....

Operation *Make More Money* is in full swing! And were it not for my recent Luggage Emergency[41] my couch kitty would be fat indeed due to my genius idea earlier this summer.

Right after the MNOW debacle,[42] I gave my millionth presentation to one of our public relations agency clients. And for the millionth time the twenty-four-year-old PR girls were too hungover to focus on my pitch. Clad entirely in black and accented by silver jewelry, this pack of anorexic ladies sat blank-faced and empty-headed in my meeting, completely oblivious to attempts to engage them in my investor relations presentation.[43]

"So, Meagan, Bethany, Kirsten, Sasha, Lynsey, and Monique,[44] do you all understand how using product X will satisfy your clients' desire to reach the institutional investor?" I asked.

"Oh, Meagan had to dash to the lav," Bethany volunteered cheerfully. "She drank a whole pitcher of frozen sangria by herself at Uncle Julio's last night and she was about to vom." I rolled my eyes in exasperation.

[41]Who can resist a set of fuchsia-and-orange-striped Kate Spade?

[42]Surprise, surprise, Kathleen was pissed.

[43]You think I'm shallow? I'm Maya-freaking-Angelou next to these girls.

[44]PR girls never have normal names like Kim or Amy.

"Ewww, please don't mention sangria or I'll totally get sick, too. Casey and I hit dollar-beer night at Barleycorn's and we totally—" began Lynsey.

"Yes, I'm *totally* sorry to hear that," I interjected. "Like I was saying, product X will—"

"Um, excuse me?" Sasha with the Cleopatra-cut bangs interrupted.

"Yes, Sasha?"

"I just wanted to tell you I love your bracelets."

Like a pack of magpies, these girls were fascinated by small, shiny objects. They probably would have paid more attention to me if I came in flashing bits of my Nanny's sterling tea set.

"*Thank you.* To continue, product X is key when your client needs to get—"

"And your big lapel flower. It's soooo *Sex in the City!*" Kirsten added.

Why did I feel like I was trying to herd a pack of cats?

"Great, thanks. AS I WAS SAYING—"

"I love *Sex in the City*! Carrie Bradshaw is my idol!" squealed Monique, her voice barely overpowering her Eternity perfume.

"Me, too!" chorused the rest of the group, looking at one another under lashes darkened by a variety of Lancôme products.

I hated these girls so very much.[45]

"If we could *please get back on topic*. PR professionals like you have found—"

"I saw you arrive when I was outside smoking. Was that your husband who dropped you off?" Lynsey asked.

"No, he's my boyfriend. In regard to institutional investors—"

Lynsey was undeterred. "He's WAY adorable! He looks just like Ed Norton, only with darker hair!"

---

[45]HATE! HATE! HATE!

"I guess he does a bit." Personally, I always thought he looked more like Ron Livingston in *Swingers*. Something about his sardonic brows, or maybe the way his eyes crinkle when he smiles.

Sasha asked, "Did you meet him here?"

"No, we met in college."

It was all I could do to not stab each of them in the neck with the sharp end of my classic Chanel camellia brooch. I wasn't there to chat about my personal life. I wanted to talk about investor relations! But if I yelled at them, they'd never buy anything from me.

"How?"

"Pardon?"

"How did you meet him?"

Incredulous, I asked, "Let me get this straight—you'd rather hear how I met my boyfriend than how these tools will make you more effective at your jobs? You're more interested in a silly, embarrassing college story from seven years ago than learning how to best serve your clients?"

"Yes!" "Definitely!" "Please!" Since any chance to educate them washed away after the third round at Barleycorn's last night, I decided to humor them in an effort to build the relationship.

"OK, it's 1994 and we both got jobs at a bar and grille on campus. After the grand opening, a group of us went out together for a new employee bonding session. Everyone ended up at my apartment after the bars closed because I had a deck. Fletch, that's his name, and no, he's NOT named after the Chevy Chase movie," I added, anticipating their next question, "made terrible martinis, drank too many of them, threw up in my shower, and finally passed out. The next morning he woke up full of regret and wanted to make it up to me. So I had him put up shelves in my apartment. He took me to dinner that night and we've been together ever since. The end."

"Ooh! That's so ro!" shrilled Bethany.

"Yes, Bethany," I replied, "because *every* romantic fairy tale ends with Prince Charming woofing up blue nacho chips on the princess' floral shower curtain from Target."

Anyway, I knew if I were going to *Make More Money*, I'd have to find a way to convince these ninnies to use my products. But since my audience was always more concerned with my accessories, they hadn't learned how to use them and, hence, didn't buy them.

I came up with a concept to educate them in a less formal setting. I created an after-hours seminar that not only gave a hands-on demonstration but also included an open bar, thus allowing the girls to booze it up while they learned. I figured this situation would neatly simulate their college careers.

I don't know if it was the show-and-tell or the chardonnay, but the seminar worked. Drunken PR monkeys lurched up to me after the program, wobbly on their stilettos, slurring, "Heeeey! Call me Mondayyyy! My client can TOTALLY ussshe thiss sshhtuff! Let'ssh do businesssh!!" To make a long story short, sales rose 35 percent in my product lines in two weeks. The vice president of sales was so impressed she sent me to roll out the program at our offices across the country. (Somehow Kathleen has been less enthusiastic about my success, but WHATEVER. She's just jealous.)

And *that's* why I've spent the summer sweating my ass off in the back of cabs.

"Gosh, I can't decide," I tell Sylvie the Dior girl, while we both scrutinize her summer line of lip glosses scattered all over the counter. Ooh, I just LOVE being at the *real* Saks on Fifth Avenue. New York is the best! We're going to move here the minute I convince Fletch it's a good idea.

Earlier I went to the adorable epicurean shop by Lincoln Center so I could stock up on Big Daddy's favorite lime marmalade. While I was juggling my bags and hailing a cab, a group of tourists asked *me* for directions. They thought *I* was a New Yorker! The best part is I actually knew how to get them to their destination.

But right this second, I'm in a major quandary. I've been working on a project with a big-time magazine and there's a chance I'm going to be on *Good Morning America*. OK, technically they want to interview the magazine's editor, but that's only because the producers haven't met ME yet.[46] That's why I'm having such a tough time choosing the proper lip gloss. Which one would look best on camera? The shimmery peach one is deliciously summery, but the iridescent petal pink one showcases my tan. I'd simply take the clear and be done with it, but it's really thick and my hair sticks to it every time I move my head. I don't want to have to pick my coif out of my mouth in front of Charlie Gibson and the rest of America.

I glance down at my watch and realize I'm twenty minutes late for my lunch date with the magazine woman. Oh, no! I hate when I lose track of time like this; it's a grievous wrong. Being late for a business meeting is practically criminal in my book. I feel awful for making such an important person wait, and I've got to wrap this up right this second. I make an executive decision.

"You know what, Sylvie? I'll take them all."

• •

I'm not back in the office from New York for two minutes when I get a call.

"Jen Lancaster speaking," I answer, lunging over my striped luggage to get to my phone.

---

[46] I am all about being telegenic.

"Jen!ItsRyanandLaurelandwe'reonaconferencecallandohmyGod youwon'tbelievewhathappened!!!" Ryan shrieks into the phone.

"Ryan, you're in full-on drama queen mode. What's the matter? Did the cute clerk at Barneys take you up on your lascivious offer?" I ask. OK, did we *not* just spend the evening drinking appletinis in the Village together last night? Why is he calling me with his panties in a bunch? What could have happened in the last twelve hours? "Or did MAC discontinue your favorite eyeliner?"

"Noooo!" he howls. "It's nothing like that!"

"Then slow down and say that whole sentence again, please," I request.

Laurel breaks in, "Jeeeen, this heah is a seeeerious cawl. Y'all, we ahh 'bout to undahgo a cohprae-muhger." When she's upset, her accent gets superthick. Whatever's happening must be bad, because I can't understand a word she's said.

"A what?"

"A COHPRAE-MUHGER," she repeats.

Now I'm aggravated and ready to kill both messengers. "What the *fuck* are you two babbling about?" I demand.

"A merger! We're about to be merged with our biggest competitor!" Ryan cries.

"My God, you're kidding me. Are you sure?" Please, please, please let them be wrong. Because if they're right, this is AWFUL news. I feel weak in the knees.

"I wish I weren't. The story just crossed the newswires and they're already talking about it on MSNBC. It's official," Ryan sadly confirms.

"Shit, what are you guys going to do?" I ask.

"Ahm goin' to mah husban's haidhuntah latah," Laurel says.

"I'm headed straight to Monster.com to post my résumé," says Ryan as I mentally revise my own CV.

"Laurel, Ryan, thanks for calling me. I've got to go. I need to start working on a contingency plan right now. I say we hope for the best but prepare for the worst."

"Lahkwise," sighs Laurel.

"Take care of yourselves, guys."

"Ditto. Bye, Laurel. Catch you on the flip side, Jen."

My hands are shaking as I hang up the phone. I went through four mergers when I worked for the insurance company, and each resulted in mass layoffs. Fortunately I was never affected, but I won't be so lucky this time. See, our competitors are much better at what my group does because we're new to the marketplace. If we merge with them, there's no way Corp. Com. will keep my team on, no matter how much past success we've had. The bottom line is *they* are the established brand. And ever since the dot-com crash, it's been harder and harder to get hired anywhere in my industry. Too many good people, not enough good jobs. This is bad. This is really bad.

. . . .

I've been working the phone like a telemarketer for the past few weeks trying to miracle up some interest. This is a lot tougher than last time I looked for a job. When I posted my résumé in June of 2000, I got ten calls a day. Now it's like I have the plague.

However, I've managed to score an interview next Tuesday at a big investor relations firm called Birchton & Co. Birchton is one of Courtney's clients and she's been talking me up to them. Yay! Although she doesn't want me to leave the company, she knows I have an expensive apartment to support. Besides, if I get in there, Courtney will count on me to throw a lot of business her way. And since it's a consulting job, the base salary is really high, so I predict I'll be parked on my new couch in no time flat.

Why was I so worried? Everything's going to be fine.

..........,.............................

The people at Birchton & Co. will hire me on the spot when they meet me because my interview outfit is just WAY TOO CUTE. After much deliberation, I decide to wear my stunning black-on-black Jones New York suit jacket with the matching tank dress underneath. I plan to wrap my citrus green leopard-print scarf around my neck for that added touch of pizzazz. And my pièce de résistance, new Kate Spade kicks! They're trimmed with a tiny bit of citrus piping and the whole look says, "Competent, Professional, and Worthy of a Six-Figure Salary."

And, yes, I remembered to shave under my arms this time. Last time I wore this outfit, it was a DISASTER. First of all, it was unseasonably hot. Retard-y Arty wrote down the wrong address and didn't realize it until we were already late and we had to RUN to the Prudential building. Between the dress, coat, each item's silk lining, panty hose, my Nancy Ganz strangulation-city slip,[47] and the client's faulty air conditioner, I baked like a meat loaf. Since I skipped the shave, I couldn't even take the jacket off. I channeled the Albert Brooks scene in *Broadcast News* with perspiration pouring rivers off my head and onto the conference table. I tried to sop it up with my notebook, but no dice. It was humiliating and I've yet to forgive Arthur.

My interview isn't until noon, but I'm so excited I was awake at five thirty this morning. I had coffee on my roof deck and watched the sun rise over the city. As I surveyed the buildings from north to south, I thought about how much I love my skyline: the Hancock Center, the AT&T building, the Merchandise Mart, Aon corporate

---

[47]OK, girdle. Again, shut up.

headquarters, 311 South Wacker, and the city's crown jewel, the Sears Tower. I must know someone on every floor of the Sears Tower. Every time I'm there, I bump into friends, clients, old classmates, etc. It's like Chicago's town square.

Today has been particularly bewitching. We had one of those glorious Indian summer dawns you never forget. Warm but not humid and the light was beautifully muted. Fat bees buzzed around my wave petunias, and the smell of rosemary and basil from my herb garden was intoxicating. I sipped and gazed and it was totally Zen.

I decide to brush up on financial news before my interview, so I head to my home office and switch on CNBC's *Squawk Box*. I love *Squawk Box*! Every morning I learn something useful from their colorful array of analysts. There's Bald Guy, Handlebar-Mustache Guy, Faboo Power Suit Gal, and Silly Accent Guy, plus a bunch of other funny, smart people who make the world of high finance interesting and accessible.

My goal someday is to be the foremost expert in my field and have big-time cutie David Faber interview me. But since I'm cool and totally a show insider from watching religiously, I'll call him by his nickname, the Brain. (Hey, maybe *I* could become one of their regular industry analysts and they'd come up with a clever moniker for me! The Wall Street Diva, perhaps?)

From the CNBC studio, it appears to be a glorious morning in New York, too. Mark Haines, the show's straight man, delivers his broadcast flawlessly, his soothing tones comforting me while I read my e-mail. Retard-y Arty has an asinine question about product features, and instead of looking them up on the shared drive, where I keep them for just such an occasion, he wants ME to find the information. Yeah, pal. I'll get right on it. What else? A couple of the Texan AEs want me to join them for lunch meetings next week. Let's see . . . YES to lunch at NoMi, and an adamant I DON'T THINK SO to lunch at Chili's. Ick . . . who takes a client to *Chili's*? Ryan's e-mail wishes me big, screaming bunches of luck today—oh, isn't he sweet? One of the stupid PR girls needs—

Wait a minute. What just happened?

. . . .

It's been a week and I've barely eaten or slept. All I can do is watch the horrifying images again and again on my television. Even when I close my eyes, I see buildings crumbling and streets filled with debris. I'm devastated. I can't stop thinking about the victims. How many other girls put on their new shoes that morning, excited to go to work in the World Trade Center on such a beautiful fall day? How many moms and dads placed hand-packed lunches they would never eat in Pentagon refrigerators? How many of my favorite *Squawk Box* analysts didn't make it out of their tower offices in time? How many children boarded planes bound for Disneyland, not knowing they'd never see Mickey's parade?

Like most Americans, I'm back at work,[48] but I'm a total zombie. I can't concentrate. Today's my first day in the office, and each time I hear a noise, I'm sure it's a plane headed for my window. I took a Xanax and I'm still shaking like a Chihuahua.

I am NOT here by choice. Kathleen's upset with our recent level of activity, so she called everyone in for a *phone blitz.* Yes, because NOTHING SIGNIFICANT happened last week on 9/11, and our meeting numbers fell because we were all goofing off. I am beyond outraged. People aren't even buried yet, and we're supposed to smile and dial, begging for business while pretending everything is just su-

---

[48]I canceled my interview on 9/11 and have since postponed my job search until I get my wits back.

per! And maybe this initiative would have been more effective a month ago when we were busy *doing her homework?*

That woman is the devil.

• •

It's been two weeks and life feels a tad more normal. Planes are flying again, prime-time television started broadcasting its fall season, and this morning I kind of yelled at a homeless guy for touching my skirt. People are beginning to bitch about how long it takes to get through the building's increased security. However, I didn't complain when armed guards spent five minutes examining the underside of my SUV for bombs. Do whatever it takes, guys. I finally went on a sales call, and it was actually fine. Of course, we spent the first fifteen minutes discussing how trite we felt talking about business, so that made it easier.[49]

I'm at my desk going over '02 business projections when my phone rings. I jump at the sound because my nerves are still on edge. The number on caller ID is unidentifiable. Ugh, these are never happy calls. They're either angry clients or clueless technicians, and I don't care to deal with either right now. I hesitate before retrieving the handset.

"Jen Lancaster speaking."

"Jen, how are you?" a voice lightly tinged with a Southern accent asks.

"I'm doing well, thanks." The voice is familiar but I can't place it.

"Listen, Jen, it's John O'Donnell, and I need to talk to you about something important."

Hmm . . . John O'Donnell is the vice president of the whole Southern sales region. Being part of the Midwest, I'm in no way under

---

[49] Apparently Kathleen is the only one without a soul.

his chain of command, so I have no clue why he's calling me and sounding so cagey.

"Sure, what's up?" I ask cautiously.

"Jen, we had to make a very difficult decision today. There's no easy way to say this, so I'm going to tell you flat out: We've eliminated Laurel's position."

You dirty rat fucks!! Laurel rocked, and you all know it! It's all I can do not to tell him off. But somehow, I manage to stay professional. Through gritted teeth, I say, "I'm really sorry to hear that. Laurel was an integral part of our group and I'll miss her. But I appreciate your telling me this yourself." *No, really, why are you telling me this? Does this mean I'm fired, too, you fat bastard?*

"You're probably wondering why I'm telling you this." *Bingo.* "Well, we can't leave the South without a product manager, so we're promoting you. As of today, you're in charge of the South and the Midwest. You've proved yourself to be a valuable asset to this organization, and we want to do whatever it takes to keep you."

"Well, John, it's gratifying to have my work recognized. Also, I spoke with Ryan yesterday, and I hear he's volunteered to take on some AE's duties where needed. If you need me to do this in Chicago, please let me know. I'll do my part to make sure we stay competitive and successful."

"Jen, I do believe you're the future of this company."

Just as I'm about to say thanks, I sneeze loudly into the phone. "Ahhchoo!"

"You're welcome. Let's touch base next week to discuss your travel schedule. Bye, Jen," he says and hangs up.

"God bless me," I reply, replacing the phone in its cradle.

And even though the speculation makes me feel like a terrible, awful, shallow person at a time like this, I wonder if I'll get a raise.

Because I kind of want that couch again.

· ·

I took my first sick day ever at Corp. Com. yesterday. After I got off the phone with John, I felt congested and achy and decided I needed a day for myself. I'm not superimmune or anything, and I get sick all the time. But I've never had the opportunity to call in and not actually still work.[50]

I rested in the morning and went to see the new John Cusack movie in the afternoon. I mixed Nestle Crunch minis with popcorn and enjoyed my salty-sweet downtime thoroughly until I saw a shot of the New York skyline. They must have reedited the movie before release last week because the towers were gone. So much for the escapist nature of movies.

I tried to get back into Birchton & Co. for another interview just in case, but they're mad at me for canceling on 9/11. Gosh, *I'm sorry.* How rude of me to be more concerned with the potential Armageddon than talking about the best cover art for your clients' annual reports. Oh, well. They're probably jerks, and I'm better off not working there. Besides, from what John said on Monday, my job is totally safe.

It's seven a.m., and as usual, I'm the only one here. After flicking on the lights, I sort through the pile of yesterday's accumulated mail on my chair. I work uninterrupted for the next hour and a half before the next employee arrives. Kathleen flounces in around nine thirty—way to set the example, BOSS. Her face darkens when she sees me and she doesn't return my greeting. *Hey, thanks for asking. I am feeling much better this morning!*

I'm knee-deep in a cost-benefit analysis spreadsheet when Kathleen approaches. "Jen, I need to talk to you."

---

[50]Thank God video phones aren't mainstream yet. I'm famous for taking conference calls in my footie pajamas.

"Sure, just a sec. I've got all this data I'm crunching, so if you don't mind, I'll finish off this column and—"

"That wasn't a request."

Bitch. Someone's off her meds again.

I follow her to her office and watch as she closes the door behind us. I haven't been able to see in here since she installed blinds. She said it was so she could use her breast pump during the day, but I suspect napping. What a mess! There are stacks and stacks of paper piled two feet high around empty filing cabinets, their drawers thrown open. Her desk is littered with textbooks, covered with discarded Starbucks cups, and smeared with nasty coffee rings. And is that a dirty *ashtray* I spy? For God's sake, she's still breast-feeding. When her kid can't do math because she smoked, she'd better not come crying to me.

Without blinking an eye, Kathleen says, "We're letting you go."

"Excuse me?" This is a joke or a prank of some sort. I surreptitiously glance around for a camera.

"We've eliminated your position."

"You're kidding, right? I spoke with O'Donnell two days ago, and he told me I was promoted. He said I was the future of this company."

"We've had a change of plans."

"What do you mean 'a change of plans'? How do I go from getting promoted to fired in forty-eight hours?!?" I am astounded. She's actually serious.

"You aren't fired. You're laid off."

"Thank you. That's a *really* comforting distinction."

"There's no reason to be snotty, especially since we're being so generous with your severance package. Now, if you'll just look here—"

"Whoa, wait a minute. Don't talk to me about my *package*. I want to hear the thought process behind this decision. And I think I have every reason to be snotty, as you so succinctly put it. I work at least sixty hours a week for you with no overtime, and I spend half my weekends in this office. I'm the first one here in the morning and the last to leave."

"Jen, you don't understand the bigger—"

"Excuse me. I'm not finished. Yesterday was my first sick day in the year I've been employed here. Sales in my lines are up one hundred sixty percent and I won the national market leadership award. I created our *entire* marketing platform. My business plan was sent out as required reading to every single sales manager in the company. In light of my accomplishments, I would really appreciate knowing exactly what went awry."

She starts, "Well, since 9/11, we don't really know what's going to happen and—"

I interrupt. "Do NOT blame this decision on terrorists, OK? If anything, the attack will INCREASE demand for my Web-based products because people will travel less. I'm sorry, but that line of reasoning simply does not compute. I demand you level with me. I'm owed that much."

"It was a business decision." She shrugs and fumbles a cigarette out of one of her piles.

"Do you know how many friends I've lost since I started working here because I didn't have time for them? Do you understand what I've given up in my personal life in order to come this far? I've gone above and beyond the line of duty in this job every single day, so I think I'm entitled to more than *'It was a business decision.'*"

"Jen, what can I say? It was a business decision, and I'm sorry."

"Don't tell me you're sorry when you're not. Your patent lack of sincerity makes me sick," I snarl. "But I don't want to leave here without an answer. Please explain where things went sideways for me. Was it because my child care issues kept me from putting in a full forty hours? Or is it that I squandered company resources doing my MBA homework? Or that I had wholly inappropriate conversations about the dissolution of my marriage to my underlings? Oh, no, wait, that was YOU. So, frankly, I don't have a fucking clue why I no longer have a job with Corp. Com. and you still do." I am livid.

Kathleen tries to stare me down, but I see the slight quiver in her chin. With a trembling hand and wavering voice, she gives me a piece of paper. "Now if you'll just sign this form saying you'll make no further claims against the company, I can release your severance check to you."

I read the document. In addition to holding the company harmless, I have to pledge never to speak ill of the organization or else they can take back my check. Fine, whatever. I sign the document because, really? I have no other choice. I push the form back with so much force a cold cup of coffee spills onto one of Kathleen's textbooks. She ignores it and hands me a thin envelope.

I tear it open and examine the enclosed check.

It's made out for one week's salary.

ONE WEEK'S SALARY?

A full year of pushing myself to the limit is worth one week's pay? I missed my niece's birth for one week's pay? I gave up my best friend's wedding for one week's pay? I skipped every major holiday with my family last year for one week's pay? I have to cough up $300 a month to cover up all the gray hair I've gotten from job stress for one week's pay??[51] I imagine I'll be violating the "not speak ill" clause very soon.

"This is bullshit and we both know it," I state in a matter-of-fact voice. "And at some point, Corp. Com. will discover exactly how worthless you are."

Her eyes damp, Kathleen barks, "We're done here. I'll give you a few minutes to clear out your desk, and then I have to escort you off the premises."

---

[51]You cheap bastards!

Silently, I stalk out of her office and return to my cubicle, where I promptly purge every single document I ever wrote from my computer. I created them on my time, and I'll be damned if someone else is going to benefit from *my* intellectual property. Zing! There go all my spreadsheets. Zap! See ya in hell, cross-referenced customer database! Bing! Good-bye, case studies! Poof! Au revoir, award-winning marketing material! And just for good measure, I wipe out my entire hard drive with a trick Fletch taught me. They're going to need computer forensics to retrieve any of my information. For a minute, I consider bringing down the entire network, but I restrain myself.[52]

I toss my cell phone, PDA, and office keys on the desk, and take a last look around. Grabbing my purse, I decide to abandon all my desk tchotchkes. It's not like I care about some stupid Dr. Evil action figure, and I refuse to I be one of those assholes you see all over the streets these days, boo-hooing and carrying a box full of shoes, plants, and kids' pictures.

Right before I'm escorted out, Courtney returns from her morning appointment. She quickly figures out what's happening and a single fat tear rolls down her cheek, cutting a path through her foundation. "How am I going to do my job without you?" she asks.

"You'll have to talk to Kathleen about that," I say. "Call me later."

In the cab on the way home I remind myself things aren't so bad. I'm smart, healthy, and talented, right? I mean, look at all I accomplished in a year with virtually *no* local management support. I kicked ass! I won the national market leadership award! Any company would be lucky to have someone as driven as me. I should be able to land another job in a minute.

You know what? Maybe I'll get an even *better* position, one

[52]Stupid moral compass (and fear of jail).

where I don't have to work with Retard-y Artys and soulless sales managers and stupid PR hacks. I'll have a nice salary and my own private office with a door and girls to get my coffee again. Everything is going to be just fine.

As the cab pulls up to my building, it hits me that I won't be able to buy my couch anytime soon.

And then I start to cry.

4

Shaken, Not Stirred

From the desk of
Miss Jennifer A. Lancaster

....

February 1, 2002

Dear Rush Limbaugh,

Not only have I been a devoted listener for ten years but your program inspired me to major in Political Science. I loved using your arguments against my Marxist professors! (Really, anyone who doesn't like Capitalism has simply never been shoe shopping at Nordstrom.) The point is I rarely disagree with you. However, I heard you clash with the President's intention to extend unemployment benefits.

How come? Do you think every unemployed person is a dirty hippie, too busy supporting Chairman Mao to seek gainful employment? Because it's totally not true.

My company laid me off at the end of September, blaming the attack on America. (Which is BS, by the way. A lot of companies used 9/11 as a convenient excuse to lay off good people without looking like ogres.) Since I've been "on the dole," I've applied for hundreds of jobs, hit dozens of networking events, registered on every single job-search portal, and hounded corporate headhunters to the point of criminal harassment. It's not like I'm sitting around the house smokin' fatties, waiting for the guv'mint to cut me my check.

I'm concerned my benefits will run out before I find work and I'll be forced to do something awful like waitressing. It's difficult for me to rationalize going from advising VPs at Fortune 500 companies to inquiring about their choice of salad dressing, you know? Because of this I believe those extra 13 weeks could really make the difference for my future.

So, please, enlighten me on why you feel this is a bad idea. I'm interested to hear your thoughts.

Many thanks,

Jen Lancaster

P.S. You look fabulous since you lost weight. Hey, why don't you talk about diet tips more often on the show? I bet it would bring in that crucial 18 to 45 female demographic.

I need some time to feel sorry for myself. Flopping down on my four-hundred-thread-count Egyptian cotton, tulip-print bedding, I kick off my Chanel slingbacks and commence moping. While staring at the rough planks of my beamed ceiling, I relive the past year. I try to figure out how I might have prevented this layoff. Could I have worked harder? Did I *really* give the company my all? My eyes trace the intricate brickwork on the wall while I wonder if I could have been more innovative. My ideas were totally fresh and original, right? I glance down at the gleaming baseboards and continue to brood. Did I take advantage of every opportunity? And didn't I always put forth my very best efforts? I scrutinize the pristine slats on the blond wood venetian blinds while I ruminate on my interpersonal interaction. Could I have built stronger relationships with my client base? Or with my team of account executives? Or with Kathleen? Was my attitude ever an issue? Looking deep within my soul in the silence of my cavernous apartment, I come to a realization . . .

. . . I was absolutely faultless. And my termination? Is their loss.

Having neatly absolved myself from any responsibility, I decide to get to work. Fortunately I transferred my customer database from my PDA to my computer a while back, so I've got a huge list of people I can call about job openings. Feeling loads better, I settle into my home office to start dialing.

λ

Unbelievable. Almost every acquaintance who could hire me has met a similar fate. The few who are still employed are waiting for the ax to fall. Apparently it's been a brutal couple of weeks for everyone in my industry. I'm at a loss as to what to do next. I've already posted on all the employment boards, applied for every single open job for which I'm qualified, and registered with scads of recruiters. In addition, the house is spotless, dinner's prepared for the next three days,

I've talked to friends and family, each of my cats has received copious amounts of catnip and chin scratchings, and let's just say any ice cream in the house is but a memory.

I'm left with no other alternative.

It's time to redecorate.

. . . .

I'm outside watering the plants when I hear the scream.

Fletch joined the Army before college, and the experience instilled in him an icy calm and the ability to maintain a cool head in a crisis. Few things rattle him, so when I hear him shriek, it means he's lost a limb. I dash down the stairs from the deck, half expecting to trip over detached bits of my beloved.

"Honey, what happened? Are you OK?" I call.

I find Fletch standing in the bathroom, mouth agape, staring at the naked wall. Uh-oh. I forgot to tell him about the wallpaper. Or, more specifically, that I removed it.

You know I live in the world's coolest pad, right? Unfortunately this doesn't extend to the bathroom. Fletch and I often debate what it reminds us of—I think it looks like a Scranton, Pennsylvania, Howard Johnson's, circa 1982, while Fletch likens it to a drug lord's lair from the *Miami Vice* set.

The bones of the bathroom are fine—white tile floors, attractive brushed chrome fixtures, clean marble counters, etc. . . . and then there's the wallpaper, obviously designed by a borderline psychotic. The only way to replicate it would be to take a roll of shiny, mirrored cream paper and have a chicken step in black paint and scale the wall like Batman. Next, invite a couple of schoolchildren over and encourage them to finger paint fuchsia-and-teal check marks. Finally, smear it all together with some dove gray Nike swooshes . . . and voilà! Welcome to my nightmare.

"I'm giving the bathroom a face-lift," I tell Fletch.

"I can see that," he replies. "What brought you to this decision?"

"Well, I was kind of bored. I decided we needed a change around here, but since you refuse to float me $6500 for the couch, I can't do a *thing* with the living room."

"Give the couch a rest already."

"It's OK. I'm totally over it. Anyway, you know how much I despised the wallpaper. We both hated it. I mean, what kind of hostess suggests her guests visit the bathroom in the bar across the street rather than use the one down the hall?"

"And?"

"And I realized I couldn't stand to look at that awful paper for one more minute. From where I stood in the shower, I saw a loose piece behind the toilet so I gave it a wee tug."

"Continue."

"And, um, nothing really happened. I pulled a little harder. Then I yanked, and finally a huge section came off in my hands. It was incredibly liberating! I got out of the shower, wrapped myself in a towel, and started ripping. A half an hour later, the walls were totally bare."

"Now what?"

"I'm going to sand down the walls and paint them."

He snorts. "*You're* going to paint?"

"Of course! I'm, like, practically an expert. Didn't I tell you in my Alpha Delta Pi days our pledge project was to refurbish the rec room, and I was in charge of painting?"

Gently he reminds me, "Jen, they kicked you out of that sorority."

"Not because of the paint job. I rocked the paint job. They booted me because of the Sigma Nu wine-and-cheese party."

"Do I know this story?"

"Remember I hated my evil pledge master, Stacey?"

"Why, again?"

"She always gave me the dirtiest chores, and I was hazed far worse than anyone else. She talked my pledge sisters out of electing me pledge class president when I SO had it in the bag. Then she assigned me more phone duty than anyone else even though I never mastered the switchboard. When I was supposed to be the chapter's nominee for Grand Prix queen, Stacey decided I couldn't do it because my GPA wasn't high enough, even though I had the most pageant experience and honestly could have won. She constantly singled me out."[53]

"Jen, if I've learned anything about you, it's these things are never one-sided. What did you do to contribute to the situation?" he asks.

"Well . . . I started dating her roommate's ex-boyfriend. Since they hadn't gone out in over a year, I wasn't violating any part of sisterhood code, especially since I met him before I pledged. Stacey and her roommate, Lisa, were just spiteful old hags. Anyway, Stacey always wore the same outfit to our functions—ugly checked cropped pants and a weird sleeveless red cowl-neck sweater that clashed audibly with her frizzy orange hair and freckles. I mean it, she wore it to every single party, and it didn't *even* look good on her.[54] On wine-and-cheese night, I had too much wine and not enough cheese and suddenly writing a check to Stacey for a new set of party clothes seemed like a capital idea."

"Which broke the camel's back."

"Yep. The one thing that really got me is the girls who kicked me out were the same ones laughing so hard at the check. What a bunch of two-faced C-U-Next-Tuesdays. Anyway, I had the last laugh when I pledged Pi Phi, especially because the Alpha Delts eventually lost their charter and were thrown off campus. HA! Served 'em right for not having a sense of humor. Anyway, what was my point?"

---

[53]Do I even need to mention how much cuter I was than her?
[54]Seriously, WAY cuter.

"You had a point?"

"Of course! My point is I'm a really good painter. As soon as you tell me where your belt sander is, I can start smoothing down the walls." Fletch has hidden all his tools from me ever since I broke his Dremel wheel a few years ago. But how could I resist using something that looked like a turbocharged pumice stone on my callused heels?

"I'll get it from storage after dinner," he says.

"Kool and the Gang. Hey, now that you're home, I'm going to take your car to Home Depot to gather paint samples. How do you feel about dark blue?"

"Anything would be better than what he had."

"Agreed. All righty, see you later!" I head toward the door.

"Hey, Jen, wait a sec. I just thought of something. . . . You *did* clear all of this with our landlord first, right?"

Oh, shit.

· ·

Apparently the gentleman in the paint department really *was* trying to help me and not just smell my hair. Perhaps if I'd listened to him and bought the deep-base primer, I wouldn't be on my twenty-seventh layer of Starry, Starry Night blue paint. Every day I put another coat on these godforsaken walls, and I can still see the light bits of the drywall peeking through. Do you have any idea the havoc this has wrought on my manicure? Fortunately yesterday's interview was a waste of time, or I'd really have been embarrassed by the giant splotch on my arm when we shook hands.

Everything started out fine—we laughed about the paint smudge, the office was pleasant, my suit was divine,[55] and the product

---

[55]Powder pink is totally the new black.

seemed OK. Although I wasn't thrilled at the prospect of selling phone book advertising, our landlord has a similar job, and she owns expensive real estate all over the city, so it must be lucrative.

Prior to meeting, we had a lovely phone interview, so I felt at ease as we spoke. Bob, the recruiter, flipped through a laminated chart while thoroughly explaining the position's responsibilities. "If you don't have any more questions about the sales process, I'd like to discuss salary," Bob said.

"Sounds good," I said, smiling. I wowed him, no doubt. This job was mine. Come on . . . big money, big money, no whammies!

"The base salary is $40,000," he said as my smile faded. "But you only receive that amount while you're in the two-week training process."

"And then it goes up," I stated confidently.

"Um, actually, no. The base is still $40,000, but you only get a portion of it after you complete the training course."

"What portion?"

He hesitated before answering, "$16,000."

"So the base is really $16,000."

"No, no, the base is considered $40,000 because that's the figure you'd report on a salary history."

"But you receive $16,000 per year once you're done with training?" I wasn't trying to be argumentative. I honestly didn't understand because surely in America you can't pay an experienced professional with a college degree $16,000. I figured I was missing something.

"Correct."

"Then why wouldn't you say the base is $16,000 but you get extra money during training?"

Bob sat quietly for a moment. I seem to have confused us both. "Listen, this is how we break out salaries around here. No one actually receives their full base salary. It's offset by commission."

"If the number you say the base salary is has no relevance to what employees put in their wallets, why not make them feel really important and tell them their base is $100,000?" I suggested. I noticed Bob's furrowed brow and white lips, so I decided to change the subject. "Um, maybe we should talk about commission."

"Yes, commission," Bob said, visibly relieved to have escaped our logical loop. "The thing about commission is you won't get any until you complete the probationary period."

"Which is how long?"

"Six months. But after six months, your income potential is practically unlimited."

I bit down on my tongue so hard I tasted blood. Yes, the initial salary is pathetic, I thought, but there must be more to the story because my landlord is loaded. They've got to include really fantastic benefits like an unlimited entertainment budget. "How do you handle the cost of taking out clients?"

"We give our account executives a company credit card for entertainment purposes after they complete the six months, but before then, we do not reimburse."

"I see." I was trying really hard to maintain my cool. "All right, so I understand the team meets in the office at eight a.m. and five p.m. daily. Do you provide a parking pass, or do people just turn in receipts?"

"You don't get reimbursed for expenses until you're off probation."

"Which means I'd pay $30 in parking fees on a daily basis." I quickly crunched the numbers in my head. "You realize that's almost $4000 out of pocket, don't you?" Funny how I can never do math unless it directly impacts my pocketbook.[56]

"You—you can write the amount off on your taxes," Bob stuttered.

---

[56]Or helps me prove a point.

"How about medical insurance and 401(k)? Surely not another six-month wait?"

"Unfortunately, yes, because—"

"Bob, exactly what led you to believe I'd buy your bait and switch? What made you think, 'Hey, this girl is a sucker'? Can you please help me understand what prompted you to waste my afternoon for a job which shakes out to approximately $1000 per month, or $250 per week, before taxes and without benefits? Bob, I'd really like to know so that I can remove that section from my résumé."

"As I stated earlier, you have the opportunity to earn big money after the probationary period."

"Unfortunately, I cannot spend the next six months living on a salary *below the national poverty line.* I don't see how anyone could."

"You'd be surprised how many people take this job," snapped Bob.

"Well, I won't be one of them. Thanks for your time, Bob, but if you'll excuse me, I have a bathroom to paint."

I can remember when the phone *used* to ring with fabulous job offers. And now . . . not so much.

Ring, ring, ring . . .

"Mr. Banfield, I'm sure death *is* a growth industry. . . . Uh-huh, I understand. . . . Regardless, I just can't see myself selling funeral services. . . . No, it's not a 'corpse thing.' I feel I lack the emotional capacity to deal with those in mourning. . . . I appreciate your contacting me, and I wish you the best of luck with your search."

Ring, ring, ring . . .

"Jack, I don't think you're hearing me. I guess I need to be more direct. How about this? I'd rather sear my own eyes out with burning hot coals than sell life insurance door to door. . . . No, I'm not willing to consider accidental death and dismemberment insurance, either. . . . OK, then, thanks for calling."

• •

Ring, ring, ring . . .

"Yes, Wally, it does sound like a 'hella good' opportunity, and I'm flattered you thought of me. . . . The problem is, I have no plans to move to Tunica County, Mississippi, in the near future. . . . Um, no, I guess I *wasn't* aware of the thriving casino boat industry down there. . . . No, no, that doesn't sway my decision. . . . Nope, not even if you throw in free passes to the buffet. . . . Aren't you sweet? I hope you keep rollin' sevens, too."

• •

My parents arrived this afternoon because they're flying to Hawaii from O'Hare airport first thing tomorrow morning. We're up on the deck enjoying the setting sun and mild October temperatures.

"I can't believe you guys are flying already," I say.

"Pfft," my mother replies. "I'm not letting a bunch of kooks ruin my trip." Of course. America wasn't hit on 9/11 because of radical Islamo-fascist ideology; we were attacked specifically to mess up my mother's vacation plans. Fortunately, she refuses to let the terrorists win.

"There was a picture of the hotel where we're staying on the cover of the *New York Times* yesterday. On a mass expanse of sand, there was one person in a lawn chair," sighs Big Daddy contentedly. My father hates crowds.

"I really think this trip is a terrible idea. I'm very concerned about the both of you being on a plane," I press.

"Oh, Jennifer, you're being ridiculous. Everything will be fine," my mother says. See what I mean? Things are fine *because she says so.* She won't let those pesky armed National Guardsmen lead her to believe air travel is anything but ducky. Noni, Mom's eccentric Sicilian mother, was exactly the same way. Everything was a statement of fact, regardless of the amount of evidence to the contrary. For example, because Noni hated artificial ingredients, she held a grudge against General Foods. She'd tell us she could make General Foods burn down if she said it three times. Of course, she'd only say it twice—she didn't want to abuse her "special powers"—so we were never able to prove her wrong.[57]

"Anyway, enough about us," she continues. "What's happening with you two? I kept expecting to get a call when you were in Vegas over Labor Day. I had my bags packed in case you decided to elope!"

"Fletch?" I ask.

Glancing at his watch, he replies, "Eighteen minutes."

Frankly I'm shocked she lasted that long.

"Every time you bug us, we postpone the engagement one month. As it stands now, don't expect nuptials till fall 2026."

"Fine, I won't pressure you." Yeah, right. "Anyway, I love what you've done to the bathroom. With your crazy work hours, when did you have time to do it? It looks like you spent day after day sanding and painting."

Fletch starts to answer, but I interrupt. He's been warned not to

---

[57] She also used to make tea from the weeds in her yard and Sunday gravy with goat meat, but that's another story.

talk about my layoff since I've yet to break the news to my parents. But I'm afraid he'll slip up and mention I've got NOTHING but time now. "Last weekend," I say quickly. "It went really fast. The walls were sized, so the paper peeled right off. Then I used a deep-base primer, so I got it done with just a couple of coats."

I covertly place my hand on my nose to see exactly how long it's grown. I hate lying to my parents. But for all her good qualities, my mother tends to obsess, and I don't want her worrying about me when she should be drinking out of hollowed coconuts on deserted beaches.

"Speaking of bathrooms, I'm going to visit yours again right now," she says, placing her soda on the table. She heads down the stairs.

Quickly, I turn to my father, "OK, Dad, here's the deal. I got laid off two weeks ago. Everything's fine, and we have plenty of money. I'm interviewing and expect to land something soon. But I'm not telling Mom until you guys get back."

Big Daddy takes a long, bracing pull of his Johnnie Walker Black on the rocks and considers what I just said. After a pause, he says, "Thank you. Airplanes don't carry the amount of Scotch it would take to drown out the sound of that woman fixated on something. Christ, she's *still* yammering about the time in 1973 that I was supposed to—"

"Excuse me, Big Daddy? Don't you have anything to say about my layoff?" I ask.

"Yes. You have no income. Remember what I used to tell you when you were a little girl? 'A fool and her money soon part.' Current-day translation? Stop pissing away your assets at Bloomingdale's," he replies. Fletch bursts out laughing, and he and my father toast each other with their cut-glass tumblers.

As much as I adore both of them, I'm not thrilled when they get together. Fletch and Dad are so much alike it's almost scary. They've both got dry, sarcastic senses of humor. They both exhibit their military roots by agonizing over their hair length (always too short), their shoes (polished to a liquid sheen), and properly folded maps . . . and just try to pull the single-malt out of either of their kung fu grips. The day Fletch dashes to the bathroom with a fresh cup of coffee and the newest issue of *Consumer Reports*, I am moving into the guest room. And when he begins sporting a belt AND suspenders? It's over.[58]

Last year, when my folks were up for Thanksgiving, Fletch and my father hid away in the den for hours, haggling over which was the very best Internet radio station for jazz. After they left, Fletch said, "I didn't know your dad killed someone."

"He WHAT?" I practically shouted. "You're teasing, right? Because I think if my dad had ENDED SOMEONE'S LIFE, I would know, especially given his propensity to tell the same story over and over. I've heard about his Mexican invasion at least four hundred times."[59]

"Jen, your dad got into hand-to-hand combat when he was stationed in Korea after the war. One night he was on patrol on the border of North and South Korea and got ambushed. It was a shoot-or-be-shot situation. He didn't have much of a choice."

"I swear I had no idea. Was he all shaken up about it?"

"Nope, he was pretty matter-of-fact."

"No surprise there. I can't believe he never used that little nugget of information to his advantage, though. Imagine how much more

---

[58]In my dad's defense, he only started with the double pants-retaining system recently. With his flat butt and heavy wallet, I suspect there may have been an *incident*.

[59]My father was the lead truck in a Marine convoy back in the early fifties. Since he refuses to ask for directions when lost, he accidentally led his entire 1,600 man division to the border of Mexico. The Mexican border guards thought it was the beginning of World War Three.

obedient I might have been had I known. 'You failed your geometry test, Jennifer? Now I have to kill you.' 'You think you're going to a Michael Jackson concert? Over *your* dead body.' 'You stayed out half an hour past curfew? Here's a shovel—start digging your grave.' What a wasted opportunity to scare me straight."

Anyway, seeing Dad and Fletch giggle about me like I'm not even sitting here makes me mad. Just then, my mother appears in the doorway.

"Hey, Mom, did Dad ever tell you about the time he killed a guy?"

. . . .

My severance and vacation pay disappear quickly. The painting project cost way more than anticipated, and my new interviewing outfits did not come cheap.[60]

"Brett and Kim want to meet at the Adobo Grill for margaritas and I don't have any money." I wave Fletch's wallet at him.

"Fool, did you part with all your money already?" Fletch asks.

"I didn't blow it, if that's what you're implying," I say. "I *invested* it in work clothes. People aren't going to hire me dressed in rags, you know. I needed a fresh new look for interviewing, and it's not like I threw away all my old stuff. I donated those huge boxes of last season's clothes to the Salvation Army so I can write the cost off my taxes. And I even remembered to get a receipt this time!"

"Congratulations. You're a true philanthropist."

"Ha, ha. Seriously, I want money for drinks, so toss the salad," I say with an extended palm.

Fletch forks over a wad of bills, but it's not as selfish as it sounds. We're pretty egalitarian around here. When Fletch was out of work

[60]But the darling Cuban-heeled patent leather shoes projected so much authority AND style that I'd have been foolish *not* to buy them.

for three months last year with no severance or unemployment insurance, I paid for everything. And not just rent, utilities, and groceries. I even covered his car note, insurance, and that sticky hair pomade he likes so much. For an entire quarter, I had no new clothes, no dinners in restaurants, or nights out with friends, and I had to trim my bangs myself. I never once complained about the situation, so if I need money for drinks now, it's payback time.

Besides, Fletch says he'd never be making the money he does if I hadn't been his cheerleader, encouraging him to go for jobs he wasn't sure he could get and urging him to demand to be paid what he was worth. Get a couple of Scotches in him and he'll prattle on about how meeting me changed his life for the better (of which I can never hear enough).

Growing up, he was always underestimated and considered a little weird. For example, there was a huge soybean field by where he lived. At six years old, when his contemporaries were totally into Bugs Bunny, Fletch was plagued by the philosophical question of why anyone would want to grow beans you couldn't eat. Instead of appreciating how bright Fletch was, his dad told him he was stupid to ask that kind of question. (And, really, what the hell purpose do soybeans serve anyway?)

"Jen, when are you going to sign up for unemployment?"

"Never," I reply.

"Why?"

"Because I'm not a deadbeat. I'm not about to suck on the government's teat. For crying out loud, I'm a Republican. They'd kick me out of the party if I went on welfare!"

"Go get your last pay stub," he instructs.

I dig around my files until I locate it. "Here you go." I hand him the sheet and perch next to him on the side of his armchair.

"Look at these lines right here. You see these dollar amounts?" I nod. "This is all the money you've had taken out in taxes this year.

Wait, maybe I should back up. You *are* aware that we have a tax system in this country, right?"

"Don't be a jerk." I whack him in the head with my handful of bills.

"OK, then you understand when you pay taxes, your money is distributed to federal and state governments. They use your tax dollars to fund a variety of items such as schools, fire departments, Medicare, Social Security, interest on the national debt, etc."

"Are you about to start singing about how a bill becomes a law?"[61]

"Wasn't planning to."

"Then will you tell me why you're giving me a civics lesson?"

"Because you need it. I'm trying to help you to understand that some of the money from right here"—he draws a circle on the page with his finger—"goes to fund unemployment claims."

"You're saying it's not welfare?"

"Exactly. When you collect unemployment, you're getting back the money YOU paid into the system for just such an occasion. It's like collecting an insurance policy. You'll particularly like this part—your ex-employer also has to pay a portion of your claim."

"Those sorry Corp. Com. bastards could be funding my tequila binge tonight instead of you?"

"Precisely."

This man knows EVERYTHING! I lunge at Fletch and knock him over with the force of my hug. "Can you love me a little less? You're crushing my windpipe," he gasps.

"Nope," I reply, squeezing harder.

$$\lambda$$

---

[61]To this day, I can only recite the preamble to the Constitution because of *Schoolhouse Rock*.

I spend the morning trying on and casting aside outfits in my walk-in closet. What does one wear to the unemployment office? Do I dress up? Shall I carry my briefcase? What's the protocol? To be honest, I don't own a lot of casual clothes. I have really dressy things for work and sleek, fun outfits for going out to chichi bistros, but not a lot of regular, weekendy stuff. I finally settle on a long skirt, sweater set, and triple strand of pearls. A quick glance in my full-length mirror confirms my suspicions. I look like a Stepford wife. Oh, well, it's better to be overdressed than underdressed, right?

I pile on the kitchen counter all the documents I'm supposed to take with me.[62] I don't feel like carrying my heavy pad folio, so I swap out my small Burberry clutch for a large Prada shopper and shove the whole lot inside of it.

I drive to the unemployment office and circle the parking lot for what feels like hours. Judging from the number of other cars trying to find a space, I'm not encouraged about the state of the economy. I finally wedge Fletch's SUV into the spot farthest from the door.

I walk up to the office, push open the glass doors, and am immediately greeted by a couple of friendly gentlemen. They usher me in and offer me coffee. How delightfully civilized! They want to know all about me, and we have a lovely chat about patriotism. This is great; I bet they find a job for me in no time. I heard all kinds of horror stories about filing for unemployment benefits, but everyone must have been exaggerating because these people are *so* helpful. Maybe it's because I look pretty today? No, I bet they're impressed with my bag.[63]

I converse with the kind men in the snazzy matching outfits

---

[62]Having once spent every Saturday for a month at the Illinois DMV trying to get my car registered, I've since learned to be prepared when dealing with bureaucracies.

[63]Quality demands respect.

about my goals and aspirations for a few more minutes. As they natter on about duty, honor, and country, it occurs to me that most government employees don't wear uniforms. Or have such short hair. Or glossy, glossy shoes. OR NEATLY FOLDED MAPS! Suddenly all the flags and pictures of tanks and submarines on the walls make sense . . . I walked into the Armed Forces recruiting center located conveniently *next door* to the unemployment office.

Like the mature adult/consummate professional I strive to be, I shriek and run away.

OK, we'll try this again. This time I walk through the doors marked with an Illinois Department of Employment Security (IDES) logo, where security personnel are already laughing at me, having just witnessed my Great Escape.

"Don't feel like being all you can be today?" a smart-mouthed guard in a shoddy security jacket asks.

"Those doors should really be marked a little more clearly. I practically enlisted, thinking I was signing up for benefits," I reply. "Or maybe that's the plan? Kind of a good idea, if you consider it. Anyway, can you please tell me where I should go to file a new claim, or would you prefer to make more fun of me first?"

The guard's cohort answers, "The few, the proud, and the unemployed need to go over to that station to fill out forms." They continue to snicker and nudge each other.

"Thank you," I say, whipping around only to slam into a short pole supporting canvas dividing ropes. I untangle myself and stomp over to the table to grab the paperwork, the guffaws barely fading from earshot. As if being here wasn't humiliation enough!

I complete reams of forms and wait my turn to bring them to the counter for a clerk's inspection. A bored man with an absurdly high voice glances at my work history and tosses the form back at me.

"You didn't complete this. Fill it out and come back," he says shrilly.

"Right here it says I can attach a résumé instead," I reply, handing my packet back. "See? Here's my résumé."

"Well, it wasn't attached," he hisses. Whoa, pal. Take it down a couple of octaves, will you? You're making the neighborhood dogs howl.

I reach across his desk and grab his stapler, attaching the pages. I give the form back to him. "It is now," I say, while batting my eyelashes prettily at him.

He sucks in his cheeks as he tears through the sheets on the prowl for more mistakes. Finding none, he smashes a stamp down a couple of times and whips another stack of questionnaires at me. "Take these and sit over there with those people until your group is called," he squeaks. Under his breath, he adds, *"Miss Prada."*

"Okey-dokey," I reply. "Best of luck shattering those wineglasses."

I soak in the atmosphere while I wait. Except for security, I've yet to see any of the IDES workers smile. This place is so depressing, no wonder everyone is cranky. The tiled ceilings are low, oppressive, and stained by rusty, leaking water pipes. Everything is industrial gray—the walls, the cubicles, the chairs, the floors, and even the employees' pallor. The few dead rubber tree plants do nothing to increase the ambience. Windows are long and smudged, affording a stunning vista of the rutted parking lot and the Dumpsters behind McDonald's. The blinding afternoon sun is not contained by the bent, filthy venetian blinds and dust motes float in the air. The only sounds are the constant drone of straining printers and a few crying children. It's like a Dilbert cartoon, minus the whimsy.

At one thirty, my group enters a small holding room for a briefing on the intricacies of making a biweekly phone call to the IDES. Ten of us shuffle in, and I take a surreptitious glance at my unemployed brethren. I notice I'm the only one not wearing a flannel shirt and construction boots. The small, angry woman running the meeting stares me up and down, her eyes narrowing when they reach the label of my bag. I get the feeling I made a bad wardrobe choice today. Finally, she snags the forms out of my hand and thumbs through the pages until she gets to my salary history. I assume her grunt is not one of pleasure, and I notice she doesn't request anyone else's paperwork. She rips away one of the sheets before returning the packet to me.

She begins her presentation.

In Spanish.

I raise my hand. "Excuse me, but did I do this wrong? Should I be in another group? I don't speak Spanish."

Small Angry Woman rolls her eyes. "No, but since everyone else here is Hispanic, I thought it would be easier for them to understand the presentation in their own language," she retorts. "But if you need to have it *your* way, fine, I speak English." Nine sets of dark, unhappy eyes glare at me. Oh, come on. It is NOT unreasonable to expect to hear my native tongue in a US government office.

With thinly veiled contempt, Small Angry Woman explains the call-in process. Every two weeks, I'll answer a litany of questions about whether I searched for a job. Apparently I'm only obligated to put in three applications every two weeks.[64] She concludes by spelling out what to do with the final form. I riffle through all my paperwork, and I can't find the sheet she's talking about. When she asks if there are any questions, I raise my hand again. "Um, hi, I don't have that form—" I start to explain.

"Then why are you in here taking up someone else's space? You were supposed to have all your paperwork completed before you came in," she roars.

"As I was saying, I don't have that form *because you tore it out of my packet.*"

---

[64]Are they kidding? I've already applied to enough places to satisfy my six-month requirement.

"No, I most certainly did—"

"Ma'am, it's sitting right in front of you." I point at the form, which is partially obscured by her pile of things, and she turns red.

"You're all done, dismissed," she says aggressively, sliding the document toward me before grabbing her binder and storming out of the room

"Oh, that's OK," I call after her. "Accidents happen. Apology accepted!"

My final hurdle is to sit at the bank of antiquated computers I may have once played Pong on in 1982 and register on the state's job search Web site. Initially, I'm happy to do so. I figured they might have opportunities not listed on places like Monster. But after an hour of encountering nothing but minimum-wage-paying jobs that require a broom and a strong back, I wave the computer area supervisor over to where I'm sitting.

"Hi, I have a question," I say.

"About what?" the supervisor replies.

"Can you tell me, am I inputting the search string correctly? Every time I add my information, I get back janitorial and manufacturing openings."

"What are you askin'?"

"I guess I'm looking for something a bit more challenging."

"Industrial cleaning is very challenging. Ever tried it?"

"Um, no, can't say that I have. I'm looking for a position commensurate with my experience, and I don't see any. Do you know if there's different criteria I should list in order to see the better jobs?"

"You sayin' you're too good to work any of these jobs? What, you too mighty to get your hands dirty? Will it mess up your nail polish?"

"No, it's just that I have a college degree and—"

"Oooh, college degree . . . so you're sayin' you're too smart to take one of these jobs? You askin' for special privileges?"

What the hell is wrong with these people? Why are they all so freaking rude? As far as I know, my only crime is carrying an expensive bag, *which I paid for myself with my old high-paying job.* It's not like my benefits checks will be coming out of their pockets, so there's no reason to be so surly, especially since I don't want to be here any more than they want me to be here.

With my most winning Miss America–style grin, I reply, "What I'm sayin' is I'm completely overqualified for every position I've come across so far. What I'm askin' is, do you have any job listings that don't suck?"

• •

Ring, ring, ring . . .

"Uh-huh . . . uh-huh . . . Let me ask you this: Is there really a demand for encyclopedias these days? According to IBM's advertising department, we have the sum total of human existence at our fingertips through the Internet. Why would anyone need to buy your book? Hello . . . hello?"

• •

Ring, ring, ring . . .

"I'm so excited you called! I've followed your company's stock for years! It's such a solid buy—you really can't go wrong with pharmaceuticals. . . . Sure, I used to visit physicians' offices all the time when I worked for the insurance company. . . . Oh, I see. . . . No, I wasn't aware . . . Um, yes, considering I get my legs waxed because I practically throw up each time I cut them with a razor, I probably *would* have a problem going into the OR to demonstrate your newest cardiac tool on a live patient. . . . OK, then, thanks for your time, and please keep me in mind if you need someone for a noninvasive product."

. . . .

"I'm home," Fletch calls as he brushes the snow off his shoulders, hangs up his coat, and stows his computer bag in the closet.

I'd been so bored with my own company over the past few months that I'd taken to pouncing on him the moment he walked in, assaulting him with verbal diarrhea on the minutiae of my day. But now I'm making a concerted effort to let him unwind for a moment before attacking him with attention. His job isn't going as well as he'd like, so I figure I should try harder to give him a relaxing home life.[65]

Recently, I've focused my energy on e-mailing friends, and it's been nice to reconnect. However, I'm always slightly disappointed when I only receive a few paragraphs in return, especially when I send them huge, multipage missives.

"How are you?" I ask. "You look cold. Do you want some of that hot chocolate you gave me for Valentine's Day?"

"Yes, please. My day was not great. The corporate brass came down on Clark about a couple of his processes, so naturally he went ballistic and spent the rest of the morning spouting off like a lunatic. Then he felt bad and took us out to lunch at his favorite hot dog joint, but once we got there, he yelled at us some more. At what point did screaming until the tendons of your neck stick out become the preferred method of talking to network engineers? I feel like I've been through the wringer."

I'm infuriated every time I hear about his boss, Clark's, unprofessional behavior. It's not that Fletch isn't tough, but every time Clark treats him like his naughty child, it brings up a slew of unpleasant adolescent memories of his abusive father. Frankly, I'm

[65]I'm not always successful, but points for trying, right?

glad the old man is dead, because I'd have an awfully hard time try-ing to be nice to him at family gatherings. Do you know he never once told Fletch he'd done a good job or that he was proud of him, even after the Army sent him to the prep school at West Point be-cause he was one of the best and brightest enlisted men? He scored almost 1400 on his SATs yet his parents still thought he'd do better at a vocational/technical trade school than at a college proper. I've spent years trying to build up the esteem his parents so causally trod upon.

"What's his problem?" I reach in the cabinet and pull out match-ing mugs and begin to heat the milk in a saucepan.

"I'm not sure. It's been much worse lately. I heard one of the women in the office filed a complaint against him because he came on to her at the Christmas party, so that may be the cause."

"Isn't he married?"

"With children."

"He's truly vile, isn't he?" I stir the milk to keep it from scalding.

"You don't know the half of it. But I don't want him ruining my night, too, so tell about your day."

"You won't believe who I heard from," I say.

"Are you going to make me guess?"

"No, I won't torture you. Actually, I heard from a couple of peo-ple. Courtney says hey and she dumped the Chadifornicator. Guess she finally got her head out of her ass, eh? She wants to know if you have any cute friends."

"I don't keep track of which of my friends are cute."

"That's OK. I bet I can think of someone. Anyway, the big news is I talked to Camille. Remember, she was the annoying granola ac-count executive at Corp. Com.? She ran into a guy who's recently launched an organization that does what Corp. Com. does. He's looking for people, and Camille thought of me—she sent me this guy's contact information. His name is Ross and he's the founder.

We chatted this afternoon, and I have an interview with him tomorrow."

"A start-up? I thought you said no start-ups. Too much risk."

I hand Fletch the steaming mug of cocoa, which I've dotted with whipped cream and covered with vanilla sprinkles. He takes a sip and smiles. I can actually see some of the tension slip away from his shoulders. "Yes and no. They *are* a start-up, but they just received millions in venture capital. They're totally funded for the next few years. The founder seems sharp and he thought my experience would be an asset. So we'll see how tomorrow goes."

"Outstanding!" he says and starts to high-five me. I try to slap his palm, and as always, I miss.

"In less exciting news, my money hasn't come yet."

"You're kidding."

For the fourth time in as many months, my unemployment check is missing. Fortunately, it happens so often I'm now a pro at refiling. The first time it didn't show up, I checked my instruction booklet. After reading and rereading, I still couldn't figure out what to do, so I called the IDES. Fifteen minutes and a dozen voice mail menus later, I finally reached a live person. When I explained who I was and what happened, the Small Angry Woman on the other end of the line said, "Oh, yes, *Miss Prada*, I remember YOU."

And right then I knew I was in for a LONG wait.

λ

My first interview with Ross at the start-up goes so well I'm invited for a second interview. The second interview is even better than the first, and I'm asked back a third time. Since Ross and I have already discussed everything under the sun at this point, I assume I'm getting an offer when I show up for my fourth interview.

Silly me.

Instead, I'm brought into a conference room, where I'm to interview with Ross *again* and his special guest . . . gah! It's WILL! I'm pretty sure my jaw hits the table when I see him.

"What are *you* doing here?" I ask before I can stop the words from leaping from my mouth. Backpedaling madly, I clarify, "I mean, how long have you worked here?"

"I started a few weeks ago," Will replies with a smug grin. "When I heard you were coming in today, I asked, um, if I could, you know, sit in on your interview."[66]

Ross allows Will to attempt to rake me over the coals for the better part of an hour. From the incendiary tone of his interview questions, it's obvious be blames me for getting fired, which is totally unfair. Did I try to buy drugs from my employees? Did I completely disregard corporate goals in order to be liked? Did I leave my résumé in a copy machine? No. He was let go due to his own lack of merit.

As we wrap up the interrogation, Ross asks Will to excuse us, and I assume that now's the time to discuss an offer.

Wrong again.

"Jen, although I'm impressed with your credentials, I'm still not one hundred percent sure how actionable your cross-platform skills are." Um, buzzword psychobabble much? What the hell does that mean? I look at him quizzically. He explains, "Before I make a decision, I need an understanding of how you'd approach this job. I want to bring you in one more time. Prepare a business plan containing tangible thirty-, sixty-, and ninety-day goals, as well as ten original marketing concepts. I also want a potential client list. To divide the PR agencies between you and the rest of the sales team, I have to know who has contacts where. On your way out, stop by Mary Ann's

[66]Fan-fucking-tastic.

desk to set up a time for later this week." He thanks me and returns to his office.

OK, this is *ridiculous*. I can't believe the hoops I'm jumping through for this job. The nerve of making me do HOMEWORK for an interview! I never wanted to tell someone to pound sand more in my life. Unfortunately, there are NO jobs out there, and I can't let this opportunity slip through my fingers. I'm incredibly aggravated to have been put in this position, but I desperately need the money. I already cashed in my 401(k)[67] and my savings account has been empty for months. Because of the missing unemployment check, I'm totally broke. I'm supposed to meet up with my family in Marco Island next week, and I had to use the money earmarked for our electric bill to pay for my ticket. I wasn't going to go, but my parents know I'm not busy, and if I told them I didn't have the money to join them, they'd completely wig out.

Looks like I have a business plan to prepare.

· ·

I spend three long days putting together the plan, stopping only for coffee and pep talks with Fletch. I create the mother of all documents—it's a forty-eight-page masterpiece. In it, I start with an industry overview, and then I segue into an analysis of the market-place and competitive landscape. My marketing plan is the meat of the proposal, with almost thirty pages devoted to sales strategy, promotion, and pitch. I wrap up the document with a framework for growth, as I detail a scalable plan encompassing management needs, legal structure, and human resources. Granted, I could have simply presented Ross with the business plan I created at my old job and

[67]Please don't tell Big Daddy.

gave to all the sales managers, but somehow I suspect Will may have already done so.

....

There's no WAY I'm not getting a job with this proposal under my belt! Seriously, I poured my whole self into the document, and it shows.

Will and Ross and a couple of other salespeople sit in rapt attention as I discuss the finer points of countering our competition. When I launch into the marketing portion of my proposal, I notice they all whip out notebooks and begin taking notes.

Like a lot of notes.

Like the kind of notes you'd take at the review session the day before the midterm when you'd skipped most of the classes.

I get a sinking feeling in the pit of my stomach. This isn't right. They should be listening and interacting, not furiously transcribing every word coming out of my mouth. I made a number of copies of my plan, but suddenly I'm hesitant to give them out. I wish I hadn't already distributed my client contact list.

The only reason these people would be more interested in my work than me is if they know they aren't going to hire me. But surely they wouldn't have put me through all these paces without honestly intending to bring me on. No one is that sleazy and unethical, right?

I finish my presentation and am summarily dismissed. No one congratulates me on my brilliant plan, except to complain about not getting a copy. No one takes me aside to discuss salary expectations. No one does anything except attempt to hustle me out of there. When I press him about next steps, all Ross says is "I'll call you to let you know our decision."

You know what? I just took it up the ass, and I didn't even get dinner first.

•••••••••••••••••••••••••••••••

What I've Learned:

1. The next time an interviewer requests a business plan, simply walk out and save yourself three days' effort, or present them with the document and a bill for consulting services. Because either way? They aren't going to hire you.

2. Com Ed does not consider travel to Florida a "medical necessity" and will have no problem cutting off your lights and leaving your boyfriend in the dark for two days while you vacation on Marco Island.

3. Never, *ever* carry a Prada bag to the unemployment office.

5

The Lobby for a Hobby

VOLUNTEERS needed to walk dogs at a no-kill animal shelter located in the Gold Coast. No experience required. Please call 312-555-2439 for more information.

With my hot new tan and super-Marco-Island-sun-streaked highlights, I'm the prettiest unemployed girl on the block. Unfortunately my good looks have gotten me nowhere. I've applied for over eight hundred positions and am still barely getting responses, though I'm not taking it personally because almost everyone I know is out of work.[68] But, still, I'm distressed that my résumé isn't standing

---

[68]My old neighbor Melissa has been laid off four times in the past year and a half. I don't understand how she hasn't yet taken a hostage out of sheer frustration.

out like a shining diamond among all the jagged, ugly rocks. So I need to do something to differentiate myself. But what? Whatever I come up with, I had better do it soon because I desperately need health insurance again.

Last time I needed my allergy medicine, I made Fletch go to the doctor and pretend to itch and sneeze. Worked like a charm. He couldn't fake asthma, though, so I have to pay full price for those meds, and they're so expensive! I'm out of my inhaler because I used the money to buy a twin set. I may be wheezing, but I'm wheezing in fuzzy, ballerina pink cashmere, baby.

I've obsessed about health care ever since I accidentally canceled my discounted medical plan through COBRA. I'd read that Fletch's employer covered domestic partners, so I figured since we lived together, he could add me to his benefits. I thought I was being so clever. Unfortunately, this was one of those almost unimaginable instances where I was completely, utterly wrong.

I marched out into the living room wearing my favorite flannel jammies with the polar bears on them and a snappy new pair of glossy black, square-toed, pilgrim-heeled boots. I danced around a bit but Fletch didn't notice. He was deeply absorbed in one of his myriad business magazines.

"A-hem." I cleared my throat. He didn't even glance in my direction. *Hello! Surely I'm more interesting than your stupid magazine! Pay attention to me, please.* I cleared my throat again and stomped back and forth.

Without looking up, he asked, "Do you need something?"

"Guess what," I said, leaning back on the arm of the couch, waggling my feet in the air.

"What?" he asked, totally engrossed in what he was reading.

"Guess what I got."

He finally peered up from his magazine and looked me up and

down. "I hope it's not new boots. Tell me it's not new boots. I thought we agreed you'd stop wasting your unemployment checks."

"We did agree. So guess how I bought them," I said in a singsong voice.

He slowly blinked at me and ran his hands through his hair in one of his getting-stressed-but-trying-not-to-show-it gestures. "Do I want to know?"

"I used my own money."

"You don't *have* any money."

"Yes, I do! I canceled my COBRA and they refunded my payment. I got the check from them today, I cashed it at the currency exchange, and that's how I bought these! Aren't they divine? Don't you *lurve* them?" I did a quick Riverdance so he could see the beauty of my boots in motion.

"Whoa, wait a minute. You *canceled* your insurance?"

"Yes, I don't have to worry about it anymore."

"I'm suddenly very afraid to ask why."

"Oh, you're being silly. Didn't you run across the article in your little magazine where they talk about all the progressive employers who insure domestic partners? Well, *your* company is one of them, and *I'm* your domestic partner. We've lived together for years. So please remember to sign me up under your plan tomorrow, sweetie."

"Jen," he said, shaking his head in disbelief, "they mean same-sex relationships."

"No, they don't. They can't. That would be discrimination."

"Yes, they do, they can, and it wouldn't."

"What about if we're the opposite sex? That counts, too, right?"

"Nope, it's just a benefit for gay couples. I know because I asked about this months ago, thinking it would save you a few bucks."

"So we get *nothing* for living together, despite the fact that you're currently the breadwinner?"

"I'm afraid not."

"Even though I do all of the laundry?"

"Ha! Even though you do *some* of the laundry."

"But that's not fair. You didn't choose to be straight! It's not your fault you were born that way. I shouldn't be punished for your heterosexuality. Maybe you should get a lawyer." I began to panic because the COBRA people were clear that once I canceled my coverage, I couldn't reinstate.

He smirked. "Yep, society's always keeping the straight man down."

"Don't be a smarty-pants. I'm serious. What if you told them I was a guy? Couldn't you go to the benefits office and, you know, swish around a bit? Tell the HR girl that her shoes are fab-u-licious? I'm sure she'd believe you were gay, especially since I taught you to wax your monobrow. You were very convincing when you lied to get my Claritin."

"A: HR is in Denver," he said, closing the magazine. "And B: it wasn't a lie: I *do* have allergies and *should* be taking Claritin."

"Even better! Seriously, there's no way they'd know I'm not a man. Ooh, you could give them my initials for the membership card, and they'll be none the wiser. J. Lancaster could totally be a dude. Correction, a gay dude."

"No."

"They wouldn't be allowed to pry into your private life. They'd never know. I'm telling you, this plan is foolproof."

"Your plan is anything *but* foolproof. What happens when they get a bill from your ob-gyn? How would I explain that, even though you're a guy, what with us being gay and all, you needed to see a women's doctor?"

Thinking on my feet,[69] I quickly came up with plan B. "OK, this

[69] And glorious new boots.

could still work. You tell them I'm a post-op transsexual. I'll wear that really dark MAC lipstick that makes me look like a drag queen, and they will absolutely believe me."

"You've got to be kidding."

With great solemnity, I told him, "Castration is no joke."

"The answer is still no."

"No, you won't pretend to be gay, or no, you won't claim that I'm a tranny?"

"No to *all* of the above."

I sensed the need to change tactics if I ever wanted to see a doctor again. "OK, Mr. I-Don't-Want-to-Help, what about this? What if I had an asthma attack and DIED because I don't have an inhaler? What would you do then, huh?"

He looked thoughtful while he paused to consider the ramifications of a world without the beauty and magic of my life force. Personally, he'd forever bear the deep wounds of tragic remembrance. On a larger scope, darkness would encompass the earth. Flowers, devastated over the loss of me, their personal sun, would wither on the vine. Trapped in perpetual darkness, owls would shriek all day long and songbirds would cease their singing. Distraught and too racked with grief to carry on, Fletch would lead a shadowy existence, wearing black every day. He'd begin the half-life of a solitary Beat poet, chain smoking in dank and depressing coffee shops on open-mike nights, while he waited for his chance to read maudlin tributes to the eternal sunshine of my soul that—

"I'd bury you with your new boots."

What? He! Oh! No! Arrgh!

I was clearly tasked to come up with the snappiest of all rejoinders for his not properly paying tribute to the possibility of my heartrending demise. But what to say? How could I express the gravity of my displeasure? How could he take the extinguishing of the light that is his darling Jennifer and turn it into a *joke*? I consulted my internal thesaurus and came up with the perfect riposte that would slash him to the bone, leaving his soul in ribbons in order to show him the folly of uttering such casually caustic words.

"Asshat!"

Fletch took off his glasses and rubbed his eyes. "I'm going to go read in the den now."

"Homophobe!"

"I will talk to you when you decide to act like an adult again."

"You suck donkey balls!" I shrieked as he retreated into his office, hands holding his temples like he always does when he feels a migraine coming on.

"You should really see a doctor about that!" I hollered as he gently closed the door behind him.

Anyway, I've yet to come up with a better way to get my asthma medicine, so I need to find a job with good prescription coverage. I put on my thinking boots[70] and brainstorm. I know that I'm a great salesperson, but how can I demonstrate this to hiring managers at good companies? Prior to 9/11, I could walk into office buildings and foot canvass, but with all the new security measures, that's out.

I was good at soliciting business over the phone before, so I should call the VPs of sales directly and market myself. And now I'd be selling a product I really love, so I think this could work. But which companies shall I call? Ooh, I know! I'll start reading the *Wall Street Journal* again. They always report on who's growing, merging, and acquiring, and that way, when I call, I'll have something to talk about. Really, with problem-solving ability like mine, who *wouldn't* hire me?

---

[70]What? Like I'd use a cap and mess up the 'do. I don't *think* so.

Ohmigod, this is going *so well*! I knew I was on the right track with the phone call business. Granted, no one's had an open position yet, but everyone I've spoken to has been very positive, and a lot of them asked me to send a résumé! Joe Thompson, national sales director at the company I've dubbed the Mother Ship,[71] wants me to touch base with him every month. Said he "liked my moxie"[72] and would speak to me in person as soon as he had an opening. Yay, me! And yay, *Wall Street Journal*! Which reminds me, I need to go downstairs and get today's issue.

I head down the four sets of crazy orange catwalks that lead to the bottom of my building's atrium. I spotted my paper down there earlier today when I kissed Fletch good-bye at the door, but now it's gone. Where is it? The atrium is through two sets of locked doors, so it's not like some deadbeat walking by could pinch my paper. One of my neighbors must have grabbed it by accident. Oh, well. I guess I'll just pick one up from the newsstand across the street. No biggie.

· ·

One missing paper? Not a problem. Two missing papers? A bit of an oversight. But FIVE missing papers? That the folks at the *Journal*'s customer service office swear they've delivered?? Fletch says I should check with our building's maintenance department, because it's probably just the cleaning people tidying up. Uh-huh. A likely explanation. But I know with every fiber of my being that one of the motherfuckers in this building is STEALING MY NEWSPA-PER. I am about to get all Sean Penn on these people. How dare they swipe a paper from a penniless unemployed girl? Everyone who

---

[71]Dubbed because I've been waiting for them to call me home for so long.
[72]I won't hold a stupid expression against him if he wants to hire me.

lives here is rich. Our parking lot looks like a BMW dealership. We've got a couple of doctors in residence, and a gaggle of attorneys. And there's that girl in 2C who's an exec officer at the only dot-com to ever turn a profit, with the Mercedes and the boob job, so I know that SHE can afford to buy her own damn paper. I just can't believe the nerve of these people. Taking someone's newspaper! How low is that??

· ·

"This needs to stop NOW," I growl at the customer service rep given the unfortunate task of trying to soothe me.

"Ma'am, again, I am so very sorry for your trouble. We've credited your account, and you won't have to pay for any of your missing papers," says the shaken representative. She's been dealing with me all week. I suspect she drew a short stick somewhere along the line.

"I do not understand why the paperboy can't just leave the paper in front of my door. I will tip him generously, so please help me comprehend the nature of the freaking problem."

"Ma'am, as I've explained, our delivery people have large routes they must cover, and they can't climb four flights of stairs just to give you your paper."

"They can't just throw it up there? The kid in *Better Off Dead* threw hard enough to break John Cusack's garage windows every day, and he was just a little boy. Are you saying that you employ a bunch of girly-armed lazy people who can't toss a paper to save their lives? Huh, is that what you're saying?"

"Ma'am. I-I don't know how to respond to that."

"OK, then answer me this. What would happen if I were to catch my neighbor in the act of pilfering my newspaper? Is that considered burglary? Could I have them arrested?"

She's quiet for a minute, and after a deep breath, she says, "Technically, I think so, but, ma'am, don't you have to live around them? Wouldn't that be kind of awkward after the fact?"

I take a quick mental inventory of the neighbors I know. Would I regret it if I were to alienate any of them? Let's see, the folks in 1A annoy me because they always put up little signs on their door to welcome guests. Sure, it sounds like a nice gesture, except they recycle paper to make said signs, so there's typing on the flip side of the sheet that shows through their glass door. Why can't they use a blank piece of paper? If they were the thieves, I wouldn't miss them OR their stupid signs.

The King of All Bad Taste just moved into 2D. He offends me because he converted his gorgeous urban loft into a faux country club full of brass trumpets and hunter green fabric and plastic ferns. Ugh! He covered the exposed brick with fake walnut paneling, drywalled the timber ceiling, and enclosed the ductwork. Why not paint a pair of leopard-skin Speedos on the David while you're at it, you barbarous philistine? So if he's the culprit? *Pas de problème!*

Mr. and Mrs. We-Like-to-Leave-Our-Trashbags-on-Our-Deck in 3F would be no great loss, as I'm convinced we're going to get raccoons because of their slovenly habits. And Brown-Thumb McKills-Them-All in 4A with the planters full of last summer's dead hibiscus bugs me, too. And don't EVEN get me started out the Too-Much-Sexingtons next door. Their busy bedsprings have forced me to sleep with earplugs. How can ANYONE do it that much? Don't they ever just feel like watching Conan? I am mortified every time I run into them at the mailboxes. Frankly, I'd love it if they were arrested. Maybe I could get one night's sleep without hearing Barry White through our communal bedroom wall. And the added bonus for them is they have a penchant for handcuffs.

"You know what?" I tell the customer service person. "That's an eventuality I'm willing to live with."

....

Lying on my belly in the front hallway, peering out the bottom part of the glass door and angled to see the atrium, I have my binoculars, the cordless phone, and a thermos of coffee handy. I'm on a stakeout and I WILL catch this thief. At daybreak, I snuck downstairs and placed an X on the bag containing my newspaper, and it's been in my sights for the past hour. I'm actually rather uncomfortable since our floors are highly polished oak, and I've had about six cups of coffee already. My bladder is so full that I can feel it pulse with every beat of my heart. How do cops handle stakeouts? Do they, like, go in a Coke can, or do they get to use a bathroom proper? God, I would so love a rest stop right now. MUST QUIT THINKING ABOUT POTTY BREAKS. I can't take my eye off the atrium.

Wait, I think I see something. . . . The guy in 3F has just left his apartment—WHY DON'T YOU PICK UP THAT GOD-DAMNED TRASH BAG—and is headed down the catwalks. I grab the phone while holding the binoculars steady, fingers itching to dial 911. Aha! He's stopping to grab a paper! Thief! Thief! You are so busted, motherfu—Oh, damn. He took the *USA Today*. At least that proves he's a moron. And I still really have to pee. However, I'll ignore the physical discomfort because I'm committed to seeing this through.

Uh-huh, here comes President Jugs out of 2C, bouncing down the stairs. Boing, boing, boing. She just bought an Audi convertible and still has her Mercedes. You'd think with all that extra cash she could afford a bra with decent support. She pauses to take a pull from her travel coffee mug. Oh, *please* don't drink that. Can't stand the idea of more liquid. Am crossing my legs at this point. But I must focus to catch this criminal. And jiggle, jiggle, jiggle, she's headed for my paper and . . . walks right past it. She heads out the door and I see her drive away. So she's innocent. For now.

A few minutes later, I hear the whoosh of water through the exposed ductwork above me, and I can't take it anymore. I dash to the nearest bathroom and the dam breaks. Sweet relief! I wash my hands lightning fast. Wiping my hands on my jammies pants as I hurriedly return to my post, I pick up the spyglasses and . . .

IT'S GONE!

MY PAPER IS GONE!

I missed my thief! I throw open the door and look around, but there's no one in sight. It's gone! And I drank all that coffee for nothing.

Oh, this means *war*.

I spend the rest of the morning pacing, plotting, cursing, and sending Fletch instant messages about the best way to seek revenge.

10:22 a.m. from allaboutjen: I know! I could get some orange paint and pour it all over the paper. Whoever steals it won't notice because the bag the paper comes in is orange. So when they open the paper they'll be covered in paint! Ha, ha! And then I will point and laugh when I see them return home in paint-splattered Mark Shale! Huzzah! Payback is a bitch!

10:26 a.m. from allaboutjen: Or, I could write in big red letters on the back of the paper "I LIKE LITTLE BOYS" so when they go to read the paper on the train, everyone will think they are a perv. Heh.

10:31 a.m. from allaboutjen: Six little words: bag full of Madagascar Hissing Cockroaches. Is that not perfect?? Victory is mine!

I send Fletch a total of forty-six IMs, my schemes getting more and more insidious, until he finally responds.

12:47 p.m. from fletch_at_work: Me=busy. You=fucking lunatic. I beg of you to put this energy to productive use. See a movie, paint the bedroom, find a hobby. But please do something.

Sheesh. He takes things so seriously.

....

I've decided to volunteer since it will get me out of the house and provide me with an excellent opportunity to wear my new boots. I tend to yell at homeless people and kids are annoying and germ-ridden, so I set my sights on working at an animal shelter. I found an opportunity in about five minutes going through the classifieds in the *Chicago Reader*. Wish it were that easy to unearth a paying job! I called the shelter, and the director sounded thrilled to hear from me, and I go to orientation today.

I show up in my luxurious $600 Mongolian lamb-trimmed coat from Bloomingdale's[73] and a flattering pair of wide-legged trousers teamed with my darling boots. I ask at the front desk for the director. She comes out and I introduce myself. "Hi, Katie. I'm Jen Lancaster. A pleasure to meet you." I try to give her my firm but

---

[73]A birthday present to myself. I'm worth it, yes?

friendly power broker shake, but she doesn't accept my proffered hand.

"Is that what you're wearing?" Katie barks by way of greeting.

"Beg pardon?"

"That," she says, gesturing at my ensemble. "Is that what you plan to wear out with the dogs?" Um, *hello*, rude much?

"Why? Is this some kind of, I don't know, *naked* shelter? Because I'll have no part of that."

"Of course not, but your outfit may not be appropriate to work with the animals."

"Why, is it illegal to walk dogs covered in dazzling accoutrements? This is the Gold Coast, for crying out loud. I may see people I know, and I am not going to be out and about dressed like a"—I eye her up and down, noting her cargo pants, work boots, giant watchband, and shapeless, faded sweatshirt . . . *don't say lesbian, don't say lesbian*—"a janitor."

Curt as can be, she snaps, "Fine. Come with me."

I follow her to the room where the rest of the new volunteers have gathered for orientation. Again, I'm the only well-dressed person here. Why is that? Do these freaks enjoy looking like the creatures from the bar scene in *Star Wars*? Regardless, it's charity, so I'm going be on my best behavior and not make fun of the mutants. Maybe I'll even try to be friendly.

Katie passes out a bunch of forms we're to complete. In an effort to be nice, I begin to chat with the earnest-looking male hippie to my right, "Why the heck are there so many waivers? I mean, how dangerous is it to play with kittens and walk dogs?" The hippie shrugs. I continue. "Besides, I have tons of experience with animals. We've had big dogs in my family my whole life. George, our Great Pyrenees, was over one hundred pounds, and so was our Newfoundland, Ted."

"Is that right?" the hippie asks, eyes transfixed on his paper-work.

"Oh, yes, and Nixon? The malamute I adopted in college? He was 130 pounds at his last checkup. Of course, he doesn't live with me anymore. I stashed him at my parents' house shortly after I got him because my landlord was showing my apartment."

"You don't say," he replies.

"Uh-huh, and as it turned out, Nixon was my father's soul mate, and Big Daddy wouldn't give him back at the end of the weekend."

The hippie shushes me before I get to tell him if Nixon could bake a decent pumpkin pie, my dad would leave my mom and marry the dog. Huh. Apparently everyone here is ugly AND socially re-tarded.

"First, you need to know what makes this organization unique. We're a no-kill shelter," Katie says, addressing the group.

"Oh, that's nice," I whisper to the dark-haired girl to my left. She looks all dot-commy with her tattoos and piercings, so I assume she's an out-of-work Web developer. "I'm so glad that I came. And I'll get exercise walking these dogs, too. Don't know about you, but I've widened a bit during my unemployment tenure."

Katie continues. "We take in animals that other shelters want to euthanize. We work with a lot of abused and abandoned dogs."

"What an honorable place this is!" I continue in hushed tones. "I'll be sure to have my boyfriend write a generous donation check." Web-dev girl flashes me a look, which is probably of approval.

"Our specialty is rescuing those used in dogfights. The bulk of the dogs we take in are pit bulls, and your job will be to rehabilitate them."

Pit bulls. *Pit bulls?* Baby-mauling, jaw-locking, people-attacking, dangerous-at-any-speed pit bulls? And ones trained to fight at that? Oh, I don't *think* so.

Just as I'm about to grab my bag and make a dash for the door,

Katie says, "I get a lot of sorority types who come in here and waste my time because they didn't understand what they were getting in to. They think this job is all romping with Lab puppies. I wish they would just LEAVE DURING ORIENTATION"—she glowers in my direction, and then continues—"rather than claim a bunch of volunteer slots and then never show up for them."

Everyone in the room is looking at me like I'm a cigarette butt in their salad bar. Great. Now I've been challenged, I'm obligated to stay. I open my purse and take out my shiny Dior compact. I figure I may as well get a good look at my face one more time before a rabid pit bull tears it off.

Want to know something weird? I'm really good at this volunteer stuff. I've only been here a few weeks and Katie already trusts me with the level two dogs. That's an honor because it usually takes six to eight weeks for the volunteers to progress past the docile, easy-to-manage level one dogs. I worked hard to prove myself because I really like the validation of a job well done, even if I'm not getting paid. Also, it's fun to show up Web-dev girl and Hippie guy, who are still languishing with the easy pups.

Now that I have my choice of dogs to walk, I gravitate toward the pit bulls. I used to believe the media hype that these are inherently bad dogs, but that's not the case at all. They LOVE people and are so eager to please, even the ones whose sweet faces are covered with scars from a hundred dogfights. They aren't evil; they're just misunderstood.

Today I waited to take Florence out last so I could spend extra time with her. She's a beautiful gray pit with a huge smile, sleek cropped ears, and kohl black–rimmed eyes. She's my favorite. I wore my pretty cashmere twin set, and I bought Florence a pink rhinestone studded collar so that we'd both look stylish cruising around the Gold Coast on our walk.

On the street we ran into an old Asian man, who took one look at her giant jaws and powerfully muscled body and said, "Oh! Pit bull! Scary!" as he backed away.

"No, no! She's very sweet! See?" To prove it, I leaned down and gave her a big kiss on her muzzle. He smiled and gave us a polite bow. Of course, she tried to disembowel a Norwich terrier a couple of blocks later, but who could blame her? I hate little rat dogs, too.[74]

When my shift is over and Florence has eaten her own weight in the special treats I brought her from the gourmet doggie bakery, I head up to the office to grab my bag. The room is so packed with pet crates, sacks of dog food, blankets, and toys that I almost don't notice Katie with her head down on the tiny desk.

"Katie, what's the matter?"

"I just agreed to take a couple more dogs, and I don't have room for them. None of the people who usually foster can help me because they all have Easter plans. I've called everyone on the list, and there's no one available. What am I going to do?" Katie asks with tears in her eyes. I'm totally over her initial rudeness. She only gets cranky because she wants to save all the stray dogs, and it's not always possible.

But maybe today it can be.

Before I have a chance to remember my beautiful new hand-woven cream-and-taupe rug, I blurt, "Do you need me to take a couple of them? I mean, just until you have space or they get adopted?"

Katie knocks her chair over in her haste to hug me. I make arrangements to come back later with the car to pick up a shepherd puppy and a tiny pit bull. I'd walked the shepherd earlier that day, and he was so cute! He looked like a bear cub, black everywhere ex-

---

[74]Cosmetics and coordinating wallets, NOT PETS, belong in purses.

cept for tiny patches of white on his chest and bunghole. As I ride home in the cab, I figure it's only for a few days and they're small, so they can't do *too* much damage.

Right?

Cost to clean deeply soiled rugs: $200.

Cost to replace shiny black, stacked-heeled, pilgrim-toed boots: $185.

Cost to fix every single delicious table and chair leg in the house: $490.

Life with two shelter dogs: Fucking priceless.

. . . .

The puppies, whom we call Bull and Bear since they are being housebroken on the *Wall Street Journal*, are equal parts endearing and destructive. We've become attached to them over the past few weeks. The five to eight minutes a day when they aren't running around biting each other like escaped mental patients are a lot of fun, though I could do without all the trips up and down the stairs. Since they're small, they have to make potty anywhere from eight to ten times a day.[75]

Bull, the shepherd, is really smart! I've already taught him to sit, stay, and shake paws. I refuse to believe that he knew those things when he came into my life and prefer to credit my training prowess.

Bear, the ten-week-old pit, is an entirely different story. All she does is pee, whine, and beg for snacks. I guess since she was found

[75]The upside is my butt is an inch higher from all the climbing.

emaciated, it makes sense that she's perpetually looking for food. Also? She is not a pretty dog. Her ears point in different directions, she's practically hairless, and she has an underbite. You know how most puppies are woolly and cute with tiny heads and giant floppy feet? Not Bear. She looks exactly like a regular pit bull, only miniature. And kind of ugly.

Behavior-wise, I admit that they're improving. We had a small setback last Tuesday, when I ran down to Starbucks for a latte. I left them out of their crates for the first time, thinking they couldn't get into much trouble in five minutes. Wrong again! They tore apart two forty-pound bags of manure-laced potting soil I'd bought and hadn't yet carried up to the deck. When I walked in, I stood there wondering when we covered the hardwood with a black rug until it registered. Two hours, one shovel, three tearful calls to Fletch, and a double helping of Xanax later, my world was back in order.

Fletch is a much bigger fan of the dogs than I am. He flies out of bed in the morning so they can roughhouse before work. Sometimes he sneaks home midday to hang out with them, and he takes them to the doggie park every evening. Twice I've caught him singing to them. His vile parents never let him have a dog, so he's loved this experience.

But the point is moot because we're taking them to an adoption event today. Cute as they are, I'm sure someone will want them, and our life (and my normally spotless home) will be back to normal.

We load the dogs in the car, packing up the various toys and accessories we've purchased for them over the past few weeks. Owning a dog is slightly less expensive than being addicted to crack. I feel a twinge of regret taking them down the stairs one last time, but I know that when I'm back to work, I won't have time for them.

The adoption event is in the far suburbs, so naturally we get stuck in heavy traffic trying to escape the city.

"Do you think there's been an accident?" I ask Fletch, scanning the rows and rows of cars stopped before us.

"This may just be typical Saturday traffic. Are you anxious to get there?" he asks.

"No." I'm quiet for a while. Fletch, unaccustomed to so little noise coming from my word hole, asks me what's the matter.

"I don't know. I've been looking forward to these guys leaving, but now that it's reality, I feel kind of guilty."

"Or maybe sad?" Fletch asks.

"No."

"You sure?"

"OK, possibly," I concede.

"Yeah, me, too."

"The only thing is, it's a shame they probably won't be adopted out to the same family. Katie said when they were found together, they cried like babies when she tried to put them in separate cages. Do you suppose they'll miss each other?"

"I don't really want to think about it. Kind of chokes me up."

We drive in silence a little farther.

I say, "Adopting these dogs ourselves is out of the question. I mean, they're so expensive and destructive. And time consuming. What would happen when I got a job?"

"That's what dog-walking services are for."

"Well, we'd probably have to replace the carpet in the bedroom and den if we kept them."

"We could always buy a carpet steamer. Or get a housekeeper."

"But that damn pit bull . . . we'd have to find a way to stop her from whining."

"All you have to do is pick her up."

"You aren't worried she'd try to kill the cats?"

"She loves the cats. Especially Tucker. Haven't you seen them stretched out on the couch together?"

"Still, keeping them is completely insane."

"Completely."

I turn around to look at the dogs in the backseat. They are spooned together in a tangle of paws and tails, sleeping peacefully. I feel something inside me break loose and suddenly my heart feels all hurty at the notion of them not being in my life. We get to the exit we're supposed to take to get off the expressway, and I turn to Fletch.

"Gimme your phone, please."

"What for?" He smiles. He knows, but he's going to make me say it anyway.

I take a deep breath. "I need to call Katie and tell her we're keeping the dogs."

....

The good news? The Sexingtons are gone! The bad news? We have the kind of stylish and cool neighbors I've been dying to meet. Why is that bad news? Because, in an ironic twist, *they* now hate *me*.

Last week I noticed a pronounced lack of *Can't Get Enough of Your Love, Baby* lately coming through the wall, and I figured the Sexingtons were on vacation. Instead, an interesting new couple had moved in next door and have managed to exist without causing me any mental or aesthetic distress. Already having scored points for being clean, quiet, and pleasant, they are carefully tending the beginnings of a lovely rooftop urban oasis. Better yet, they bought their patio furniture at the same place as us, so our decks are simpatico! We could be in a Crate & Barrel ad together.

Intrigued by their obvious good taste, yesterday, I began chatting with them over our shared deck railing. I discovered that we have many common interests, such as a passion for animal rescue and a love of Coen brothers' movies. Rarely do I meet people so articulate and erudite, so I put aside my usual neighbor-hating stance, and on a mad impulse, I invited them over to watch *The Big Lebowski* with us. Keeping in theme with the movie, we decided to serve White Russians.

I zipped around the place, making sure everything was perfect for their arrival. The floors were waxed, the couches sucked free of pet hair, the toilet was so clean I could use it to serve punch, and the whole place was delectably fragrant, thanks to my special mélange of tulip, clean cotton, and lilac Yankee Candles. Fletch set up the bar and somehow scraped together four matching rocks glasses. They sparkled and twinkled in the candlelight, ready to be filled with our evening's libations.

We took great pains at getting ourselves ready for the night, too. Fletch's khakis had a knifelike crease down the front, and he sported a jaunty Joseph Abboud shirt. I chose a pair of linen Capri overalls and paired them with a nautical-striped, summer-weight Ralph Lauren turtleneck and Joan & David loafers. The look said, "When not in the courtroom, I enjoy a day of yachting." Perfection! I even managed to arrange my hair in a straightened pageboy, with just the right amount of body. (My trademark pearls completed the look, of course.)

The dogs, renamed Maisy and Loki because *Bull* and *Bear* didn't flow properly, sensed the night was important and fell fast asleep in their crates. I didn't trust the cats not to lick their genitals openly, so I gave them extra rations of catnip; it seemed to do the trick.

Lisette and Jake rang our doorbell bearing those mouthwatering little shell-shaped Belgian chocolates and an impressive bottle of wine. I told you they had class! Jake shook Fletch's hand and kissed my cheek, and Lisette complimented me on our decor. I knew that this was to be the kind of mature, urbane evening we'd hoped to spend ever since we moved to Bucktown.

Fletch chilled the wine and expertly mixed the cocktails. We chatted for a bit, and our conversation was that same snappy repartee generally found in Woody Allen movies or the *New Yorker*. I, in particular, was witty and debonair, and I could already envision the fashionable soirees we would throw ensemble with our new best friends.[76]

We settled in to watch the movie, and Fletch served the first round of White Russians. I adore White Russians because they dare to combine my favorite ingredients: sugar, fat, caffeine, and alcohol. I do so love empty carbohydrates. Anyway, I slugged my first drink down a trifle quickly, but I couldn't help it. It was creamily delicious, and I was a touch nervous. Caring whether someone likes me is definitely new territory.

Fletch obliged to make me another, and I chugged it down as well. Ah, the velvety-smooth coffee mellowness . . . And, my goodness! The second one disappeared before Jeff Bridges' rug was stolen! But I figured they were White Russians—how strong could they be? I mean, it's just a dash of Kahlua and mostly cream and ice—so, yes, please, sweetie, I would have another. Mmm, that's the stuff. . . .

After I downed my fourth, I began to experience profound thoughts. Naturally, I had to immediately and loudly share these trenchant ideas with the group. For example, Fletch and I don't want children, so I suddenly decided it would be good to announce that I was going to have Fletch "fixed" and he should "get me a steak knife. I can do it right now!"

I noticed that the room had grown quite warm, so after declaring I was "sweatin' like a whore on dollar day" I proceeded to the bedroom and stripped off my turtleneck, although I left on my Capri overalls and bra. I looked at myself in the mirror and decided I was

[76]In this particular fantasy, we're sitting on my dream couch.

almost a dead-ringer for one of the cute girls in Bananarama's "Cruel Summer" video. But there was something missing. . . .

I remembered the long clip-on ponytail, which I had been so pleased to find the month before, as it had been an ideal match for my highlights and hair texture. I could simply clip this to my existing 'do, and the long tresses would cover up any part of my bra peeking through my overalls. But instead of making my own small ponytail and then tucking it inside the fake one, I fastened it to the top of my head so that it flowed over my existing hair, creating some sort of long, perverse mullet or a hairy dorsal fin.

"Oh, yes," I said to my reflection, "this is the Look to Impress." And the Queen of Entertaining went out to address her minions.

I made my grand reentrance to what I thought was applause, but in the harsh light of day now realize was laughter. I basked in my company's adoration and slammed another White Russian. At this point, the room, which had grown warmer despite my abbreviated outfit, became a virtual oven, and worse yet, it was spinning. I politely excused myself and headed to the bathroom, where I filled up my squeaky-clean commode approximately fourteen times.

I woke up shivering on cold tile floors the next morning at five a.m., completely disheveled in my stained and tatty overalls. For a moment, I thought my vision had magically been restored to 20/20, but then realized I'd passed out in my contact lenses. I extricated the fake ponytail from my nest of hair, washed my face, brushed my teeth, and crawled off to bed.

I wake again later in the day. I don't know what time it is, but I do know that Fletch is poking me with a wooden spoon.

"Why are you using a kitchen utensil to wake me up?" I ask.

"Because you're too ripe for me to touch with my bare skin," he replies.

"I feel like death," I say. "My hair hurts. My cuticles are dizzy.

My pores are nauseous. I sprained my spleen. Every inch of me is in distress right now."

He snickers. "That's nothing compared to the smell."

"How come you didn't put me in bed after I passed out?"

"I tried, but you wouldn't budge. When you woke up, you wouldn't stop jabbering about your minions, so I left you there."

"Fletch, I can't figure out why I had such a bad reaction to those stupid White Russians. Yeah, they went down a little fast, but don't you remember how I could knock them back in college? I could drink fraternity guys under the table, and I was the only twenty-one-year-old girl at Harry's Bar who properly appreciated Johnnie Walker Black Scotch. So why on earth did a little Kahlua and cream give me such a kick in the ass?"

"Because they were *White Russians*, Jen. They're Kahlua, milk, and a double shot of vodka."

"So how much liquor is that?" I am too hungover to do math.

"About nineteen ounces."

"Sweet Jesus."

"Yeah."

"Do you think Lisette and Jake noticed?"

"Um, Jen, I don't know how to tell you this, but they probably aren't going to come over again. Ever."

"Shit."

"I do have some good news for you, though."

Hopefully, I suggest, "Scientists have discovered a cure for a coffee-liqueur hangover?"

"Better. I found out what's been happening to your newspapers."

I sit up so fast I get vertigo. "Who was it? Was it President Jugs? Or the Trashmores? Tell me!!"

Trying to keep a straight face, he says, "Well, I ran into the main-

tenance guy this morning when I was out with the dogs." Unsuccessful, he shakes and sputters with suppressed laughter. "And he
told me that in an effort to keep the atrium clean, he tosses out any
leftover newspapers at nine a.m."

I want to die. Or kill.

6

Who Says Romance Is Dead?

```
To: SweetMelissa
From: jen_lancaster@hotmail.com
Date: August 27, 2002
Subject: Goin' to the Chapel

Melissa,

For your amusement, here's a list
of people I have yelled at in the
past 24 hours.

1)  Fletch

2)  The idiot at Walsh Park who
thought it was a good idea to bring
her toddler in the gated dog run
and then got mad when dogs (OK,
```

Maisy) jumped on the child. IT'S A DOGGIE PARK—
WHAT THE FUCK DO YOU EXPECT THE DOGS TO DO? PLAY
GIN RUMMY?

3) Fletch

4) The Mandalay Bay reservations people. They
tried to make me believe the Honeymoon Suites
would only be available on a one-off basis, and
we'd have to swap rooms every day, and was that
all right? (BTW, if you repeat, "Not acceptable;
find a way to make it happen" enough times, you
will get what you want.)

5) Fletch

6) Our landlord. I do not care if a central
air-conditioning unit is really expensive to
replace. We pay thousands of dollars a month in
rent precisely so we DON'T have to worry about
replacement costs. Again, our apartment is 89
degrees so FIND A WAY TO MAKE IT HAPPEN.

7) My mother. I am NOT driving out to your
hotel by O'Hare the day before we leave for the
wedding simply so you can see/criticize my
dress because I am busy GETTING READY TO LEAVE
FOR MY WEDDING.

8) Fletch

```
9) The vet. Did I not pay you HANDFULS OF $100
BILLS to get all the dogs' medical needs
addressed, only to find you forgot to give Maisy
the Kennel Cough shot and Chicago Club Canine
initially wouldn't board her without it?


Anyway, see you soon, provided I don't wind up in
jail first.

Jen
```

"Maisy, we're fucked."

Always the optimist, Maisy responds to the sound of my voice with a full-on body wag, shaking her spotted backside so hard that she falls over. Undaunted, she rights herself and nibbles my toes with a vengeance. Ugh. I don't know how she can stand to look at them, let alone lick them. My disastrous attempt at a home pedicure left me with two oozing ingrown nails and, until they heal, a slight limp. Now on top of being unemployed, I'm a gimp, too. Fabulous.

"Maisy, I'm serious. We are in deep financial shit here. How are we going to fix this?"

Maisy's idea is to lick my deeply gashed knees. Ahh, the joys of shaving. When I tried waxing them myself—following my esthetician Petra's motions exactly, mind you—the pain was unbearable. I wanted to slap myself for hurting me, and I yanked up more flesh than hair. The wax she uses at Molto Bene must be different from the el cheapo brand I bought at the drugstore. Raising dogs is way more expensive than we'd anticipated, and we've already blown a couple of grand just on vet bills and hundreds more on supplies. So I've been forced to give up all nonessential spa services. I'm down to professional cut and color only. When I see everyone else at Bene walking around in robes and pedicure flip-flops between treatments, I feel an actual ache in my chest.[77]

We've been in a financial pinch ever since the Justice Department launched an investigation into Fletch's employer's accounting practices. His five-figure monthly commissions have shriveled down to nothing over the past couple of months. Apparently, nobody wants to do business with the organization they see testifying on C-SPAN every day. Go figure. He says if our financial situation doesn't change before my unemployment checks run out, we might not be able to keep our apartment. When he told me that, I ran to the bedroom and pulled the covers over my head. The thought of living anywhere else chills me to the bone. The very idea of moving to some tawdry little two-flat out in the unfashionable suburbs makes me want to drink bleach.

I HAVE to stay here. I simply have to. To be honest, too much of my identity comes from possessing this space. As my job used to define me, living here's all I have left. This apartment makes it OK that I can't buy Prada's newest anymore. I can be content going on lousy interviews and begging for positions that pay half of what I used to earn as long as I know at the end of the day my glorious penthouse awaits. The minute I climb into my Jacuzzi tub, all the day's unpleasantness is rinsed down the drain. When I step onto my deck and survey the city, I feel like anything is possible. This apartment keeps me centered; it keeps me sane. Without this place, I'm just another nobody from Indiana with a worthless state college degree.

Before I was laid off, we talked about buying our apartment. Now it's possible we won't even be able to live out our lease. It boggles my mind but, like Scarlett O'Hara says, I'll think about that tomorrow when I can stand it.

---

[77]I even envied the dogs last week when the vet trimmed their dew claws.

Instead, I'll wallow in depression because today is Cinco de Mayo, and I'm stuck here in Illinois. It's the first time in years that I haven't spent this weekend recharging my batteries in Las Vegas, gaming, relaxing, and jump-starting my summer tan. How can I carry off the citrus green color I love so much if I'm not deeply bronzed? Self-tanner just makes me look like an Oompa Loompa. Sure, I've caught a few rays this spring while outside with the dogs, but it's not the same. I look in the mirror and think, *Hi, Casper, it's nice to see you.* Had I the opportunity to lounge poolside in Vegas, I'd be positively *homeless* tan by now. Sadly, Fletch curtailed my travel plans, reminding me of the Marco Island/Com Ed debacle.

Everything would be resolved if I could just land a decent job. However, I'm finding it almost impossible to get an outside sales position that doesn't require owning a car. The coolio travel management company was all set to make me an offer until I told them I didn't have wheels. At my Corp. Com. and Midwest IR Co., my meetings entailed plane tickets, and the few that didn't were a cab ride away. Before that, I had a company car, so I haven't needed my own vehicle in almost five years.

Obviously buying a new car is out of the question, given our recent financial straits. I'd previously planned to purchase my parents' Cadillac. When the Caddy was brand-new, my dad loved it so much that he'd contemplated having it buried next to him in the family plot. "After all," he'd say, "your mother is nice, but Bavarian engineering like this only comes around once in a lifetime." However, he finally agreed to sell it to me after Mom started driving it. She quickly turned his pristine baby into a Bavarian garbage barge, its backseat brimming with leaking bags of potting soil, gas station cappuccino cups, dog fur, shoes, umbrellas, and therapy journals.[78]

I loved the Caddy from the minute I settled into the creamy

---

[78]Despite her tacit denial, Dad and I both know the sabotage was deliberate.

French vanilla leather interior and cooed over the golden glow of its vanity mirrors. When I took it on the open road, I found myself— Little Miss Safety First—flying along at ninety miles per hour, windows ajar while Courtney Love wailed on about skies made of amethyst. When I saw my reflection in a shiny-sided passing truck, I realized that I looked as thin, rich, and cute as I felt. The Caddy isn't a car; it's a magic carpet!

I imagined how cool I'd be, casually toying with my key ring when approaching the checkout counter at the grocery store. The other plebes would see the Cadillac logo and know they were in the Presence of Greatness. Naturally they'd insist I go to the head of the line, where I belonged. Just thinking about its emerald green paint job, heated adjustable seats, and twelve-disk changer makes me weak in the scabby knees. I mourn for the car that I can no longer buy.

"Maisy, this sucks. I have no Cadillac, no esthetician services, no Vegas trip, no tan, and no damn job. My life is a country music song." I exhale loudly. Maisy snaps at the stream of air I expel. "If something doesn't change soon, we're going to have to move in to a cardboard box."

The prospect of fresh air and outdoor living sends Maisy into peals of delight, and she wriggles, writhes, and nips at my callused heels. Why the hell is this dog so happy all the time? And hopeful? She's grinning one of those big-assed pit bull smiles, complete with a curl at the end of her tongue. Temporarily licked out, she's panting contentedly. Does she not understand that our situation is bleak? We need money and a car, and no one's just going to give those things to us.

Or . . . or . . . would they?

I'm struck by an epiphany that takes me a minute to wrap my mind around, what with it being so brilliant and all.

OH, MY GOD, I AM A GENIUS!

I know how to fix *everything*!

I will GET MARRIED!!

People always receive lots of cash and prizes at weddings, right? Foldable wedding presents would definitely get us out of debt, and maybe we'd even get enough money to buy a car. No, better yet, if we only did a small wedding, my parents might *give* us the Caddy in lieu of a big shindig. A huge ballroom full of well-wishers *would* be fun, but it's not necessary, especially since I'm no longer obligated to invite business associates. Intimate could still be cool, right? And if abandoning the idea of lobster tails at the Drake means I'd have the tools to get a proper job, then selfish trumps shellfish!

Wait, I'm having *another* brainstorm! Call the *Guinness Book* folks because I may just be the smartest person alive! We could have the wedding in LAS VEGAS! Since marriage would mean the culmination of her lifelong dream, I'm sure Mom would spring for all the spa services I'd need to prep for the wedding. And, ooh . . . a honeymoon in Vegas sounds just dandy!

But when? My beleaguered pores can't wait much longer for a facial, so I think we should do it soon.[79] More guests—and their gifts—would show up if we did it on a three-day weekend. Memorial Day is too soon, so scratch that. Hmm, if we got married over Labor Day weekend, I'd have the whole summer to pull a wedding together. People have awesome weddings there on the spur of the moment, and with four months' lead time, it could be magnificent! And not cheesy! *This is the best idea EVER!*

A terrible thought derails my happy train. What about my cherished and deserved princess-cut Tiffany bauble? I look forlornly at my self-manicured, naked left finger. There's no way Fletch could buy my beloved multicarat ring before the end of the summer with our present rent burden. We're barely scraping by now. Could I live without it? I fantasize about jewelry the way other girls do about Brad Pitt. Forget chiseled abs and a square jaw. It takes platinum and

---

[79]Honestly? I'd sell my unexfoliated soul for a salt glow right about now.

baguettes to make me swoon. I wouldn't be ringless, though. I do have the small diamond from Nanny's engagement ring that I'd planned to make into a pendant. *Could* I be satisfied with an engagement ring that didn't require a full-time bodyguard? I wonder.

I ponder while gazing at the city displayed before me from the best vantage point in town. The sun is setting, and the reflection on the buildings is a hundred shades of gold, pink, and blue. As I enjoy the spectacular view for the thousandth time, I decide that if a smaller ring meant keeping the dot-com palace, then . . . yes. Yes, I could.

I guess that covers all the bases, which means . . . *Holy cats, I'm getting married!*

I begin to hoot and hop around on the deck while Maisy, unaccustomed to such a vigorous outpouring of emotion, dances and yips along beside me as I shout[80] out across the rooftops.

"Hey, Bucktown, I'm getting married! And keeping my house! And getting a Cadillac! Then I can get a job so I'll get paychecks! Big, fat, happy paychecks! So I'll be rich again and I can go to Neiman Marcus and buy those shoes with the cherries hand painted on the wooden heels that made me cry when my credit card was declined! Yay!!"

I gather steam while Maisy leaps and turns semicircles in the air. "Pedicures! I'll be able to afford pedicures again! No more limping for me! And there will be a big party and I'll look amazing and I'll wear a gorgeous dress and I'll see all my favorite people in my favorite place and maybe play a few slots! I might even win a jackpot! And people will give me presents! Lots and lots of wonderful presents! I wonder if I can register for cosmetics. Ooh, or possibly the cherry shoes? Regardless, it doesn't matter, because I'M GETTING MARRIED!!! Hooray!"

[80]Literally.

I sit down to catch my breath. I wonder who I should tell first. Obviously I want to talk to my parents and their checkbook, but Shayla will be dying to know, too. What about Carol? I was the first person she talked to about her engagement. Is there some sort of quid pro quo protocol I'm supposed to follow?

Should I tell my brother? No, he'll just squeal to my parents and wreck the surprise because he's a jerk like that. Or how about Melissa? Will she be mad if she doesn't hear the news first? She's my best girlfriend around here, but Andy is *really* my best friend, but he lives in Indiana and we hardly ever see him. Michael and Amy are our closest married friends, but we're also tight with Brett, and especially with Chris, even though he's not dating Shayla anymore and—

Oh, wait. I should probably tell Fletch first.

. . . .

Maisy and I hobble down the spiral stairs from the roof deck. She landed wrong while we were jumping for joy upstairs and now has a sore paw. Hopefully she'll be OK in a few minutes. If not, I'll run her over to the emergency vet. For once I'm not concerned about price, because, given the size of their initial medical bills, Maisy and Loki now have doggie insurance. How ironic is it that my puppies have health coverage and I don't?

"Where are you?" He's supposed to be in the kitchen making salsa for our Cinco de Mayo gathering, but he's not there. Now that I'm getting married, I have calls to make, bridal magazines to buy, menus to plan, etc. I'd like to start right this minute, but I really ought to confirm he's my betrothed before I book a chapel.

From the bathroom, I hear, "I'm on the mug. What do you need?"

"Come out here!"

"I'm kind of busy."

"Well, how much longer will you be?"

"I don't know. I think the enchiladas last night were bad. Give me a couple of minutes."

The enchiladas and not the twelve Coronas he had with dinner are to blame? Right. But now is not the time to criticize; now is the time to quietly wait.

And wait.

After five interminable minutes, I am unable to contain myself, and I bang on the door. "Hurry up!" Patience is not one of my virtues.

"Why don't you just use the other bathroom?"

"I don't need to go."

"Then stop bothering me. I'll be done soon."

"Why is it taking you so long? What are you doing in there?"

"Euclidian geometry. GO AWAY."

I'm antsy but figure that marriage proposals are better when not yelled through bathroom doors, so I loiter in the hallway for what feels like an eternity. Actually, it's only another two minutes. He soon emerges in a cloud of crisp cotton air freshener, holding this week's *Crain's Chicago Business* magazine. I practically leap on him.

"What is wrong with you?" he asks in exasperation.

"I need to talk to you. Come over here and sit with me," I say, gesturing from the couch.

He blanches because no good conversation starts with those words. Never in recorded history has the dread *I need to talk to you* phrase been followed by something a man *wants* to hear like "I think we should have a threesome with my hot friend" or "I'm buying you a 1969 Camaro, and is black OK?" Fletch is understandably nervous.

I can practically see the cogs moving in his head as he scans his mental Rolodex for recent transgressions. Sometimes I worry I'm too hard on him. On the other hand, he says I'm worth the aggravation and he *did* consent to follow the Jen Commandments, so it's not like he wasn't warned.

The Jen Commandments

One: I loathe cooking. Therefore anytime I am forced into meal preparation, expect it to be done as loudly, profanely, and grudgingly as possible. (Angry: It's what's for dinner.)

Two: I hate holding anything heavier than my purse. If I have something in my hands, I will attempt to trick you into carrying it for me.

Three: I am not a great listener, although I might appear to be. Sure, I may be nodding and saying, "Mmm hmm," but usually I'm just trying to think of a way to steer the conversation back to being about me.

Four: It is *always* all about me.

Five: I complain. A lot. Be particularly cautious if I am hungry, hot, or tired. May God have mercy on your soul if I am all three.

Six: I am fashionably late for social obligations. The only exception is when I brunch with Melissa. You must chauffeur me to the restaurant and I will shriek at you the entire time for dawdling, also known as obeying traffic signals. If it means getting me there on time, you *will* be expected to drive on the sidewalk.

Seven: Speaking of friends, many of them are cuter or thinner than me. You are not allowed to notice this.

Eight: There will be occasions when you breathe too loudly for my liking. Ditto on chewing.

Nine: All men's socks look the same to me. If you care
about wearing a matching set, please double-check them yourself before crossing your legs at a business meeting.

Ten: I enjoy rearranging furniture. You need to enjoy
moving bookcases.

"Stop looking nervous. I promise this is good," I say. Warily, he
sits down while I lay out my proposal. In the same calm, convincing
voice that I used to sell $10 million worth of goods and services back
in the day, I highlight the pros and dispel the cons of the plan.[81] The
more I talk, the more he nods and verbalizes his agreement. Turns
out that he's amenable to everything from Cadillac to Calphalon.

Although he concurs with each point, I sense reluctance.

"Fletch, make sure this is something you absolutely, positively,
one hundred percent want. Don't say yes because I'm a good salesperson. Say yes because you think it's the right thing for us to do," I
plead.

"I do want to do this. You've nicely laid out all the business reasons that this is a good idea." His voice is full of reticence.

"Honey, I know when you're holding something back. Say whatever's on your mind. If you're not ready for this, you have to be honest."

"No, no, that's not it. Overall, I think a Vegas wedding is a great
idea."

"Fletch, I can hear the hesitation in your voice. What is it? Are
you disappointed we aren't going to get married here in the city? Or
is it the timing? I thought with my not working and so few prospects,
this summer is the perfect opportunity to do it. But if you aren't
sure, then we'll forget about it for now." Fletch doesn't say anything.

[81]Had I more time to think about it, I would have prepared a PowerPoint presentation.

"Or is it because of how I look? Dear God, tell me it's not because I've put on a few pounds." A few pounds? Try almost twenty. I can't fit into half of my wardrobe anymore.

"Jen, you look fine. The thing is, I'm excited and I wish we'd have gotten married years ago."

"So you don't think I'm too fat to be a bride?"

"Now you *are* being ridiculous."

"Then what's the problem?"

"In terms of romance, this stinks on ice. It feels like a business deal, not a proposal. Like I should shake your hand instead of kissing you."

"What do you mean?"

"I've been thinking about how I'd propose for a long time. In all the scenarios I'd imagined, none of then included being ambushed in the bathroom after a bout with bad Mexican food."

"Oh. Did I steal your thunder?"

"No. Not really. Well, yes. Seems like I should have been the one to propose."

Dammit, I forgot that he might have a stake in this whole marriage thing. It didn't occur to me that he may have had expectations, too. I've got to return his thunder because I hate seeing him disappointed. I suggest, "Why don't you officially propose once you get a setting for Nanny's diamond?"

He brightens immediately. "That's a good idea! I'll do that. But I won't tell you when, because I want it to be a surprise. How about I take the day off tomorrow to go to Jewelers' Row and look at settings?"

"Sounds like a plan." We smile at each other. As he leans in for a kiss, Maisy jumps up between us and gives him a once-over with her tongue. She's small but determined, so the easiest thing is to simply let her finish. Fortunately, she tires quickly, and he returns his attention to me, drying his face with the tail of his shirt.

"We're really going to do this, huh?"

"As long as my parents are cool with the finances, and we can get a nice space booked some time over Labor Day weekend, then, yeah, I think so."

We seal the deal with a dog-free peck. Just as I'm about to get up from the couch, he stops me.

"Can I ask you something?"

He wants to ask me something? OHMIGOD! He's going to propose *right now*! I bet he was planning to do this all along! It all makes sense. . . . We *are* having people over tonight, and we never have guests on a Sunday. . . . I think our barbecue is really supposed to be a surprise engagement party. Woo-hoo! He's going to ask me to marry him!

Yes, I know we've technically just agreed to marry, but I wasn't expecting my big, romantic proposal today. No wonder he got squirrelly for a minute there. HE was going to propose, and I beat him to the punch! What an unbelievable coincidence that we *both* decided to do it today! Are we in unison or what? We are SO meant to be together.

With my heart in my throat and hands shaking, I look adoringly into his eyes and say, "Fletcher, you can ask me anything."

He stops to catch his breath. Aww, he's trying to work up his confidence for what is the biggest moment in his life. We both pause. OK, here we go!!

"What's wrong with Maisy's foot?"

Courtney, Brett, Kim, and Biola are here for our Cinco de Mayo gathering, and the wedding announcement has put everyone in a particularly festive mood. We're all drinking margaritas and woofing down guacamole while Fletch tends to the rib eyes sizzling away on the grill.

"Fletch, when did you know Jen was *the one*?" asks Biola.

Fletch closes the lid to the grill and sits down with us. Cracking open a Miller High Life, he says, "I knew years ago." He takes a sip and reflects for a minute. "Specifically, it was our first Valentine's Day, and we'd been together about three months. We went to the nicest restaurant in our college town and had the best dinner of my life. Jen picked out everything—the wine, the appetizers, our entrées, etc. I was so impressed by her confidence and the way she handled herself I began to think she was out of my league."

I laugh. "Didn't last long, did it?"

"We finished dinner and went to her apartment. When we got there, her cats were acting strange. They normally sleep twenty-three hours a day, so to find them awake and alert was really unusual. They were fixated on this black spot on the wall. Upon closer inspection, I realized it was a small bat."

"How did you get a bat in your apartment?" Brett asks me, but his eyes never leave Courtney's direction. Hmm, I may have to try my hand at matchmaking. I bet they'd make a nice couple, especially since Court's finally rid of the Chadifornicator.

"I lived in an incredibly scary building but it was almost the only place on campus that would allow pets. The creaky old fireplace flue had come open and the bat let itself in." I'm not kidding—that place was a dump. Once I even persuaded a local news crew to do a broadcast from my apartment because it was so cold. My landlord practically had a heart attack when he saw his building on TV, but you know what? When you don't respond to twenty-five consecutive calls about a heat problem, I take matters into my own hands.

"Yeah, and Jen lost it," Fletch says. "LOST IT. She began running around, screaming about cats getting rabies. I helped her examine them, we determined they were untouched, and we put them in their carriers. But Jen was still pushing the panic button because of a *Far Side* cartoon. A disheveled bat with a briefcase walks into his house and tells his bat wife, 'I musta been tangled up in that bimbo's hair all day.' She had really long hair at the time and was sure the bat was going to nose-dive into it. She kept yelling about bimbos, and then she put a wicker basket on her head and closed off the opening at the bottom by wrapping a sheet around her neck. Suddenly, I understood the sophisticated girl in the restaurant was just an act, and the real Jen was standing in front of me, wearing a garbage can on her head. And I knew at that moment if I married her, life would never be boring."

"How did you get the bat out of your place?" Kim inquires.

"I called my fraternity brother Tim. He brought over my lacrosse sticks and umpire mask. Between the two of us, we caught the bat and let him free outside," Fletch finishes.

Disappointed, Courtney says, "That's possibly the least romantic thing I've ever heard."

"Think so? Then wait till you hear how Jen proposed."

• •

I told my parents about getting married, careful not to mention anyone else knew before they did.[82] Surprisingly, my mother was totally rational and didn't cry or carry on like I expected. I figured she'd be all clingy and emotional. Perhaps the idea of writing all those checks was a sobering thought. My parents decided if Dad agreed to give us the car, he'd be off the hook for financing the wedding. (Of course, if he had his way, the wedding would be in the backyard, hot dogs on this side of the pool, hamburgers on that side, and try not to step in Nixon's towers o' dog poop.)

In only two weeks, I've managed to plan and book almost everything. Armed with my mother's MasterCard and a promise to "not

---

[82]Like I want to be cut out of the will?

go completely crazy," I started researching Las Vegas wedding venues. I thought it would be a riot to be married by Elvis but Fletch flatly refused, so I looked into hotel wedding chapels. I picked Mandalay Bay because it's classy and private. The Venetian had a lovely wedding spot on the Ponte al di Piazza bridge, but I didn't want a bunch of strangers gawping at me while I exchanged vows. You want to watch a show? Buy a ticket.

As Mandalay Bay's chapel is located in a building outside of the hotel, I figured there'd be less danger of people wandering in during the ceremony, looking for the buffet. And thus, I'll neatly eliminate the danger of my head whirling around like Linda Blair in the *Exorcist*, yelling, "Excuse me, but I am making a solemn promise in front of God and everyone, so could you kindly get the fuck out?" at an innocent stranger.[83]

We decided we wanted a nontraditional event. You see, a while back, my friends Michael and Amy had the most spectacular wedding. First, the decor was amazing. Everything took place in the Chicago Cultural Center. It used to be the Chicago Public Library, and the main room had a vaulted ceiling much like a church. Every surface was mosaicked, but instead of religious iconography, all the designs were literature-based. The rooms had sweeping three-story windows and breathtaking views up and down Michigan Avenue, and without one piece of ornamentation, it was among the most beautiful places I'd ever seen. Add thousands of dollars' worth of flowers, crystal, and linen in a roomful of folks in black tie, and the whole scene was something out of a Martha Stewart book. Then include a forty-foot dessert table with at least a hundred different treats,[84] gracious hosts, a top-shelf open bar, and you have my fantasy wedding. During the bride's speech, Amy told a touching story

---

[83]This is also why we're not inviting any children. Beautiful noise? I think not.
[84]Yes, I tried one of each. Shut up.

of being in her late thirties and having given up on love. But one wrong number later, she and Michael found each other and the rest was history. And at that moment, Navy Pier's fireworks began exploding in the giant window right behind them with nary a dry eye in the house.

I figured I'd never be able to compete with what I considered the most perfect wedding in existence, so I concentrated on making mine superfun. I booked our reception in Rum Jungle, a Brazilian-themed nightclub at Mandalay Bay, complete with walls of fire and water, rum bottles stacked fifty feet high, and cages full of go-go dancers.[85] Since the music in Rum Jungle is all Latin techno, I don't have to bother booking a DJ and, subsequently, threaten his life for playing "YMCA" and the chicken dance song. We're encouraging people to dress resort-casual, and I bought my dad an adorable Hawaiian print shirt for the occasion. We're skipping silly old practices, such as feeding each other cake. Also, I refuse to toss the bouquet because rounding up and pointing out all the single women is cruel and unusual punishment.

Since I'm sure I'd turn into a Bridezilla, I decided not to have wedding attendants. It recently occurred to me it's all well and good to be a bridesmaid in your twenties, but by the time you hit your thirties, it's less of an honor and more of a chore. Besides, Carol has three kids, Shayla is finishing grad school, and Melissa just started a new job after being unemployed for a few months. I like them all too much to stick them with the financial and emotional burdens involved. And this way, I won't have to attend any bridal showers. I'd rather receive fewer gifts than be forced to craft a gown out of toilet paper.

I admit I cheated a bit while making wedding arrangements. When planning, I knew I wouldn't have the two to three hours it takes to keep Maisy and Loki entertained and happy, so I shipped

---

[85]Seriously, what's more fun than go-go dancers?

them off to a doggie day care from eight a.m. to five p.m. Although we can barely afford it, having that much uninterrupted time made all the difference. Plus they get so much exercise while at Doggie Day, they come home happy and exhausted. And everyone knows, a tired dog is not a dog that will dig around in your closet, find your precious Chanel slingbacks, and EAT BOTH OF THEM WHOLE.[86] Now I'm sending them a couple of days a week since the bulk of the planning is done.

My only remaining task is to find a dress, and really, as much as I like to shop, how hard can it be?

$$\lambda$$

Hate stupid dresses.

Hate stupid bridal shops.

Hate stupid bridal shop employees.

Hate stupid bridal shop owners.

Hate stupid entire bridal industry.

Hate stupid *Modern Bride*, *Bride's Magazine*, and *Chicago Bride*.

Hate stupid salesgirls at Escada, Saks, and Neiman's, who eyed my waist and clucked their tongues, saying, "Nope, sorry, nothing over a size twelve. But good luck to you."

Hate stupid fat self who can't fit into any pretty designer gowns.

Hate stupid weddings.

. . . .

Apparently it pays to have a nervous breakdown in the middle of Bloomingdale's.

While my favorite clerk got me a glass of water, an exceptionally

[86]Don't ask. It was a really bad day.

stylish plus-sized society woman dug around in her bag until she found a card for Dress Doctor. So now I'm getting my gown made by an exclusive seamstress, and all those anorexic whores on Michigan Avenue and Oak Street who made me feel like I was the Goodyear blimp can kiss the very fattest part of my ass.

I have my first appointment with Soheila at Dress Doctor this afternoon. Her assistant answers the door and leads me into the showroom. Her shop is more like an office, and it's quiet, private, and orderly. While I wait, I scrutinize the intricate stitching on one of her design displays and find her work to be flawless.

Soheila enters from the back of the shop and greets me warmly. I suspect I'm in capable hands. I show her pictures of dresses I like, and we discuss what features I want. Immediately we rule out strapless because with the recent addition of fat on my broad shoulders, I look like more of a linebacker and less of a fairy princess.[87] I prefer classic design and eschew anything with ruffles or sequins. Also, my ankles are surprisingly shapely and I want them to show because I plan to get great shoes.

While flipping through a design book, Soheila asks me a series of "do you prefer this or this" questions and it reminds me of visiting the eye doctor. But within minutes, she shows me a dress in a vintage *Vogue* pattern book, and it encompasses everything I love. It's retro and glamorous without being weighed down with extraneous lace or beading. Its perfection is its simplicity. I gaze adoringly at a glorious A-line, tea-length gown with a short tulle bustle and a portrait collar and I fall in love. And yet . . .

"This is it, Soheila," I say, tapping the page.

"Yes. Are you quite sure? I have many books and we can look at them until you are positive you have found the perfect dress," replies Soheila kindly.

---

[87]I'm totally losing the weight just as soon as my stress level decreases.

"No, this is it. I'm sure. It's just . . ." I trail off.

"Just what? Jennifer, is this truly your choice? Please do not rush your decision. I will have plenty of time to make whatever you want."

"It is, I do, I love the dress. I'm just not sure of the color."

"If you do not care for the snowy white, we can use ivory or eggshell."

"No, those colors don't really do it for me, either," I respond. Soheila retrieves a book of fabrics and lays it across my knees.

"What do you envision? Here is a beautiful ecru dupioni silk. The heavy texture would work well with the lines of the dress. Or perhaps you would prefer something softer with an undertone of blush?" she asks, holding out a baby pink taffeta swatch.

"Yeah, these are nice, but . . ."

"Jennifer, this is a once-in-a-lifetime event. Tell me what you see when you picture your wedding in your dreams."

I close my eyes and try to envision the day. Fletch, happy and handsome in his white dinner jacket, gracefully twirls me around the parquet floor.[88] With his short hair and funky horn-rimmed glasses, Fletch reminds me of an old-school astronaut. My whole look is Jacqueline Bouvier Kennedy of the Camelot era, and I'm sporting an adorably bubble-shaped up 'do with gardenias in my hair. On my face, I'm wearing thick black eyeliner, doelike false lashes, and frosty pink lipstick. No, scratch that. Light lipstick makes me look like I've been eating powdered donuts.[89] We resemble Barbie and Ken, circa 1962. I float in his arms, swirling around in a fitted—I'VE GOT IT!

"Black! That's it! I see myself in a black dress." I pause, waiting

---

[88]In my dreams, I'm an excellent dancer, and not a left-footed Frankenstein, clomping into other people.

[89]It's my dream, so I can wear the updated Dior Brun Swing shade if I want.

for her reaction. I have never heard of anyone wearing black to her wedding, particularly in the case of a first marriage.

Soheila stares into the distance for a moment before starting to nod her head. "A black wedding dress. Yes. Yes, I think this is a good idea. It will be striking, but nontraditional."

"Exactly!"

"Then we shall take your measurements now," she says.

....

My mother launches straight into negotiation mode. "But you'd look so beautiful in a white dress. I've always pictured you getting married in a pristine white strapless dress with a long train and intricate beading on the bodice." I'm home to address wedding invitations and to pick up the Cadillac. Every time we spoke on the phone for the past month, I changed the subject when she asked about the dress. I purposefully didn't tell her specifics about it until today, since it's now too late to make changes. She is less than enthused with my choice.

"Not one bit of what you just said is appealing or would look good on me," I reply. I use my feet to push off the side of the pool and I paddle my raft toward the sunny part of the deep end. With less than two months to go, I'm coated in SPF 0 oil, fully committing myself to tanorexia. I might not be skinny on my wedding day, so I'll compensate by being dark.

"What if you had the dress made in white for the ceremony and wore the black one for the reception?" she suggests, swimming right along behind me.

"How many times do we have to go over this? I already told you I'm wearing the black dress. I want nontraditional," I argue. Except for wardrobe, my mother has been delightfully hands-off in regard to wedding choices. Her only suggestion involved the invitations. I thought something Vegasy would be appropriate, but both Mom and the stationer convinced me otherwise. I ended up selecting a thick cream William Arthur card with flaps that fold open like doors to expose embossed vellum over a painting of a topiary. The invitation ties together with a green tulle ribbon and comes with a green parchment-lined envelope. They are truly stunning.[90]

"But I'll pay for both dresses."

"Which is exceptionally generous of you," I reply. "Although it's a waste of a thousand dollars. With that money, I'd rather keep the bar open for an extra hour or give each of the guests a gift basket. Remember, you're the one who says a wedding is as much about the guests as it is about the couple."

"Jennifer, don't worry about the money. We can extend the reception time and get the second dress if you want."

I peer at her over the edge of my raft. "Who are you and what have you done with my mother?" I ask. Having grown up struggling, Mom's always kept a tight grip on her cash. This woman would rather die than pay retail.

"All I want is for you to have a wonderful wedding," she huffs. "Is that so wrong?"

"No, Mom. It's a lovely thought, and I'm very thankful for your offer, but having to change dresses midstream will be nothing but a hassle, so it's not happening."

"What about wearing that green color you like so much? Or maybe pink? Why does it have to be black?" she badgers.

"Because I *like* and look good in black. What's nice is I'll actually be able to eat, drink, and circulate at the reception without worrying about someone spilling a tropical drink on my white dress. My outfit will be pretty *and* functional, so I know I'll be comfortable. Besides,

---

[90]Considering they cost more than a year's tuition, they'd better be.

I've always wanted a fancy black cocktail dress, and this gown is something I can wear again."

She snorts. "To my funeral, maybe."

"Mom, *let it go*. You were the one who allowed a saleslady to talk you into a wedding dress you didn't like. You said every time you see your wedding photos, you get mad. You've held a grudge against Priscilla's of Boston for the past forty years. That's not going to happen with me. The black dress is what I'm getting, and it's not going to change."

"I just want you to be happy," she says, creeping dangerously close to the border of the Maternal Martyr Zone.

"And I am, so thank you again. I couldn't have done any of this without you. Oh, I almost forgot—I didn't tell you about the shoes I bought."

"Did you get the open-toe sandals I suggested?"

"No, they were too high and the straps bit into my ankles. I got a really cute pair of Enzos with a heel style I've never seen before. There's a small notch taken out of the back of them, but they're still sturdy enough that they won't hurt, and they make my legs look great."

"Black?"

"Um . . . no."

"You didn't get black shoes? But what else could you wear with a black dress?"

"Well, they were on sale, which should make you happy. As for color, they're . . . well, they're actually leopard print and . . ." My mother suddenly disappears. "Mom? Mom? Mother, where are you? Mom! MOM! It's just a pair of shoes. STOP TRYING TO DROWN YOURSELF!"

"Do you have any regrets that we aren't inviting any of your family to the wedding?" I ask Fletch.

"Jen, what have I told you about attacking me with conversation the second I come in?" Fletch stows his computer bag in the front hall closet and enters the kitchen.

"I'm sorry. I forgot. Anyway, are you sad that we aren't having any of your *people* at the wedding?"

Fletch grabs a cold Miller High Life out of the fridge and joins me in the living area, where I'm working on guest lists. "Not one bit. All my friends are coming, and they feel more like family than my sister or mother ever did. We'd have to seat them at their very own table to accommodate all the crazy they'd bring."

"I know, but I want to make doubly sure you're OK with it. I can call your mom and apologize if I have to." Perhaps telling his mother the last time we spoke that it's taken me years to undo all the damage she caused wasn't my most diplomatic course of action. (Mentioning to his sister there was nothing wrong with her a little Haldol[91] couldn't cure didn't make me popular, either.)

"Do that and I won't marry you. Think about it, Jen. My mother spent her whole life sitting idly by, allowing my father to make me believe I was worthless and I'd never amount to anything." Fletch stands and begins to pace across the floor. Whenever we discuss his lousy family, he gets agitated.

"For the longest time, I didn't realize her inaction was just as damaging as my dad's abuse. Although the Army taught me I had potential, *you* were the first person who truly believed in me. *You* were the one who convinced me anything was possible. If I hadn't met you, I'd have taken my telecom degree and gotten a job as a $10/hour technician in some small, shitty radio station in Nowhere, Indiana."

[91] An antipsychotic drug. WHICH SHE NEEDS.

"Oh, come on. You're the second-smartest person I know.[92] You'd have become successful without me." Seriously? He can do long division. IN HIS HEAD!

"No, I'd never have achieved all that I have if I didn't have you beside me. So for her to say, 'You can do better,' the day I call to tell her we're getting married, especially as kind as you'd been to her? No way. Unconscionable. Unforgivable. If you hadn't grabbed the phone out of my hand and said all those things, I would have done so myself."

"So you don't mind if I put big black X's through their names on the guest list? I'm using a marker, so it's permanent."

"Strike away. They were toxic, and I'm glad they're out of my life."

I stow my guest lists and sit on the ottoman across from him. "What kind of day did you have?"

"Better than usual. Clark's been out of the office. He didn't mention why he'd be gone, but Ernesto told me it's because the sexual harassment charge against him is finally going to court."

"Cool. Can he go to jail because of it?"

"No, Jen, it's civil court, not criminal."

"What's the difference?"

"Do you really want to know?

"Not really." Blunt honestly is the cornerstone of our relationship.

"And how did your day go?"

"Fan-fucking-tastic. You'll love this—I got dinged for the dog-walking job Marta at the park referred me for. The owner said although he respected my credentials, he needed someone who was more 'responsible.' Then when I called that media company, they told me they were moving in a different direction. I tried to press

[92]My dad is the first.

them by asking, 'What direction might that be?' and the girl got all shitty and said, 'Not yours.'"

"Heh. Sorry about that, though. I know you're trying."

"Well, I hope we get a lot of cash for wedding presents because it doesn't seem like I'm going to get a job anytime soon."

....

I'm at the Dress Doctor for our weekly fitting. Soheila has constructed my entire wedding gown out of muslin first to get the size exactly right. Once we have the perfect fit, she'll cut apart the cheap fabric and use it as a pattern for the lush black dupioni we've chosen for the actual dress.

It's about 90 degrees outside and I happily shed my sticky street clothes. I stand in the dressing room in my underwear for a couple of minutes to cool down. Finally chilled, I strip out of my regular bra and put on my special wedding foundation garments. The last time I was here, Sohelia pointed at my bustline, grabbed my bra straps, and said, "These? Need to be up here," while yanking everything skyward. The new bra she had me buy makes me look like the prow of a ship, and I can practically rest my chin on my own rack. However, Soheila's been right about everything so far, and I trust her implicitly. If she says I need to wear a steel-plated bra, so be it. She hands me the bleached muslin dress, and I slip into it.

When I exit, Sohelia makes the final adjustments before leading me over to the three-way mirror. I step up on the platform and give myself a once-over, and I don't notice my messy ponytail or smeared mascara.

I gasp, "I look like a real bride!"

Sohelia grins a quiet smile. "You are a real bride, my friend."

"I mean, I knew the fit would be great, but I didn't realize the muslin would be so pretty. It's almost a shame you have to cut it up."

"You will love the finished product. The black will take your breath away."

"It will if it's even half as nice as this." I admire myself for a minute, twirling and inspecting the gown from all angles. I bend and stretch, and holding an imaginary bouquet, I do the retarded step-together, step-together walk I vowed would not take place on my wedding day. "Soheila, do me a favor?"

"Of course."

"Promise if she calls again you won't tell my mother how nice the dress looked in white."

人

I'm getting married in a week and am still technically not en-gaged. Surely Fletch didn't forget about getting my diamond set, right? He's been really bogged down with work lately because his charming boss thought it would be a good idea to start sending Fletch to Milwaukee three days a week. Although it's a two-hour commute each way, Clark expects Fletch to be in the Milwaukee of-fice during business hours, so he's gone from six a.m. to eight p.m. on those days.[93]

Fortunately, Fletch is on vacation for the next two and a half weeks, so hopefully he can finally unclench. He was all weird and hyper earlier and gave me the third degree about where I was going. I told him I was getting my hair colored this afternoon, and I'd be back before dinner, and to kindly chill the hell out. He's normally such a rock that when he gets tense it impacts not only me but also

---

[93]Fletch says Clark is going through a divorce now, hence the tyranny. The next boss I have had better be single or come with a clean bill of marital health from his or her therapist. This divorce business makes people way too irrational.

the cats and dogs. Tucker kept nuzzling Fletch's ankles and Loki pranced and whined.

I'm at the bottom of the half flight of stairs leading to my apartment when Maisy's head appears at the door. She's got something pink by her mouth and my heart practically stops because I think it's a Kate Spade sandal. Lately Fletch leaves the house in such a daze that he sometimes forgets to shut the closet door. While I sleep, Maisy engages in a leather-goods holocaust. I'm down three purses, one piece of luggage, four of my most expensive pairs of shoes, and even though they weren't leather, my Gucci sunglasses. When we bought Bitter Apple antichew spray, Maisy simply ate the bottle.[94]

I leap up five steps and burst into the house. "Oh, no, Maisy, what have you done now?" I yelp, leaning over to survey the damage. But Maisy doesn't have a shoe. Instead, she has a piece of pink paper tied around her neck with a plaid ribbon, and in blocky, backward script it says, *DeAr MuMMy, PleeAzE mArrY my DadDY . . .*

"Fletch, Fletch, where are you? What's going on?" I call. Loki comes trotting over and he's also wearing a note. I bend down to read it: *. . . becuZ I DoN'T wanNa B a bAStard 4ever.*

It takes me a minute to figure out what just happened.

How cute is this? We have a proposal! I'm really engaged now! Yay! Except I seem to be missing a fiancé.

And a ring.

Where is the ring?

I look at Maisy again and I notice her ribbon is wet and frayed, like she's been chewing on it. Please, God, tell me I'm not going to have to wait twelve to fourteen hours to see my engagement ring. It's bad enough watching bits of my favorite accessories shoot out her

---

[94]Loki, the "good dog," much prefers to nibble mission-style furniture. He's a sixty-pound termite with a puffy tail.

backside. Are we going to have to hover over her, rooting through her poop to make everything official?

"Fletch, WHERE ARE YOU?" I hear a telltale flush and Fletch exits the bathroom looking sheepish.

"You're early. I wasn't supposed to be in the bathroom when you got back."

"Rory only did a partial highlight, which takes less time."

"I guess you saw the notes?"

"I did, and my answer is yes."

"I sort of assumed you'd say that, what with our leaving for Vegas in two days and all." Fletch notices I'm not cheering and dancing around like he expected. "Jen, aren't you happy? You said you wanted a surprise and you got it. What's with the giant puss on your face?"

My chin begins to quiver. "I was happy until I realized Maisy ate my ring."

"No, she didn't."

"Yes, she did—look!" I show him the tattered ribbon.

"No, she didn't," he says gently. He pulls me toward him. "She didn't eat your ring. She tried, but she didn't get it. See?" From his pocket, he pulls out a small velvet pouch and shakes out the contents. A band of white-and-yellow gold with my Nanny's lovely round diamond channel-set in the center sparkles in his palm. I snatch it right up. It's not what I expected yet it's *exactly* my style.

"How did you know what I like when I only ever talked about big, fat square stones and multiple baguettes? Did one of my friends help you shop?"

"No, I found it on my own. I saw hundreds of settings, but this one looked the most like you, so that's the one I chose. Now would you like some champagne so we can toast properly?"

"We don't have any. I think we've just got that one sticky bottle of Baileys at the back of the fridge left over from Christmas."

"Jen, we have champagne." He lifts a bottle of Moët & Chandon out of an ice bucket in the freezer.

"It's my favorite kind!" I exclaim.

Diamonds *and* champagne? I should get married more often.

. . . .

After a long, hot, stressful week, we're finally in Vegas. My parents, Fletch, and I came out on the same flight, although we weren't seated together. Fortunately when we checked in at the gate, an exceptionally sensitive airline employee heard our conversation, noticed the addition of crazy about mother's eyes, and placed us at opposite ends of the plane.[95]

You see, the previous evening, my mom morphed from a licensed professional therapist with a master's degree and widely varied interests into some sort of horrific, bat-shit-crazy Japanese anime character named Momzilla. The minute she Velcroed herself to me in the car on the way to the airport, second-guessing every single one of my carefully detailed wedding plans, I knew I was in trouble.

"Mom, what is the matter with you? Why are you so stressed?" I asked.

"There are just so many details to manage," she replied, her foot tapping out one hundred beats per minute while she clutched my hand.

"Yes, and I've already managed them. What do you think I was doing all summer with your credit card? This week has been orchestrated to a T. I told you not to worry about the details. It will be perfect, so please just sit back and enjoy it. All the hard work is done."

[95]When we get home, I am totally sending that flight attendant flowers.

"What about the flowers? You haven't even seen them. How do you know they're going to look good at the reception?" she fretted.

"Mom, I appreciate your concern, but it's unnecessary. The florist told me she does events at Rum Jungle every single week and we discussed the arrangements at length. Between the orchids, birds of paradise, gardenias, and ginger blossoms, they'll look and smell exquisite."

"The first thing we have to do once we get there is to check out the reception site. I want to make sure I like where they put us. What if they place us by the fire pit? It will feel like sitting in a greasy garage. Also, we must make place cards."

"Again, Mom, I've worked with the manager at length. Everything is confirmed, and it's going to be great. And I've told you a dozen times, seating charts and caged go-go dancers DO NOT GO TOGETHER. I want casual and informal. Place cards will go against the whole 'bucking tradition' theme of the wedding."

"What if the service is bad? My sisters will never let me hear the end of it." With eight children in the family, most of my mother's siblings have been locked in a lifelong competition with one another. Usually my mother doesn't play along, but she's finally thrown her hat in the ring with this event.

"First of all, it's Vegas and there's no such thing as bad service. Second, I actually spoke to the waiters working our event, and they were really enthusiastic. Stop obsessing, please."

"What about your dress? Are you sure you packed it? And how are you going to get it pressed the day of the ceremony?"[96]

"Mom, we're going to *Las Vegas*. They have EVERYTHING

---

[96]She's still pissed I wouldn't let her iron my high school graduation gown. However, I was only seventeen at the time and have since come to embrace the virtues of a properly pressed garment.

there, OK? I could call the concierge and request a crack pipe and a thirteen-year-old male prostitute, and both would be delivered to the room within the hour. Getting help ironing my dress will not pose a problem."

"NOW YOU'RE TAKING DRUGS?"

"Mom, I'm using hyperbole. You HAVE to lighten up."

"What about your hair and your makeup?"

"Have you even *looked* at the itinerary I prepared for you? Our salon appointments start at noon on the day of the wedding. I booked them two months ago at Robert Cromeans. It's one of the best salons in the country." My mother had clenched fists and a line of perspiration over her top lip. "When I booked our appointments, I told them the time of the wedding, and we spaced out our services accordingly. Remember, they have brides in there every day, and they know what they're doing."

This news did not seem to soothe her. I continued. "Mom, please, please, please calm down. You're going to make *me* nervous."

"There are just so many details," she repeated.

"Yes, I KNOW. And I took care of ALL OF THEM. As I see it, you have a choice. You can travel back in time and actually become involved in the planning process instead of having me do everything, or you can simply have faith in me and trust my level of competence." At this point, we reached the airline's check-in desk. Slyly the attendant raised her left hand at me and gestured to her own engagement ring. We exchanged a quick flash of understanding—with one glance, she appreciated my valiant fight in the Battle for Black, and I immediately recognized the loss she suffered in the Great Salmon Debacle. Without uttering a word, she assigned us separate seats.

On the bright side, for once I wasn't worried about terrorists commandeering the plane. If Al Qaeda attempted to disrupt our scheduled flight path, I was confident Momzilla would swat any hijackers down like flies.

Fletch and I sit back by the galley, and another nice flight attendant keeps us in free Bloody Marys the whole way. She even situates the drinks cart between us and the aisle so my mother can't get to us. By the time we hit the tarmac, my Mom-induced tension has melted away.[97]

We meet up in baggage claim, and my father is completely frazzled, unusual because he used to defuse land mines in Korea because of his unwavering calm. But denied the opportunity to obsess at me, Momzilla turned her attention to Big Daddy. They bickered for three and a half hours about the twenty pounds of chocolate coins we special-ordered as guest favors.[98] Dad didn't see why he wasn't allowed to check the coins, and Momzilla couldn't understand why a man with crippling arthritis in his shoulders couldn't just carry the candy and be quiet about it already. Momzilla would have carried them herself, if she hadn't insisted on transporting my dress.

Their underlying tension begins to affect Fletch, and my lovely calm evaporates. I'm forced to throw down the Bride Card and I demand détente. Under a tentative truce, we make our way out to the limousine. Our driver greets us warmly and starts grabbing our luggage, although my mother refuses to turn over the bag of coins.

"So how is everyone today?" he asks.

"Sick of talking about goddamned chocolate," mutters Dad.

"Contemplating homicide." Mom glares in Dad's direction.

"Not nearly drunk enough," Fletch responds.

"We're all great, thanks," I say, shooting everyone the dirtiest of looks. The driver arranges our bags in the trunk while we climb in the limo. The second we're seated, Mom begins to second-guess the

---

[97]Seriously, I'd marry *you*, American Airlines, if I weren't already engaged.
[98]Which are way too cute. The stamp in the candy says, "Jen and Fletch, Bucking Tradition Since 1994" on one side and it has our wedding date on the other, and they're wrapped to look like casino chips.

dinner menu, Fletch whines about needing a martini, and Dad complains about poor Mr. Nixon staying all by himself in the kennel.

And I? Have had *enough.*

"People? GET IT TOGETHER. We're here, OK? We're about to see fifty of our closest friends and family, and we WILL have a good time. Why? Because every single detail has been thoroughly orchestrated and lovingly micromanaged by my own hand," I shout. Gaining steam, I continue. "This wedding is going to be PERFECTION, *so I do not want to hear one more word about chocolate or catering or flowers or anything else.* As of right now, all the bitching and complaining stops. We are going to paste big, fat smiles on our faces, and we are going to be a happy, normal, functional family IF IT KILLS US. Nothing can go wrong because I have addressed every single possible contingency. So, please, everyone, cease and desist. It's going to be great." Everyone whispers timorous apologies, and I settle back with a triumphant smile on my face.

"Where to?" the chauffeur asks as he slides into the front seat.

"To Mandalay Bay, please," I reply.

"Should be a pretty wild weekend at Mandalay," he says, as we merge onto Paradise Road.

"Really," I say magnanimously. Normally it annoys me to have a chatty driver, especially when I'm with other people, but I'm trying to demonstrate to my family what it means to be a good sport. "Why is that?" I ask, feigning interest.

"That hotel always gets freaky this weekend."

"Because of the holiday, I assume."

"Partially, but mostly it's because of the strippers and porn stars."

A confused silence emanates from the backseat.

"You folks ARE aware the Adult Entertainment Expo is being held at your hotel, right?"

My father spends the next three days hiding from my mother. And, coincidentally, as she's barely left my side, Fletch also disappears. We catch glimpses of them occasionally in the hotel's restaurants and bars, whooping it up with their friends who got here early. I'm glad the men are having a good time. My mother's anxiety has reached dizzying new heights and we've squabbled nonstop about everything. (*"Walking to Treasure Island will take an hour even if we do get on the people movers."* "No, it won't." *"YES, IT WILL."* "Why aren't you using sunscreen?" *"I want to get really dark."* "You'll get cancer." *"I'm sure heart disease will kill me first."* "Should you really be wasting all your money in the slot machines?" *"It was $5 worth of nickels!"*) Fortunately, my brother arrived last night, and even though he's usually an ass, he helps defuse the situation. He and Mom are off somewhere right now. I don't know or care what they're doing because I am finally, blissfully alone.

Because we're on a budget and I haven't gotten any presents yet, I can't take advantage of my precious downtime by doing my usual Vegas activities. Denied the opportunity to shop and gamble, I'm working on my tan. I love it here because Mandalay Bay's outside area is second to none. Scattered throughout the lush landscaping are scads of regular pools and hot tubs, although I prefer to lie on the gigantic natural sand beach by the wave pool.

However, I'm not having a good time today. Apparently I'm the only one poolside without an *Anal Pirates II* screen credit, and I am more than a little uncomfortable. I don't mean to stare, but I can't help it. Seriously, I've never seen so much plastic in my life! The sleeping gal to my right appears to be carrying flesh-colored watermelons under her eye patches, and on my left, the woman is wearing two thimbles attached by dental floss. Earlier, a gentleman smuggling a flotation device in his pants had a chat *right next to me at eye level* with Thimbleina regarding their most recent film. I feared one wrong move could put my eye out, so I didn't hear everything they talked about, although I believe it included something called a "rim job."[99]

Strained from too much stimulus, I close my eyes and keep them closed until a large shadow passes over me. When I look up, instead of a seeing a puffy cumulus cloud, I spy a hairy, fat, yet somehow comfortingly familiar belly.

"Hey, Peeg!" my brother calls cheerfully.

"Todd! What are you doing here?" His plane got in so late last night, I'd already gone to bed and hadn't yet seen him.

"Gimme $20."

"For what?" My brother has plenty of money and wants for nothing. However, he takes great pleasure in attempting to squeeze cash out of me and has perfected his craft over the years.

"I kept Mom out of your hair all morning, and I just sent her off to lunch with Auntie Virginia so you won't see her until the rehearsal dinner tonight." I told you he was good.

"Done," I reply, grabbing my beach bag. I give him my last $20 bill. "Thanks. I consider this money well spent."

Thimbleina offers Todd her chair because she's off to her own lunch with the Astroglide people. I thank her, because, really, what else do you say? Todd eases into his chair with a *Sports Illustrated*, a *Sporting News*, a *Baseball Digest*, a *Golf Magazine*, today's sports page, and a towel.

"I'm honestly surprised you made it out here. Don't you need to be writing about how some athlete threw some sort of projectile through some sort of apparatus?" My brother is the sports editor at

---

[99] I don't know what it is, so don't ask. (AND DON'T EXPLAIN IT TO ME.)

his paper, and he works constantly. What his employers don't understand is he'd pay *them* to be able to write about sports all day.

"Nope, got an intern to cover my page for a few days, so I'm good. Hey, how do I get one of those foot-long strawberry margaritas?"

"You flip the flag up in the back like this." I demonstrate on my own chair.

The waitress retrieves our drink order, and Todd is soon taking contented sips, alternating his glances between the Red Sox article and the porn queens frolicking with one another in the surf.

"I hope they're using extra chlorine this weekend," Todd snickers.

"No kidding. This convention is making me nuts. Last night Mom and I were waiting in line for a cab next to a woman in an outfit fabricated from a Mylar balloon. Her dress was short enough to be worn as a tank top. A couple of men behind us made a big fuss over how nice she smelled, and it made me mad. Excuse me, but *I'm* the one who showered, moisturized, and perfumed myself with J'Adore Dior minutes before. *She* smelled like crab dip."

"When I called Jean last night, she wasn't pleased to hear about the strippers, either." Hmm, Jean's at home managing three children under the age of six, and her husband's at a hotel full of adult entertainers. I can't imagine why she'd be upset.

"Did Mom tell you about the guy with the greasy tan and a ton of gold necklaces who asked me if *I* was here for the convention? I said to him, 'Pal, I'm wearing a pink Lacoste, green Capri pants, and a triple strand of pearls. Exactly what part of my countenance says, 'I have sex with strangers on film' to you?"

"After a bunch of strippers got off the elevator this morning, Mom made the comment, 'I can't stop looking at boobs.' I don't think she realized other the people in the elevator were listening,"

Todd tells me with a laugh. My mother and I both lack the internal firewall that keeps us from saying almost everything we think.

"If I didn't know better, I'd guess you were enjoying yourself. How many times have I heard you say you hated Vegas and would never, ever come out here?"

He shrugs. "I say a lot of things I don't mean in order to make you mad."[100]

"Once I'm married, will you'll finally start treating me like an adult? And quit writing mean articles about me? Maybe not try to extort money every time we see each other?"

"Can't see it happening, but because of your wedding, I'll make you a deal. If you give me $5, I'll be nice to you for the rest of the week."

"You're truly a prince among men."

"Yeah."

I hand him five singles. "Hey, Todd, how did you find me out here? The beach itself is something like eleven acres, not including the rest of the pool area."

"I looked out the window up in Mom and Dad's room, and I tried to spot the fattest person. I saw a big blob, figured it was you, and here I am."

I hold out my palm and demand he return my $5.

He complies. "It was worth it."

"Mom, come *on*. Our appointments start in a few minutes." It's my wedding day, and I'm standing in the hallway outside my parents' room, banging on the door and trying to get my mother out of bed. I can't believe I have to rally her. As anxious and excited as

---

[100]See? See what I mean? He's an ASS.

she's been about today, I figured she'd have been up since dawn. "If we don't get down to the spa now, we won't have time for coffee and muffins."

My mother opens the door and I'm taken aback at how green she is. "Oh, my God! What happened to you?" I exclaim.

"Shh, sick. Very, very sick," she whispers, leaning on my shoulder for support. "I don't know why. I only had one glass of wine."

"Mom? It's not considered *one glass* if the waiter keeps refilling it."

She gasps. "Jennifer, that's a lie! I don't drink! Besides, I only had one glass. I'm sure this is a bad reaction to the tannins because it was red wine."

"You were sitting next to me at the table, and I saw the waiter top off your goblet at least fifteen times. Do the math: We had twenty guests at the rehearsal dinner, yet we went through fifty bottles of wine. That's an average of about ten glasses apiece."

"I do not have a hangover! I'm sick! I ate too many rich foods last night, and they interacted with the tannins."

"Really? If you're not hungover, you wouldn't mind if I talked about a fatty pork chop covered with fried onions, served in a dirty ash tray?"

"No!" she yells, dashing to the trash can by the elevator.

"Ready to change that *one glass* answer?"

"Well, maybe I had two glasses, but no more than that," she claims. While our elevator descends to the spa level, my mother places both hands on the walls to steady herself.

"Oh, look, it's Julia, Queen of Denial! Mom, do you recall why Fletch and I left the rehearsal dinner so early last night?"

"Actually, no."

"Remember when you and cousin Karla started singing 'Show Me the Way to Go Home,' and I begged you to stop? And you looked at me with your hair all disheveled and your blazer hanging off your shoulder and replied, 'Itsch my daaay, annnd I'll do whats I wantsss,' so I turned to Fletch and said, 'We're leaving.'"

"I would never say such a thing. And it was only one glass. Possibly two."

"Tell yourself that enough and it will eventually begin to feel true."

I check us into the spa. "Hi, I'm here for a sugar glow and this radiant mother of the bride is here for a massage." I gesture toward my mother, who is practically grass green at this point. I collect our robes and keys, and we head to the locker room to change.

In the waiting area, I indulge in muffins, fruit, and a mimosa while my mother clings to her bottle of water. I shake my glass at her. "Care for a little hair of the dog?" She winces and places her head in her hands. When my esthetician comes to get me, I follow her to the treatment room, calling over my shoulder, "Don't yack on the massage table!"

When my sugar glow ends, I rinse off and look for my mother. We planned to spend some time in the eucalyptus steam room and then the sauna before we have our manicures.

"Jennifer?" asks the woman behind the counter.

"Yes?"

"Your mother said she'd meet you at the salon later. I think she went back upstairs to lie down."

"Thanks for telling me."

"Is she going to be OK? She looked pretty bad."

"She'll be fine," I reply. "After all, she only had one glass of wine."

* *

I've pictured my wedding day a hundred thousand times. In none of these scenarios was my teetotaling mother too hungover to help me get ready. Because I didn't want to impinge on any of my friends, I'm completely alone right now. Fletch is getting buffed and polished in the men's spa, so it's just me in my room, finishing a club sandwich and a Coke while watching a *Real World San Francisco* re-run.[101]

I have to be at the chapel in a half an hour, so it's time to put on my dress. After washing the mayo off my hands and fixing my lip-stick, I slip on my gown and attempt to zip it. Because of the zipper's placement, I can only get it up halfway. I struggle to the point of breaking a sweat and then I give up. My bridal magazines lied to me: This does *not* feel like the best day of my life.

Fortunately, it *looks* like the best day of my life. The stylist pinned my hair in a messy up 'do, festooned with baby orchids and it's all tousled and Brigette Bardot–like. My makeup is unbelievable, too— the artist used some kind of iridescent powder on my cheekbones, and they look amazing. I ate my lunch in front of the mirror because I couldn't stop gazing adoringly at myself. I am one hot bride.

I call my parents' room, seeking help. In an amused voice, Dad informs me they'll be over as soon as my mother finishes dry heav-ing. Then he starts grousing about his cummerbund. He's mad at my mother because she insisted he wear a white dinner jacket instead of a blazer and the Hawaiian shirt I'd bought him for the ceremony. Apparently I'm not the only one with a Mom-induced wardrobe dilemma.

Half-dressed, but radiant, I sit on the bed and wait. Surely I won't have to go down the aisle with my steel-plated bra showing, right?

λ

---

[101]Oh, Puck, you scamp. I shall never tire of your snot rockets and homophobia.

Here I am, about to make a covenant before God and the most important people in my life, and all I can think is the minister looks exactly like the Father Guido Sarducci character from *Saturday Night Live.*

"Fletch, Guido Sarducci! He looks like Father Guido Sarducci," I whisper without moving my lips.

"That's exactly what I was thinking," he whispers back.

"I wonder if it's really him. When was the last time you saw him on TV? Hey, did you notice the gangbanger getting married right before us? His child bride looked about fourteen years old, and they already had a baby! And did you see the tattoo on his neck? He must have—"

The minister begins the ceremony. Oh. We should probably not be talking. I already kind of got in trouble for stopping to chat with a couple of people on my way down the aisle.

We opted for the religious ceremony today. I mean, just because I'm getting married in a casino doesn't mean I'm a pagan. Even with God included, the whole thing should take less than fifteen minutes, which should be a new record for weddings I've attended. In high school, Carol and I went to this girl Janine's wedding and it was sixteen minutes long. Of course, she was seventeen years old and heavily pregnant, but still . . . I win.

Ever been to a Catholic ceremony with a full mass? Oy. You could grow old and die before that service ends. With a fifteen-minute ceremony, there's no time for all the extraneous foolishness that bores everyone at weddings, like that awful "Love Is" reading or the hideous "Today I Marry My Friend" poem. Ugh. I'd rather repeat Homer Simpson's vows from the "Milhouse Divided" episode: "Do you, Marge, take Homer, in richness and poorness—poorness is underlined—in impotence and in potence, in quiet solitude or blasting across the alkali flats in a jet-powered, monkey-navigated—"

Fletch pokes me. Huh? "Oh, um, yes, I do come before you today on my own free will," I tell Father Guido.

"Excellent," he replies. "And now I shall read for you a verse from First Corinthians." Father Guido whips off his glasses and I inadvertently roll my eyes. Excuse me, padre? You perform this ceremony twenty times a day and I'm willing to bet you've got this stuff down cold. I appreciate the dramatic effect of removing your eyewear, but your theatrics really aren't needed. We've already agreed to buy the video—no need to thespian things up, all right?

"Ahem. Love is patient, love is kind . . ."

GAH!!

. . . .

After the ceremony, Fletch and I pose for at least a thousand photos. My brother does some photography for his newspaper, so he's also taking pictures. Todd and our photographer are having some sort of professional pissing match, seeing who can use the most lenses and capture the most angles.

"Yo, Ansel Adams, Annie Leibovitz, can we please wrap this up? There will be plenty more photo ops during the reception and I'm melting out here," I complain. When it's 105 degrees, a dry heat is still awfully hot, especially in my stupid scuba-suit girdle. "I'm marinating like a pork chop. Let's GO!"

"These are memories you'll cherish for a lifetime," the hired photographer replies.

"No, my memories are taking place INDOORS, where my friends and family are enjoying air-conditioning and cold drinks. The only memory I have right now is of sweat rolling down the crack of my ass. Can we please go inside?"

Our hired photographer replies, "Of course!" Finally! "As soon as we shoot you by the mosaic fountains."

"And by the elephant statues!" my brother adds.

"Don't forget the iron gates!"

"And what about those huge palm trees?"

"Hey, you know what would be a great shot? Through the foliage. Let's just get a couple more. . . ."[102]

I'm at least ten pounds thinner by the time we're allowed indoors. While waiting for us, the guests have been drinking almost two hours, and a couple of our friends are completely trashed. Fletch's old Army buddy Joel is in such rough shape that Fletch takes him upstairs to lie down in our room.

Since everyone else has been at the reception for DAYS, we get the last two seats, against the wall, sandwiched neatly between my mother and father, and across from a couple of their neighbors. My mother insisted other guests sit at what looked like the open and accessible head table, forcing us into a tiny marital box, where it's virtually impossible A) to get up, and B) for anyone to come over to talk to us. Momzilla has conquered her hangover and glommed on to me again. She finally appreciates all my hard work, and the second-guessing has morphed into an outpouring of physical affection. My dinner conversation consists of phrases like: *"I can't hold my glass and your hand at the same time, Mom." "You're smothering me! Please sit on your own chair." "You've kissed me more times than my husband today. KNOCK IT OFF."* I'm actually delighted at the prospect of taking more pictures just to escape my mother-loving veal pen.

I spend a sum total of thirty-six seconds with my friends at the reception, so we make plans to meet up after I change out of my dress. Somehow I get roped into carrying cake and flowers back to my parents' room.[103]

---

[102]HATE!

[103]The cake is the best part of the reception. It had layers of mocha hazelnut, white chocolate–raspberry, lemon–Bavarian cream, and the topper was cream cheese–carrot cake, all covered with white modeling chocolate. By the way, did you know fifty guests can't consume twenty-five pounds of cake? I didn't, hence the trip upstairs.

A good thirty minutes passes by the time I make it back down to Rum Jungle. A line has gathered outside the club but I ignore it. As I let myself in the velvet rope and walk in the door, an enormous slab of beef wearing a suit and a headset throws a meaty arm in front of me.

"Excuse me," I say, attempting to walk around him.

"We're closed until ten o'clock."

"Yeah, I know. You were shut down for a private party—mine."

"Party's over. We're closed till they finish tearing down the tables to convert it from restaurant seating to nightclub seating."

"But I see all my guests in there at the bar right now. It's obviously not closed if they're still having drinks."

"Sorry. I can't let you in until ten p.m."

"Can I at least run in and tell my friends I'm here? They've got to wonder where I am."

"Sure." I start to walk in the door, and he blocks me again.

"At ten o'clock."

I see what's happening. This ham-fisted, steroid-addled, genetic freak of nature is *toying* with me. Pal, today is *not* the day for this.

"Are you trying to tell me that my parents spent *thousands of dollars* here this evening and I, *the bride*, am not allowed to JOIN THE REST OF MY WEDDING PARTY?"

"Oh, you can join them." He cracks the knuckles on his dinner plate–sized hands.

"Thank you."

"At ten o'clock."

"Am I missing something here? Because I am obviously not effectively communicating with you. Tell me, should I dip into my wedding present money—*which I need to keep my home*—and find a nice big bill to give to you for the privilege of attending my own wedding reception?"

A muscle tenses in his enormous square jaw, and he gives me a mean little grin. He shifts his eyes from side to side and leans in to quietly inform me, "Wouldn't hurt."

"Trust me, it would." I address the line of waiting patrons. "Hey, everyone? This gentleman expects me to BRIBE him to get into my own reception. Can you believe someone would stoop so low as to extort cash from a *bride* on her *wedding day*? However, I choose not to BRIBE him, but I wanted to let you all know it sounds like he's willing to accept money under the table for early entry!" I return the bouncer's mean smile and revel in the fact he's gone completely pale under his tan. "How 'bout I run in and get my friends now?"

As we exit, I wish the bouncer best of luck with the graft and let him know we'll never be back. He doesn't care, but it certainly makes me feel better.

Somewhere in the past half an hour, I seem to have lost my groom. He and a few fraternity brothers took off to look for me while I was on cake duty. Our remaining group heads to one of the lounges, and we stake out a bunch of couches. After a couple of drinks, I realize how tired I am, but I don't want to leave until Fletch finds us. I wait and wait but he doesn't show up. Around eleven thirty p.m., I tell my brother to make sure Fletch knows I've gone up to the room and to join me there.

As I let myself into the room, the first thing I notice is the crib . . . but not until after I've fallen into it.

Frantically, I dial the concierge. "Hi, this is Jennifer Lancaster in one of the honeymoon suites. . . . Fine, thanks. No, wait, I'm actually not fine. Housekeeping set up a CRIB in my room, I tripped over it, and I want it removed. . . . Uh-huh, yes. . . . You know, all the other couples I saw at the chapel today already had children, so I assume it was meant for one of their rooms. . . . I suggest you try Child Bride and Tattoo Neck's room first. I'm pretty sure they don't make a lot of good choices, and I bet they kept the baby with them tonight. . . . Great. Thank you."

Rubbing my hip where I bruised it on the crib, I survey the rest of the room. The bed is disheveled from where Joel passed out on it earlier, but not before spilling what I *hope* was his beer. Nice. OK, I'm not going to freak out about this because Fletch did the right thing by having him sleep it off. I don't know why he didn't station Joel on the COUCH, but I'm not going to get mad. It's my special day, and everything was perfect. Granted, I didn't get much of a chance to enjoy any of it, but everyone else did, so I guess that's what's important.

Then I notice exactly how smoky the room is. Fletch must have been up here looking for me because everyone in his entourage smokes when they drink. All the ashtrays in the suite are clean so I wonder what happened to the cigarette butts. The smell of stale smoke is nauseatingly prevalent.

Oh . . . I see. They chose to stub them out *in the remains of my room service tray.* I am trying very hard not to get mad. I repeat to myself *special day, happy guests, looked pretty eating a sandwich, everything's OK.*

I toss the cigarette-laden tray into the hall and housekeeping finally arrives to collect the crib. I roam around the suite waiting for Fletch to come up. We're going to open presents together and finally have a few minutes alone. Frankly, it sounds like heaven.

A half hour passes with no sign of Fletcher . . . and another half hour . . . and then an hour.

By two thirty a.m., I am beyond furious. This is my wedding night—so where exactly is my groom? The one thing I asked him today was not to drink to excess because I didn't want to get mad at him. I *begged* him, actually, and he *promised* he'd behave himself. By my calculations, he's had access to cocktails for over ten hours, so chances are excellent he's drunk as a monkey.

An hour ago, I changed into a VERY unsexy pair of gray flannel pajamas, took down my elaborate wedding up 'do, and washed off my $180 makeup application. Since he's NOT going to be sleeping in this bed with me anytime soon, he can just forget any notion of a romantic wedding night.

I'm watching the only thing on TV—a Britney Spears movie—when Todd, Carol, and my friend Jen carry Fletch in the door around three a.m.

"Hi! Happpppy Weddinnnng!" Fletch greets me, stumbling into the room.

"WHERE THE FUCK HAVE YOU BEEN?" Steam is blowing out my ears. I crossed from *angry* into *bloodlust* about fifteen minutes ago.

Todd answers, "He was downstairs with us. Hey, Jen, I need to borrow a—"

"I have been sitting up here alone for almost four hours waiting for you," I seethe. "Did it occur to you to check on me? Perhaps call me and see what I was doing?" I stomp around the room and begin to slam things.

"Whaaaat?" Fletch slurs.

"Oh, I thought you went to bed, so we figured it was OK for him to hang out with us," Todd adds helpfully.

"Is that the message I gave you? No. I told you to tell him to come upstairs," I reply. "By the way, Fletch, thanks for letting your friends trash the room. There's nothing more inviting in a honeymoon suite than a bunch of cigarettes mashed out in an old sandwich. And you'd better hope it's just beer spilled on the comforter, because you are sleeping with it on the couch." I pick up my bouquet and hurl it at him. It bounces off his chest, but not before a few of the gardenias explode.

While I rage, Carol and Jen slowly back out the door. "Bye, Jen." "Good night, Jen." "We'll talk to you when you get back." "Thanks for everything."

"Hey, calm down. We told Fletch it was OK, and we all had a

really good time together. Really, you should be mad at us," my brother says.

"Todd, Fletch made up his own mind. He decided to get liquored up with his buddies rather than BE WITH HIS NEW WIFE. And that? Is not acceptable."

"OK, I'm going to go, but first give me—"

"GET OUT! GET OUT! GET OUT!" I scream while my brother skitters out of the room.

Fletch loosens his bow tie and falls forward on the bed, attempting to cover himself with the blankets.

"Oh, no, you don't! YOU! COUCH! NOW!"

"No, wanna schhhleeep heeeeere becaussshe itsch a haaaapy weddding," he mumbles.

"Not bloody likely," I spit before rolling him off the bed.

"Ooof. Owww. Hitsch my headdd. You're a baaaad wiiiife. Shun't a gotten marrieeeeed."

Can you honestly blame me for hurling his laptop at him?

PART TWO

Pandora

7

Opening the Box

From the desk of
Miss Jennifer A. Lancaster

Jen's Post-Wedding To-Do List:
  * Find a job!
  * Stop frivolous spending.
  * Lose weight.
  * Fix up Courtney and Brett.

*I*t's the first day of my honeymoon, and the phone is ringing. I've barely slept. Fletch passed out immediately after our fight, but I was too mad to sleep and only dozed off as the sun rose. Groggily, I pick up the receiver. "Someone better be dead."

"Jennifer!" Oh, great. It's my mother and I can

already tell she's in a *state*. "Todd told us what happened! Are you getting a divorce?"

"Excuse me?"

"Todd's here and he said you had a huge fight with Fletch."

This has got to be a joke. "Why are you calling me at"—I lift my head and squint at the digital clock, "seven a.m. to pry into my day-old marriage? I'm going back to sleep now. GOOD-BYE." I bang down the phone.

Two minutes later, the phone rings again. *"What?"*

"GOOD MORNING, FLETCH'S WIFE! HOW THE HELL ARE YA?" Five foot ten, 225 pounds, steroid-free, and without an ounce of fat, Joel is the toughest guy I've ever met. But all that extra testosterone means he tends to speak in capital letters, and right now I'm not in the mood for a (VERY LOUD) chat. At some point while I slept, Fletch—still wearing most of his wedding garb—crawled into bed with me. I shake him and hand him the phone. "Deal with this."

Fletch doesn't dare defy me. "Hello? Oh, hey, Joel . . . Yeah, thanks . . . What? I'm not sure. . . . Sorry, I don't think that's a good idea. . . . You know, you missed the whole reception? You're kidding. . . . You're kidding! That's unbelievable. . . . OK . . . OK . . . All right, see you at home. Bye."

Curiosity supersedes my fury, and I demand to know what Joel said.

"You're speaking to me?" Fletch asks tentatively.

"For now."

"First he called to tell us he's in the lobby. He wants to spend the day together."

"No fucking way."

"I assumed as much. Then he told me what happened to him last night after he left our room. He tried to get back in the reception but the bouncers wouldn't let him—they said he was too drunk—so he decided to take a nap again. In the landscaping. The police found him, and they brought him back to his hotel."

"Maybe when the police here find someone passed out in the bushes, they figure, 'This guy has thoroughly enjoyed everything Vegas has to offer' and they're nice to him."

"I think he got lucky."

Funny, but just having a simple conversation reminds me how much I love Fletch. Even though I'm still upset, I decide to forgive him for last night. I'm not happy with some of the choices he made, but I may have let my mother's situational insanity (and that bovine bouncer) unduly influence my mood.

Also, I did ruin his laptop. "Fletch?"

"Yeah?" He takes off the rest of his tuxedo and changes for bed. The sight of him in his SpongeBob jammies pants completely thaws my heart.

"I'm sorry for throwing your computer."

"That's OK."

"And I'm sorry for overreacting."

"You didn't overreact. You were completely justified. I did exactly what you asked me not to do and I'm really, really sorry."

"Listen, I don't want to start our married life this way. Let's say we were both at fault and declare it a clean slate."

"You sure?"

"Sweetie, think about how many episodes of *COPS* we've watched together. Technically you could have me arrested for felony assault. Granted, we were in a luxury suite and not a trailer, and you were wearing a dinner jacket and not jeans without a shirt, but the concept is the same."

He considers this for so long, I start contemplating my life behind bars. On the one hand, I'm a delicate flower who'd wilt without access to a hairdryer and MTV. On the other, I bet I'd be Queen of the Prison in no time. Although I'd eschew those awful jail tattoos, I could see my way to allowing the other inmates to give me a flattering but powerful nickname. I'm thinking "Her Majesty" might be nice— I can already picture the other inmates bowing before me to kiss my ring while I dole out cigarettes and favors—

"Agreed."

Perhaps avoiding jail is for the best. We exchange our first marital kiss sans audience and settle in to our respective sides of the bed to sleep.

"Hey, I have a good idea. When we look back on our wedding day, why don't we just blame everything on my mother?"

My mom shows up at noon while I'm drinking coffee and recounting wedding loot. I'd expected to become rich, but I guess when you only invite a handful of people you only get a handful of gifts. Bummer. However, I *am* the proud owner of a Cadillac and now am allowed—nay, *obligated*—to start bugging my single friends about when they're "going to settle down already."[104]

"I thought you'd want some of the centerpieces," Mom says, nudging her way into the room. Bullshit. She's here to get the dirt on last night. She settles into the suite's sofa and kicks up her feet. "We missed you at breakfast." I am SO not buying her faux-casual attitude.

"I told you from the get-go I wasn't attending a nine a.m. brunch the day after my wedding."

"Everyone had a wonderful time. My sisters said it was one of the best weddings they've ever attended."

"I'm glad."

"The whole family is going home today. Todd left for the airport

---

[104] I had to put up with it for seven years—it's payback time.

a few minutes ago." She toys with an obscenely large calla lily on my bouquet until she can't contain herself anymore. Wait for it. . . . Wait for it. . . . "So where's your husband?"

"Showering."

"Are you getting a divorce?"

"Don't be ridiculous."

"Then are you going to share what happened with me?"

"Mom, I already told you it's none of your business, and I'd appreciate it if you respected my privacy."

"But Todd said—"

"I don't care what Todd said. Everything is fine. Don't waste one minute worrying about us. This isn't the first scrap we've had, and it won't be the last. But we're generally pretty good about communicating, and when things boil up, they pass quickly. Now we're cool like Fonzie, OK?"

"I'm glad to hear it." By the way she's fidgeting, I can tell she's not satisfied with my explanation, but she wisely drops the subject anyway. "What's on our itinerary today?"

"When Fletch is done, we're going to the photography office to look at our proofs."

"The pictures are done already?"

"Mom, this is *Vegas*."

"I'll come with you."

"Buzzzzzt, wrong answer."

"But I want to see them!"

"Today is the first day of my honeymoon and I am spending it *alone* with my husband—meaning without *you*. I'll run the photos by your room later."

"Then where are we having dinner tonight?"

"Mom, I don't mean to hurt your feelings, but the mother-daughter togetherness part of this trip is over. Fletch and I are having dinner in the Foundation Room at the House of Blues. Alone.

It's supposed to be all funky and rock and roll and I'm sure you wouldn't like it."[105]

She pouts. "Well, you certainly don't seem very grateful after—"

"I told you I can't thank you enough for everything you've done for us. You truly gave us everything we'd want in a wedding, and we're incredibly grateful. And as soon as I start working, I'll start paying you back."

"Jennifer, that's not necessary."

"I want to. But my point is, as thankful as we are, it IS the first day of our new lives together, and we want time alone. And stop smirking, I don't mean that in a *naked* sense because I will DIE before I ever discuss sex with you. Think about it—would you have wanted Noni and Grampa tagging along on your honeymoon?"

"I guess it would have been awkward having my parents there the first time your father and I—"

"Shh, stop, too much information. Say any more and I'll have to wash my brain with vodka. Why don't you go have a nice day with Dad? That is, if he isn't still hiding from you."

"He did mention wanting to see the Hoover Dam."

"Sounds like a plan. I'll see you later," I say, shooing her toward the door. When I hug her, I notice she's still wearing yesterday's false eyelashes.

"Mom? You know those come off with a little makeup remover and a cotton pad?"

"I'm not taking them off."

"Why not?"

"I spent $180 on that makeup job and I refuse to wash my face until I get my money's worth."

• •

---

[105]She actually might like it but I DON'T CARE.

Since neither Courtney nor Brett could make it to the wedding, I've had to wait till we got home to get them together, and now we're in one of the horseshoe-shaped booths at Piece on North Avenue. While I should be wolfing down their trademark white pizza and slyly building my case about why Courtney and Brett would make a perfect couple, I'm making a scene.

"That is such horseshit! HORSESHIT!!" I pound the table so hard that our microbrews slosh out of our glasses. "So that bitch—that breast-pumping, nanny-trouble-having, divorcee LYING BITCH told you I turned down the job?"

After almost a year, Corp. Com. has decided to reinstate my position and relaunch my old product line. Since I'd been laid off, I *should* have been first in line for consideration. All my old AEs assumed I'd come back, but Kathleen told them I'd rejected their offer.

"Courtney, she never called me."

"She probably couldn't reach you."

"I'm home twenty-three hours a day. And if I'm not around, I have caller ID, voice mail, and call-waiting. Even if she called and didn't leave a message, I'd have a record of it. She didn't call, end of story." For some strange reason, Courtney likes Kathleen and tries to make excuses for her. "Face it, Court. She lied."

"Are you *sure* you never talked to her? I just can't see that she'd—"

"Um, *hello*? We're having dinner at a freaking pizza place instead of Morton's. I'm drinking BEER and not martinis or champagne. For God's sake, I'M CLIPPING COUPONS in an effort to conserve money. Don't believe me? I've got one in my bag *right now*."

I notice the stricken look on Courtney's face and try to speak in a calmer voice. "I don't mean to take it out on you, and I'm really sorry, but does someone concerned about saving thirty-five cents on a can of Friskies strike you as the kind of person with the luxury of being choosy? The last thing I'd do would be to turn down a well-paying job, even if it meant sucking up to Kathleen." Suddenly I'm struck with an idea. "Court, give me your phone. I'll call her right now and tell her I'm still available. I promise I'll be nice."

Courtney blanches and toys with a stray pizza crust. "I don't think that's a good idea."

"Why not? I can prove to her that I'm still as much of a go-getter as I ever was."

Courtney won't look me in the eye. She takes a bite of her pizza and chews it at least a hundred times before swallowing. "She already hired someone."

THAT BITCH.

I grit my teeth. "May I ask exactly who was more qualified to do my job than me?"[106]

"I'm afraid to say." Courtney shrinks in her seat.

"Come on, tell me. I'm not going to get mad at *you*."

"Don't you believe her," Brett interjects. "She has a long history of killing the messenger." OK, so I *may* have yelled at him once or twice for giving me bad news when we worked together at Midwest IR. But when his tech team couldn't deliver the solution I sold in the time they'd promised and the lost commission was the equivalent of an upscale SUV, what did he expect?

"Vroom, vroom, what'd you say, Brett, vroom, vroom? I can't hear you over the roar of my new Range Rover, vroom, vroom." I pretend to steer the car I SHOULD have been able to buy had his team not been comprised of ham-fisted Luddites.

"I'm never going to live that down, am I?"

"Not in this lifetime," Fletch replies.

"Will you just tell me already?" I huff.

"OK, OK. She hired . . . Taggart." Courtney winces as if she's anticipating a blow.

---

[106]Correct answer? NO ONE.

"*Taggart*? What's a *Taggart*? Wait a minute, is Taggart her goofy, bucktoothed sister?"

"Yes."

"Wasn't she one of those weirdo, home-schooling, hippie moms? She has something like seven kids, doesn't she?"

"She has four."

"And how is she going to educate a stable full of rug rats, work an incredibly time-consuming job, and churn her own organic butter at the same time?"

"Kathleen got her permission to work from home," Courtney whispers. She's slid halfway under the table at this point.

I whip out my cat-food coupon and wave it at Courtney. "*This*! *This* is what I have to resort to because some bulgur-wheat-eating, hairy-legged, über-breeding RELATIVE got the job that should have been mine?" I bang my mug down on the table so hard it shatters, causing our server to inquire if I wouldn't prefer sitting in the shouting section.

Oh, terrific, now *pizza joint* waitresses are making fun of me.

Brett interjects, "Jen, I didn't mention it because I assumed you wouldn't be interested, but your cat-food coupon is a cry for help." Brett flicks a stray shard of glass off his sweater. "Clearly, Julie has an open position on her team."

"Which one was Julie? I thought you only worked with the Joshes," Fletch says.

"Julie joined Midwest IR a few months after I left. She runs my old division." And probably not nearly as well as I did.

"Lizzie quit to move to San Francisco, so Julie needs another marketing person. The job is still the same as when Lizzie worked for you—mostly writing Web site copy and monitoring advertisers' traffic stats. The base is about $50K plus quarterly bonuses. Do you want me to talk to Julie about you or are you looking for more?"

"A $50K salary is WAY less insulting than I used to believe, especially since it's about $50K more than I make at the moment. Honestly? It sounds like a godsend."

Brett asks, "Would you feel weird working a coordinator's job in the department you used to run?"

"Probably, but I guarantee you it would be less uncomfortable than the conversations I've had with my student loan officer lately. Brett, you're awesome. Thanks so much." I lean over to hug him.

Fletch pops his head under the table. "Courtney, crisis averted. You can come out now." He turns his attention to Brett. "Looks like you may finally be forgiven, vroom, vroom."

. . . .

"I *so* nailed it," I tell Brett. We're sitting in his corner office doing a postmortem on my interview with Julie. If nothing else, my cute outfit should guarantee me the job—I'm wearing a fitted taupe jacket with a swirly skirt and matching camisole with spectator slingbacks. Sure, add a flower-strewn hat, and I'd fit in perfectly at the Kentucky Derby, but since I'm not applying for VP, I figured a less traditional suit would be appropriate. "Seriously, it could not have gone better. After all, I created the product—the portfolio management tool was my baby. I decided on the level of interactivity, the features, even the colors on the interface. How could I *not* be the perfect person to write marketing copy about it?"

"How'd you explain your willingness to accept a lesser position?" Brett asks.

"I told Julie my life was different now. I'm married, I have dogs, I have a whole new set of responsibilities. I said I don't want to spend sixty hours a week in the office."

"Which, because I know you, is a lie."

"I figured if talked up my work ethic too much, she'd worry I was bucking for her job."

"When will she make a decision?"

"A couple of days. But she's going to say yes, I'm sure of it."

"Cool. By the way, have you, um, spoken with Courtney lately?"

"Of course, Brett. I talk to Court all the time. Was there something specific you'd like to know?" A bright pink flush spreads across Brett's cheeks. "You're blushing! You *like* her! Oh, that's darling! I knew you guys would connect. You have so much in common like your triathlete competition things and predilection for Dave Matthews.[107] It just so happens she asked me to give you her number." I root around in my purse until I locate her digits. I place her business card in front of Brett.

"Thanks, Jen. I owe you."

A phone number in exchange for the opportunity to earn fifty large? "Brett, I'm pretty sure we're even."

• •

I'm finishing reading all the day's new job postings when Fletch walks in. "Hey, sweetie, what's up? You're home *really* early." Maisy and Loki bark and spin, delighted at their dad's unexpected arrival. I am too because I'm dying for a little human interaction. I talk to those damn dogs all day long. Someday they're going to start talking back, and I am simply not prepared for that.

Then I notice that Fletch is carrying a huge paper box full of personal effects. *Uh-oh.*

"You want the good news or the bad news first?"

I take a deep breath. "Bad, please."

"I was laid off."

I gesture toward his box. "I figured. But you know what? It's not your fault. I know how hard you worked, and I'm very proud of the

[107]HATE! Dave Matthews makes me want to kick puppies.

job you did there. Are you OK?" I fight my way through the dogs to give Fletch a big hug. After seeing his employer on C-SPAN every day for the past month, we suspected this might happen.

"Actually, I am. They gave me a decent severance package, and I'll still get my year-end bonus. Plus I'm eligible for unemployment insurance, so we'll be OK for a little while."

"That's the good news?"

"Nope. When Clark told me my position was eliminated, he could barely keep from smiling. Miserable son of a bitch. While I'm packing up my stuff and commiserating with everyone else—Lisa, Bill, and Ernesto are also gone—the regional VP goes into Clark's office and closes the door. Two minutes later we hear shouting and slamming. Apparently Clark got canned, too."

"He didn't know it was coming?"

"Completely blindsided him."

"That's hilarious."

"Yeah, but I didn't tell you the best part. Right before I walked out, I poked my head in his door and said, 'I'll save you a place in line at the unemployment office.' Must have been the last straw because he lunged out of his chair and *took a swing at me!*"

"No way!"

"I kid you not. Ernesto called the police, and the whole team got to enjoy watching Clark being escorted out in handcuffs. Best day of work ever." A malevolent grin plays across his face.

"You baited him." I'm always secretly delighted when Fletch gets in touch with his inner evil streak.

"You bet I did. That man made me miserable for three years with his explosive rage. He was so much like my dad. As I never had the pleasure of seeing my father arrested, this was the next best thing. I should be upset about losing my job, but I feel great."

The phone rings and I peer at the caller ID. "Fletch, hold that thought—it's Midwest IR. I'm crossing my fingers that it's an offer."

I take a deep breath before grabbing the phone. "Good afternoon. Jennifer speaking."

"Hi, Jennifer. It's Julie from Midwest IR. How are you?"

"Terrific, thanks! What's up?" I'm trying to sound cool, but really I'm a basket case. I need this job now more than ever. After an entire YEAR off, I'm dying to get back to work. I'm even thrilled at the prospect of wearing panty hose again. Shoot, I'll take public transportation if I need to. This way Fletch can be on *my* health insurance so he doesn't have to worry about COBRA. Ooh, and I'll start another 401(k) and begin to feel like a real adult again.[108]

So what if it's a step down? With my work ethic, I'll be back on top in no time. I predict a promotion in six months or less. After all, the other VPs loved me at Midwest IR. And when—

"I'm calling to say we've decided to go in a different direction."

"I'm sorry. Can you repeat that?" The dogs are still yipping and whining, so I must have heard her wrong.

"We've decided not to extend an offer. But I really enjoyed our interview after hearing so many good things about you."

"I don't understand. I promise I wouldn't be bored if that's your concern. I know I worked on more advanced projects before, but—"

"You just don't have the kind of experience we need in this department."

"Cut the crap, Julie. I created the very product your department supports, so don't tell me I'm not experienced. Level with me. When Corp. Com. laid me off, they never gave me a reason, and it's driven me nuts for a whole year. Be honest. Was I overconfident? Arrogant? Whatever was wrong, please tell me so I can fix it before I interview anywhere else."

Julie sighs and lowers her voice. "Jen, you did everything right

---

[108] Thank God.

and I really lobbied for your hire. But Ben won't let me bring you back. He says you're too unprofessional."

Oh, that is *rich*. "Julie, do you know why I left Midwest IR in the first place? It's not solely because I got a better offer. Ben threw a cup of coffee at me during a board meeting while screaming, 'If you can't give me the fucking answers I want, then fucking lie to me!' But as I was not about to let that old bastard see me cry, I replied, 'Come on, sir, you're the president of this place—get it together.' I should have thrown coffee back at him. Instead, I went home to change clothes and post my résumé."

"I heard a rumor about that." Ben's unprofessional behavior is legendary. "I swear I didn't know it was you. Things must really be tough out there if you were willing to come back here."

"You don't know the half of it."

"God, I'm *so* sorry. Take care, and if you need a reference? Call me."

Before I even hang up the phone, Fletch is by my side. "No luck?"

"What are we going to do? A minute ago I was elated because I thought that job was mine. Now I'm scared to death because no one in this household has an income. How are we going to pay for this place? How are we going to keep up with our bills? How am I ever going to get my hair colored again?" I begin to pace and wring my hands.

"You know what we should do right now?" Fletch asks.

"Pray? Cry? Move back to Indiana so I can work at Hardee's, as my brother keeps helpfully suggesting?"

"No. We're going to the Four Seasons."

"Are you *insane*?"

"I say we celebrate the end of the dot-com era by going out with a bang. Our days of posing at their bar are over, so why not celebrate with a couple of $15 martinis?"

"You *are* insane."

Brief silence.

"And I'll be ready in ten minutes."

Four Seasons esss DELICIOUSSS Jack Frost marteeenneees pepperminty chocolaty. . . . 100 percent YUMMM! Pooor but haaaaappppeee!! Fletchhhss is SCHMARTEST MOST HANDD-SUM MAN ALIVE even wiscch his pancake butt. Mmmm . . . pancakes! Sommebuddy buuuy me pancakes? Pleeeeease?

Drunkety. Most, most excccelent drunkety.[109]

. . . .

"Jen, it's a simple favor," Fletch says.

"But I don't want to," I reply.

"Come on, it'll be easy. And you'll get to drive the Cadillac."

"I can drive the Caddy anytime I want."

"But you never have anywhere to go."

"So? I can still use it to take the dogs to the park."

"Last time you drove them it took a week to scrub all the mud off the seats. Admit it. There's no good reason not to do this for Carol."

"Then *you* do it."

"Number one, she didn't ask me. Number two, I have an interview that afternoon. And number three, she's the only nonrelative you have who's been able to stand you for more than a decade."

God, I hate when he's right.

A couple of days ago, Carol e-mailed to ask a favor. Her family's coming up from Indianapolis this weekend. Carol and her small children are visiting friends and her husband, Pete, is running the

---

[109]Six hours and $250 later.

Chicago marathon. As their time here is limited, Carol asked if I could go to the convention center and pick up Pete's official race pack. Since I've got NOTHING going on right now, there's no good reason I can't do this simple task for my oldest friend . . . except that I don't want to because according to Fletch I can be a trifle torpid and a bit selfish.[110]

"Jen, think about it. How often does Carol ask you to do anything for her?"

"Almost never," I concede.

"And how many times has she done something unpleasant for you?"

"Well . . . there was that time in high school when I insisted we see *Desperately Seeking Susan* in full-on Wannabe-like-Madonna gear." Poor Carol. Warily she cast aside her Bonne Belle Dr Pepper Lip Smackers for heavy kohl eyeliner and her Topsiders for torn fishnets. And when I yanked her out of her seat to dance in the aisle with me to "Get into the Groove," she never once complained, even when I accidentally stabbed her with an oversized cross.[111]

"Is that it?"

"No. She also used to let me ride to our speech meets in the back of her car and do Queen Elizabeth waves."

"And?"

"Once when I was a sophomore, she came up from IU, and we met these Alpha Sigs at a party. I got to make out with the cute one with the Flock of Seagulls haircut while she patiently listened to his roommate prattle on in painstaking detail about the musical genius of Jethro Tull."[112]

"Uh-huh. Anything else?"

---

[110]He is SO sleeping on the couch tonight.
[111]It was a very brief phase. I was back to tartan plaid within the week.
[112]The roommate's nickname was Zitty-Zitty Bang-Bang.

"Um . . . she never judged me in my junior year when I thought it would be fun to live my life like a character in a Bret Easton Ellis novel."[113]

"Are you forgetting her wedding?"

Actually, I had. On Carol's wedding day—the one time I should have shaken myself out of my perpetual narcissistic haze and paid her special attention—Carol had to come to my hotel room to hustle me down to the ceremony. I'd lost track of time while grooming myself and almost delayed the start of the wedding.

Looking back at our lives together, I realize in the Big Book of Favors, I'm woefully lacking credit. I've always taken more than I've given. I'm not sure I deserve a friend like Carol. Defeated, I admit, "OK, OK. You've got me. I'll do it."

· ·

4:46 p.m. from allaboutjen: I'm in. Gimme the deets.

4:48 p.m. from carol_and_pete: Thanks, you're a lifesaver! Any time tomorrow between 8-6 PM, go to McCormick Place (you know where that is, right?) to pick up Pete's race information pack at the pre-marathon health and fitness fair. Among other things, the pack will contain the microchip Pete needs to wear so his time will be recorded. It's crucial he has this before the race. You'll have to have the chip activated and grab his t-shirt, but it shouldn't be a big deal.

4:50 p.m. from allaboutjen: I can't believe anyone would voluntarily run 26 miles. Sometimes I sit on the couch crosslegged because I don't feel like walking to the bathroom.

---

[113] A *very bad* phase. Don't ask.

4:51 p.m. from carol_n_pete: Yeah, I remember you peeing in the pool on more than one occasion, too. Gross. As for running, Pete turns 40 this year, so this may be a mid-life thing. It's OK with me—marathon running beats him having an affair or buying a sports car we can't afford.

4:52 p.m. from allaboutjen: Word. See you this weekend.

. . . .

The convention center is five miles round-trip from my apartment, which means the whole trip is less than half the distance Pete is running on Sunday. How bad can it be? *Trading Spaces* is on in an hour, and I figure it will take me fifteen minutes to get down there, ten to pick up the pack, and then fifteen more to get back . . . and bing! I'm home in time to see a shirtless Ty build a bookcase. I planned to leave earlier but I got sucked into a particularly sleazy episode of *Elimidate*.[114]

I quickly assess myself in the hall mirror before walking out the door. My honey caramel highlights are magnificent as always, and I have the remnants of summer freckles still sprinkled across my nose. Too cute. I'm ravishing in an all-black Ralph Lauren Capri pant and cotton sweater ensemble. Yes, it's plus-sized but I'm sure with the hair, jewelry, and Chanel bag, the size of my ass is barely noticeable.[115] I appraise myself long and hard and conclude that,

---

[114]What's the deal with straight girls tongue kissing other straight girls these days? I mean, gay is cool, bi isn't scandalous, but I have trouble dealing with this *Girls Gone Wild* foolishness.

[115]Recently a man stopped me at Star Bar when I was clad in a similar outfit and told me, "Honey, I'm gay, but I would totally do you. You're fabulous!!" This is possibly the greatest compliment I've received in my entire life.

caboose be damned, I *am* fabulous. I grab a Twix for the road and I'm off.

I saddle up the Caddy and ride .6 miles to the expressway . . . and get stuck for an hour and fifteen minutes. Since I don't commute anymore, I completely forgot about Friday afternoon traffic. Dammit, I should have know this was going to happen. Why did I even agree to this stupid errand? I put James' "Laid" on the CD player and listen to it at full blast in an attempt to soothe my traffic-addled nerves.[116]

I finally get to a point where I can turn off the expressway. Because I'm such a savvy Chicago girl, I'll just take a short cut and beat the rest of the traffic to McCormick. HA! Look at all the lemming tourists going the long way! Suckers!

Note to self: NEVER, EVER, EVER attempt to take a shortcut on the way to McCormick Place.

OK, picture a bunch of bombed-out storefronts, garbage-strewn roadways, and sad-looking people drinking brown liquid out of brown paper bags while assessing Carbohydrate Barbie FREAKING THE HELL OUT in her deluxe sedan, and you'll get an accurate snapshot of the last half hour of my life.[117] As stopping for directions was NOT an option, I did the only thing I knew how—I turned my fear into anger and I blamed the whole situation on other people. *Stupid Pete. Why couldn't he run the Boston marathon? Stupid Carol. By all rights she should hate me by now. Why did she have to keep liking me? Stupid Fletch. How does he always know how to make me feel*

---

[116]This used to be my big stress-relieving song when I worked at Corp. Com. I'd play it over and over again and it always managed to calm me. Positive K's "I Got a Man" and English Beat's "Save It for Later" are also excellent release valves.
[117]Which, fortunately, was not the LAST half hour of my life, although I couldn't be sure at the time.

guilty? I should be watching Hildy staple kittens to a home owner's wall right about now, not driving around the world's scariest neighborhood. Stupid Mayor Daley. Why didn't he post signs saying that clueless ex-sorority girls should not be cruising around in luxury cars through the Robert Taylor projects, like, ever?

I purposefully blew every light hoping the cops would notice and thus escort me out, but no luck. *Stupid police.* Somehow I made it to the convention center in one piece, although I cannot speak of the various traffic laws I violated to do so.

Anyway, here's an interesting fact about the convention center. It's big.

Awfully big.

Like a million square feet of exhibit space big.

As I walk the 1.2 miles from the parking garage to the main hallway, I curse Carol's name a little more. Had I realized it was so far, I wouldn't have worn such strappy shoes. With each step I take, the buckle embeds itself deeper into my skin. As I hobble along, I decide people-watching will take my mind off the pain. *Hmm . . . ugly . . . ugly . . . scrawny . . . ooh, lotta ear hair on that one . . . ugly . . . Chic jeans—ha! 1984 called and they want their pants back . . . blech, it's cologne after shower, not instead of, sir . . . boring . . . wow, that person has amazing calf muscles . . . hmm, so does that one . . . nice mullet, jackass . . . yikes, it's called* rhinoplasty, *look into it . . . too skinny . . . too skinny . . . ma'am, seriously, eat a sandwich or something, you're WAY too thin. . . .*

There are a lot of really toned people jogging past me. That's kind of weird—am I late? I consult my Coach Tank watch and see that we have another whole hour, so why is everyone rushing? More people with whippet-slim waists careen by. Funny because Chicago isn't really a "skinny" city, and that's why I like it here. So what if I've put on a few[118] pounds since I got laid off? An extra layer of fat

[118]Fifty.

is exactly what a gal needs to get through those chilly Chicago winters. A bit of excess weight is practically a necessity—it's like I'm more evolved than these lollipop heads.

A group of girls with six-pack abs whizz by me so fast I almost get dragged along in their tailwind. *C'mon, ladies. Bulimia is going to ruin your teeth. Who cares how trim you are if you've got a mouthful of rotting canines and molars? And, God, look at that girl in the spandex shorts—she has thighs like a baby giraffe.* Self-consciously, I place hand on my own thigh. Definitely not baby giraffe material. The closer I get to the main hallway, the denser the crowd grows. There are six-packs and perfectly toned calves everywhere I look. Gah, what's with these people? Why are they all so tall and thin??

All of a sudden it hits me. . . . This is a health and fitness fair . . . *AND I AM THE ONLY FAT PERSON HERE.*

I break into a cold sweat, as it dawns on me that everyone else in this building is planning to run 26.2 miles on Sunday . . . which means these people never perspire while eating dinner. Or have to stop for a breather when climbing the stairs. They use their exercise bikes for exercise and not just to dry hand-knit sweaters and— HOLY CRAP!—they're looking at me wondering *how on earth I'm going to compete in this race*!

At this moment, I realize all the Chanel handbags in the world aren't going to camouflage the simple reality that I am grossly out of shape. This is SO much worse than being the only non–porn star at my hotel during my wedding. How am I supposed to lord myself over a bunch of clean-living fitness nuts? Impossible! These are the kind of people who think whole milk is a sin against nature and would rather DIE than put half-and-half on their Count Chocula.[119] All I want to do is get the hell out of here, but if I don't claim Pete's

---

[119]So wrong and yet so good.

chip, he can't race and that's six months of training down the drain. Plus there's a discrepancy in the Big Book of Favors, so I force myself to press on.

Though normally superconfident, I am not prepared for the judgmental stares of the ultrafit. They don't know me and have no idea of my prowess in the boardroom. They're unfamiliar with my shoe collection and unaware that I live in the Dot-Com Palace. And they didn't notice me pulling up in the Caddy. All they can see is how much space I occupy.

With each step I take, I feel cellulite blossoming on my arms, my stomach, and my calves. *Stop it!* I think my chin just multiplied and my thighs inflated. *No! Deflate! Deflate!* And I'm pretty sure I can see my own ass out of the corner of my eye. *Gah! Cut it out!!* Am I imagining things, or do my footsteps sound like those of the giant who stomped though the city in the beginning of *Underdog*? *And how did I go from aging-but-still-kind-of-hot ex-sorority girl to horrific, stompy cartoon monster in less than an hour?*

My sleek and sexy python sandals have morphed into cloven hooves by the time I reach the line for the race packet. While I wait, the air is abuzz with tales of other marathons while many sets of eyes cut in my direction. Eventually an asshat in a JUST DO IT T-shirt asks me, "How's *your* training going?"

"Great. I find carb-loading Big Macs and Hershey bars right before the race really helps me achieve my personal best," I reply. An awkward silence falls over the group while they stare down at their hundred dollar running shoes.

"You guys understand I'm kidding, right? I'm just picking up the packet for a friend," I add. They break out into relieved (and highly insulting) laughter. "Yes, haw, haw, haw, aren't all fat people funny?" I snap. I whip out a Dior compact and aggressively powder my nose. The line grows silent. We continue to shuffle forward and eventually

I get to the counter. I hand over my redemption brochure, and the spry old man in a high-tech track suit does a double-take when he sees me.

With much trepidation, he inquires, "This isn't for you, is it?"

"Do I look like Peter Kohrs?" I tersely reply. "Let me assure you, I got suckered into this errand and will *not* be running this weekend. So you can take the EMS unit off of speed dial, Jack LaLanne."

The fact I don't choke him when he mutters, "Thank heavens," is a testament to my remarkable self-restraint.[120]

I haul my ponderous bulk to the next station and try to make sure no small children topple in my wake. The wide-eyed stares at my midsection are making my self-consciousness almost unbearable. I want to shout at the top of my lungs, *"The average American woman is size fourteen! Jim Fixx died while jogging! You wish you had hair like this! And sometimes I eat salad for dinner!"* but I don't for fear of drawing any additional attention.

When I get to the place where I have to activate the microchip, another misguided do-gooder tries to warn me about the health risks of overexertion. I politely thank him[121] and move on to the main part of the fair, where I have to redeem the stupid T-shirt voucher.

And thus I enter the belly of the beast.

As I descend into the depths of the fair, I see not a few dozen fit people, not a couple hundred, but multiple thousands of sinewy hard bodies. I doubt anyone's body fat percentage here is above 5 percent. I can't help but notice all the beady eyes that narrow as I descend the escalator. Of course, the runners are all zooming down the adjacent stairs, so it's just me on the machine, floating down like a Ralph Lauren–designed Goodyear blimp.

---

[120]I would have punched him in the neck had I not thought everyone would point and titter, "What's the fracas with the fat girl over there?"
[121]Tell him to "fuck off."

When Lara Flynn Boyle's evil twin remarks to a wafer-thin friend, "I thought this was a *fitness* fair, not Lane Bryant," I reach my breaking point. I whip around to face her.

"Listen, you anorexic bitch, how *dare* you make fun of me for being chunky? I'd think you'd be happy that a porky chick is running against you. I mean, you're a competitive person, right? Shouldn't you be *glad* to race someone you can beat? And where exactly is the great love and camaraderie that runners are supposed to have for each other? Or does that only apply to the thin and cute participants? Shouldn't all those endorphins in your system make you happy to the point that you wouldn't attack a total stranger? And you know what? If our plane crashed in the Andes? You'd *wish* I was there because I guarantee you that all this extra fat would make me ABSOLUTELY DELICIOUS," I hiss approximately three inches from her face. I find when being confrontational you're a lot scarier up close and quiet than loud and distant.

She and her friend sprint away from me while I shout, "Maybe if you run that fast on Sunday, you'll win! Good luck!"

At this point, every single person on the south end of the exhibit hall is watching me. So I pull the Twix bar out of my bag and begin to masticate loudly and obnoxiously. I do an exaggerated waddle up to the T-shirt area and see the lines are broken down by size. I wave a chocolate-coated hand at the volunteer and shout in a faux–New York accent, "Yo, yuh, you, little girlie. You got dese shirts in triple XLs? Gotta make sure it covers all my beauty-ful curves." Karen Carpenter II meekly raises an emaciated finger in the direction of the biggest shirts and I'm off.[122]

I shove the rest of the candy bar in my mouth, lick my chops

---

[122]I don't care if the shirt doesn't fit Pete. This is not about a shirt. This is about not going quietly into that good night. Just because they don't eat refined sugar does not make these people morally superior.

noisily, and wipe my chocolaty paw on the Studebaker also known as my ass. I announce, "Damn. Them Twixes aahh tasty!" to the New Balance–clad Ally McBeal behind me. "Hey, I need me a smoke wicked bad. You got a light?" I ask her.

She's beyond appalled. "Smoking is not allowed in the convention center. And furthermore, it's very bad for you."

"So's Jack Daniel's shooters and my boyfriend Snake, but that don't mean it ain't fun!" I reply, punctuating the statement with a resounding smack on my own butt and a quick pelvic thrust.

The look on her gaunt little face is priceless.

Dignity *and* T-shirt redeemed, I exit.[123] I'm so glad to be away from the health and fitness Nazis that I don't even mind the next hour on the expressway.

Because in the Big Book of Favors, Carol and I are now even.

• •

Now that Fletch has his days free, we have plenty of time to take Maisy and Loki to the park. Chicago is a dog-friendly city, and there are tons of specific areas that are double-gated and completely enclosed so dogs can run to their hearts' content. The parks have low doggie drinking fountains, benches for their owners, and gratis poop bags.[124] Our dogs adore jaunts to the park because they can get the kind of exercise their fat primary caregiver can't give them. I tried to run with them a couple of times but with them clotheslining my legs with their leashes and stopping short to sniff and causing me to tumble over them, and my own exertion-based stabbing chest pains, I figured it was too dangerous.

The best part about the doggie park is the interaction. Even

---

[123]Ironically, I actually jog back to the parking garage at an admirable clip.
[124]If they had a coffee cart, I might never leave.

for someone like me who has a hard time being friendly, it's easy to break the ice—all you have to do is talk about your dogs! I've met a ton of interesting people at Walsh Park, and we've totally bonded.

Blending seamlessly with the cool, tattooed, band-having, this-is-just-my-day-job professional dog walkers are ex–marketing gurus, unemployed MBAs, and laid-off project managers. It's an eclectic mix of people, but we seem to mesh. When someone new joins our group, we always ask, "What did you used to do for a living?" For a while we even had a Tuesday Afternoon Drinking Club—exactly what it sounds like—but finding us shit-faced at four p.m. annoyed too many of our respective employed significant others and band members. Going to the park has been like group therapy for me, and the only downside is all the doody touching.

Lately Fletch and I have taken the dogs to Churchill Park—it's brand-new and right around the corner from our loft. I still prefer Walsh Park, but it's a half hour walk,[125] and the dogs are just as happy.

The people aren't as friendly, though, probably because instead of being unemployed, most of them are consultants with flexible schedules. And whereas Walsh Park is an interesting potpourri of people and mixed-breed mutts, Churchill is all about purebreds and their humorless Lexus SUV–driving, Accenture-working, North Face–clad owners.

We're here on Saturday afternoon, and it's like a Westminster Kennel Club competition. There's easily $15,000 worth of dogs dashing up and down the gravel run.

"Uh-oh," I say to Fletch, gesturing toward the south gate. "Here comes THAT guy." A small, tidy, fussy man wearing those weird Donald J. Pliner elf shoes and immaculate chinos saunters

---

[125]Who am I kidding? It's a five-minute drive.

into the park, being towed by his gigantic, gay boxers Marcel and Gilbert.[126]

"What's wrong with him?" Fletch asks.

"You'll see."

As soon as they're released, Marcel and *Zhjill-BEHR* begin to humpity-pumpity every dog that crosses their path, particularly disturbing because the dogs still possess their *factory-installed* equipment. Icky. Small Tidy Fussy man simply reads his *Paris Match* and, instead of disciplining his dogs, ignores the whole scene. While Loki romps with Maisy, Marcel sneaks up behind him and climbs aboard. Loki growls and snaps at Marcel and then continues to play.

"Pardonnez-moi," yells Small Tidy Fussy man. "Your dog, he attacked mine. You should get your violent dogs out of here." At the moment, Maisy's on her back letting a Jack Russell lick her goodies while Fletch attaches her leash. Loki sits at attention, waiting his turn.

"Wait a minute. You have the nerve to let your dogs hump and jump, doing nothing about it, and then you blame *my* dog for following his instinct?"

"Every time I come here, your dog attacks mine, no?"

"That's because every time your dogs *corn hole* mine. Given the choice, my dogs prefer *not* to be date-raped. Maybe if you'd actually follow park rules and neuter them, we wouldn't have this problem."

"Do you know how much my boxers are worth? I need their seed for breeding purposes. It is *most* important. And I can't have your aggressive"—he pauses to sneer—"*junkyard dogs* marring their looks by biting them."

OK, that does it. You can insult my parentage, intelligence, or taste but you DO NOT say disparaging things about my dogs. "It's

---

[126]That's pronounced *Zhjill-BEHR—God forbid* you read the tags and assume the English pronunciation. I thought he was going to sic the French Ministry of Language on me.

obvious you're worried about protecting your investment, not your dogs. And anyone who considers his pets to be an investment is simply loathsome." I look to the crowd for their support. At Walsh Park, my entire posse would be standing behind me. But here? No one will even meet my gaze.

"Well, yes, I can see where your dogs get their violent streak," he snorts.

I whip off my mittens and toss them to the ground, shouting, "Violent? You think these sweet, loving creatures are violent? OH, I WILL *SHOW* YOU VIOLENCE, YOU FROGGY LITTLE—" Then Fletch yanks me and the dogs out of the park.

As I'm dragged down Winchester Avenue, Fletch clears his throat. "So that went well."

I am hopping mad. "How dare that Francophile accuse our dogs of being violent? They're afraid of the cats *and* the vacuum. And why is everyone at Churchill Park such a jerk anyway? Why can't they be cool like my friends at Walsh?"

"It's the neighborhood—it's changed. When we moved here, there was an equal mix of dot-commers, artists, and immigrants. Now developers are paying top dollar for lots, and the Mexican and Polish families are moving out of the area. Prices are escalating so fast it's only consultants and brokers who can live here. Plus, they're snapping up the spaces vacated by the dot-com refugees because they all moved home to Wheaton to live with their parents."

"I hate how different everything is now."

"I do, too. The neighborhood's so sanitized. Remember when we first moved here how dangerous it was to be on the street at night? Now when I walk the dogs after dark, I run into yuppie families holding children eating gelato on their shoulders. The whole place has been Disneyfied and the worst part is we can barely afford it anymore."

"Do you"—I try to swallow the lump in my throat—"do you

think it might be time for us to move?" We walk silently for a minute until we get to the front door of our building. We wait to enter while a mother—talking on her cell phone—navigates a high-tech stroller containing a child wearing Gore-Tex and tiny Merrell snow clogs. An off-leash chocolate lab trails obediently along at her side.

Fletch sighs. "Maybe so."

8

Temporary Insanity

It won't kill you," Shayla says.

"It might," I reply.

"You're being a big baby. I did it every summer during grad school, and it was easy money. Why don't you give it a try? It may be the answer to your problems. Not only would it give you an income now—it could lead to a full-time position."

"But isn't it degrading?"

"No, not so much. But assuming it were, which is more degrading in the long run: working a temp job and earning some pin money, or bitching about unemployment while sitting around in your pajamas drinking wine from a box at three in the afternoon?"

"These aren't pajamas. They're *lounge pants*." I smooth out my pant legs and adjust the zipper on my gray hoodie. "Granted, they're burgundy flannel, polar bear–print lounge pants with an open fly that I occasionally sleep in, but I also wear them to the grocery store and when I walk the dogs."

"Saying they aren't pajamas doesn't make them not pajamas."

"Whatever. Anyway, this box wine is a lot better than you'd expect. Have some."

"I would but I've got to teach a class in the morning. I'll stick to hot tea, thanks." Shayla just got her PhD and is now an assistant professor, yet still finds time to play in an alt-country band called Brother Lowdown and, on occasion, swill wine with me in the afternoon. Shayla rocks on so many levels.

"When does Brother Lowdown have their next gig?"

"We're doing a show Friday at the Abbey Pub."

"Cool. We'll try to be there."

"If you come, will you behave yourself? They still talk about you there."

This isn't completely my fault. Earlier that day I had a minor meltdown over an expensive car repair, so I took a couple Xanax, forgetting about going out later. For some reason, Brother Lowdown was only on stage for half an hour, much to my dismay. Another local band called Butterside Down played after them. Their only fault was not being Brother Lowdown, yet in my addled condition, I blamed them for Brother Lowdown's short set. Apparently antianxiety medicine and Stoli Razberi and soda don't mix. Two bouncers forcibly removed me from the establishment for standing by the stage and shouting epithets like "Butterside Sucks! Buttersuck Sucks! Suckyside Down!"

Or so I'm told.

I woke up fully dressed in my bathtub fifteen hours later with no memory of the evening, and an odd craving for toast.

"I'll be good," I promise.

"By the way, nice attempt at changing the subject. Fletch said you'd try to weasel out of this chat. You brought me over here to brainstorm, yet you reject the most expedient solution. I'm telling you, temping is not that bad."

"How about this? If—and that's a big if—if I have an interview and I'm slated to be at a temp job, what do I do?"

Shayla whorls honey into her tea while explaining, "Unlike traditional employers, the temp agencies and their respective clients not only don't care if you're looking for permanent work, they expect it. If you need to go to an interview, you simply tell them in advance and they'll get someone to cover your shift." She squeezes a slice of fresh lemon and stirs again. "Why do you ask? Is this an issue? Have you had a lot of interviews lately?"

I sigh deeply and rub Maisy's ears. As usual, the dogs and cats are piled all around me. I've cranked the heat down to 60 degrees in an effort to conserve money, and the freezing-cold critters are drawn to my body warmth. When Shayla arrived, I told her to come in, but suggested she leave her coat on. "Not even a nibble in almost two months. At this point, I'm applying for jobs that pay my starting salary out of college."[127]

"Yikes. Have you gone to any networking events?"

"Dozens. The only people I've networked with are unemployed, too."

"How many résumés have you sent?"

"Hundreds upon hundreds. I now apply for every single job I see.[128] The few employers I've spoken with say they get so many résumés, they don't even bother sending form-letter rejections anymore. But if you ask me, I think these employers are enjoying the change of economy. It's like the ultimate payback from when all the

---

[127]Twenty-five thousand dollars, and yes, thanks, I *do* want to cry.
[128]So what if I don't know how to repair an airplane? They pay A LOT and I'm willing to learn.

good people left to work for Internet companies. 'Your oh-so-important leg-wear-by-mail company didn't work out? And now you want to come back? HA!' They love that it's a buyer's market."

"Still, sounds like you're doing everything right, so what's the problem?"

"There are a few factors working against me. First off, thousands of other jobless people are doing everything right, too. Plus, it's the end of the year, and no one's hiring until they get their budgets in January. And rumors about war certainly aren't helping the overall employment situation. For lateral positions, I used to make too much money and priced myself out of the market."

"Maybe your résumé is too good? What about downplaying your experience just to get a foot in the door?"

"I already dumbed-down my résumé, but it hasn't helped. For better jobs, employers can snatch up formerly expensive, experienced people for a song. Thus my services aren't wanted." I fortify myself with another giant slug of wine. "And when I interviewed for lesser jobs, employers are convinced I'll be bored. I even tried to get a part-time position with a dog-walking company, figuring the exercise would help me lose weight, and the owner said if I couldn't give him a year's commitment, he wasn't interested. So here I sit in my pajamas, drinking bargain wine, completely out of ideas."

Shayla opens her backpack and takes out a business card. "Here's my temp agency's owner's number. His name is Chuck and he's a nice guy. Tell him I sent you, and you'll probably get a placement right away." Shayla tries to hand me the card, but I'm hesitant to touch it. "Take it. It won't bite you. Call him." She looks me up and down before adding, "Now."

With much reluctance, I accept the card. "I remember a time when I used to like you."

"Self-pity and elastic waist pants do not suit you. Call them. You'll thank me when you cash your first check."

Fletch and I discussed it and determined I should give temping a whirl.[129] What it boils down to is I temp or we'll have no choice but to move to a cheaper neighborhood. Yes, we've talked about moving, but we should move because we *want* to, not because we *have* to. Our rent is taking a huge bite out of Fletch's severance package and our strict budget doesn't allow for extras like Christmas presents or wine in bottles.

I sucked it up and called Shayla's temp agency. And here I am, going through the intake process, ready to take my timed typing test. For the first time, I feel fortunate to have attended a shitty high school that taught typing on IBM Selectrics and not computers. I just watched the last two people blow their tests because they didn't know where to place the paper or how to operate the return carriage. Plus, they showed up for their intake assessment wearing JEANS, while I'm clad in a striking pin-striped pantsuit with a starchy white collar and my hair's in a fabulous French twist. HA! I'm about to blow these kids out of the water.

I position myself in front of the typewriter, hands poised over the keys. Jill, the office's receptionist, stands behind me with a stopwatch. "OK, you're going to type for the next sixty seconds. If you make a mistake, just keep going. And . . . three, two, one—go!" she says.

I'm off! My fingers fly across the familiar old keys, and I bang out entire paragraphs in record time. Smoke practically rises from the machine and the motor hums while the printwheel strikes perfectly *againandagainandagainandagain* in rapid succession. The whole desk vibrates with intensity, each stroke bringing me closer to the title of Miss Typewriter 2002. By the time Jill calls stop, I'm spent with the exertion of having transposed the entire Gutenberg Bible.

---

[129]I'll not detail the tears shed and tantrums thrown in reaching this decision.

Victoriously, I rip the sheet out and hand it to her, waiting for my accolades. She examines my work.

"Well?" I ask expectantly. My dad's old secretary could type 120 words per minute. He'd beg her to type more slowly because she'd burn through a typewriter per month.[130] As fast as I just went, I'm sure I've tied her record.

"Looks like you can do about thirty words per minute," Jill says.

LIES! Tremendous lies! Acknowledge my prowess! "That's impossible. I *flew* through those paragraphs."

"Yes, and they're riddled with errors. You'd have been better off going a little slower. Subtracting typos, you're at about thirty words per minute, and honestly, I'm being generous. I'm sorry to tell you that you won't be eligible for a lot of our open jobs—most require at least forty-five words per minute. But you're welcome to come to our office anytime so you can practice and improve."

Pfft—I should get extra credit for even knowing what an IBM Selectric *is*. Whatever. "What's next?" I ask.

"We're on to the computer-skills assessment now. If you want to grab your briefcase and follow me, we can get started."

Maybe I didn't rock the typing test. Big deal. I will OWN the computer part. I am the reigning Queen of Spreadsheets. Sorting? I can ascend or descend by make, model, and serial number. Summation? Child's play. You want a formula to add a 37 percent margin to base pricing, but only on select column items? Bring. It. On. And, shoot, I can do things with an Access Database that would make the baby Jesus cry. Or how about a Web page? I've got the *mad* HTML skillz, yo. I taught myself how to program back in the Midwest IR days when I designed the portfolio management interface. Feel free to call me Jennifer Lancaster Gates from now on.

---

[130]For a while, Dad's corporate office thought he was selling typewriters on the black market.

Jill boots up the computer and opens Microsoft Word. Once we're in the program, she hands me a heavily formatted document and tells me to replicate it. Ugh, why? I'd rather die than allow a hideous note like this go out under my letterhead. There are inserted tables and graphs and columns and about fifteen different type styles and sizes, along with breaks and footnotes and page numbers.

"Okeydokey, I'll be back in five minutes." Jill returns to the reception desk. I proceed cautiously, relying heavily on the happy animated Microsoft paperclip. The assignment's not hard—it's just tedious. If my boss ever handed me something like this, I'd sit him down to discuss aesthetics and the concept of *less is more*, rather than allow him to endorse such a schizophrenic mess.

A nanosecond later, Jill is standing over my shoulder. She prints out my work and examines it. "This is terrible! I can't believe how bad this is! And you're so slow. Your Word skills are negligible. Have you even *worked* in an office before?"

"Yes, I have," I reply with a clenched jaw. I just tried my hardest and now a *receptionist* is dogging to me? I don't *think* so. "Of course, I was a vice president, and I used to have girls *like you* who did this for me."

....

Luckily Shayla placed a call to Chuck, and her recommendation is the only reason I get a placement. For the next week, I'll be supporting the advertising sales manager of a huge home decor magazine. OK, how lucky is this? I would love to do advertising sales. My friend Kim is VP of advertising at Midwest IR, and she's always flying somewhere fun to entertain potential clients at high-end bars and restaurants. I'm witty and charming, and clients find me delightful—I could easily sell ads. Not only am I superpersuasive, but I love this magazine. I would be a perfect fit here, and I'm going to work my hardest to make sure the sales manager takes notice.

I arrive promptly at the reception desk at eight forty-five a.m. and am greeted by a cranky old smoker named Pat. She looks and sounds exactly like Marge Simpson's sisters, and I notice she keeps her cigarettes in their own needlepoint carrier attached with a plastic chain around her neck. "I'll take you back to where you're working, but first, you can put your coat in here." She gestures to a walk-in closet that smells like a stale ashtray, so I assume this is where Pat stows her coat, too.[131]

I follow Pat to the end of a long hallway and she shows me my work space. "You'll be filling in for Kathy while she recovers."

"So she's sick, not on vacation?" I ask, in an effort to make friendly conversation.

"I'm sure that's none of your business," Pat replies. OK, so much for conversation. "You'll support Jerry, the advertising sales manager. Mainly you'll answer the phone. Here, let me show you how to work it."

"This is a Lucent PBX with Audix voice mail, right? I used this kind at all of my old jobs, so I'm pretty familiar with them."

Completely ignoring me, Pat continues to demonstrate every single one of the phone's features, half of which she describes incorrectly. I don't bother taking notes because I've used this system a thousand times. I have no need to transcribe an erroneous refresher course. "Hey, you should be writing this down."

"Like I said, I've used this system extensively and—"

"WRITE IT DOWN," Pat growls. "If you screw up the phone, Jerry's gonna be on my ass."

"No problem." I'm slowly learning to choose my battles and figure this isn't the hill I want to die on. I pull a portfolio out of my briefcase and begin to take notes.

---

[131] Am I suddenly psychic? Because I see a $15 dry-cleaning bill in my future.

"When the phone rings and Jerry isn't there to answer, you pick it up and hold it to your mouth like this. You say, 'Hello, Jerry Jenkins' office.'"

I write: *When phone rings, place receiver next to your word hole and not your hoo-hoo or other bodily aperture, and say, "Shalom."*

"Then you say, 'I'm sorry. Jerry isn't available. Would you like to leave a message?' If they do, you have to ask them who they are, what they want, and find out their phone number."

I write: *Tell them Jerry went for a massage, and here's my phone number.*

"Then you have to make sure to give Jerry the message."

I write: *Tell Jerry someone called about something important, and they sounded mad, so I hung up on them.*

"That's about it on the phone. Now Jerry might need you to make copies. If so, the machine is right there." She points to a copier located directly outside Jerry's door.

"It's a standard Xerox, right? Copies go here, the prints come out here, lift the glass to create an enlargement, refill paper here, press this button if you want to collate and this one for staples?" I point to each feature as I describe it.

"This is the copy machine. If you want to make a copy . . ."

Warily, I open my portfolio while Pat drones on, repeating each of the copier's aspects I'd just described. *Tell Jerry when Xeroxing his butt, cheek definition will be most crisp if he wipes the glass with Windex first.*

Pat details a litany of other absurdly easy tasks I may be called upon to perform, and I'm a bit incredulous that I'm going to earn $12/hour for doing what amounts to a trained monkey's job. Having successfully unloaded her dearth of knowledge, Pat says we're finished and she starts to head back to her desk.[132]

---

[132]Outside to smoke.

"Wait. Is that it? There's nothing else? What should I be doing when I'm not answering the phone or making copies?"

"I dunno. I guess try to look busy. Oh, one more thing. The bathroom is down the hall. To get there, you take a right, then a left, and then a right."

"Yeah, thanks. I saw it when I came in."

"Better write that down. Most of our temps get lost trying to find it."

Does she think I'm completely stupid? I may have arrived here in a yellow vehicle today, but it was a cab, not the short bus. Is she afraid if I can't find the bathroom, I'll whiz in the coat closet? I want to slap the nicotine out of her while shouting, "I used to be a vice president!" but I don't. Instead, I write: *If nature calls, tell them Jerry went for a massage, and here's my number.*

. . . .

I sit at my desk employing perfect posture so that I'll make the best possible impression when Jerry gets to the office. Head up, shoulders squared, stomach sucked in, I look poised and professional. I wait.

And wait. And wait.

Oh, my God, is this ever boring and uncomfortable.

The clock on my PC is crawling along, and I'm desperate for something to do. I can't bear to hold the pose anymore, so I ask a couple of the other assistants if they need help with anything. Unfortunately, they seem to be managing their personal phone calls and nail filing just fine, thanks. Excuse me, ladies? This is why you *are* and will always *be* secretaries.

I need a project, and if no one will give me one, I'll just have to create something to do. Yes! Capital idea! That way, when Jerry comes in, he'll see what an industrious self-starter I am and will find room for me on his team. But what can I do?

I peer around the room. The coffeemaker is full, the copier area is tidy, and the community work space is neat. The only section in need of attention is Kathy's desk, and it's a filthy mess.

I begin Operation Clean Sweep by sanitizing. Her keyboard is full of crud, and I don't want to use it, lest I catch her cooties. She must have eaten sandwiches over this thing every day for the past ten years. I blow it with a can of compressed air and crusty tumbleweeds explode out of it. I try to suppress my gag reflex.

I scrub the desk's surface, drawers, and cabinets with the unopened bottle of Fantastik I found buried under a pile of month-old newspapers in the corner of her work space. The paper towels turn black with my very first pass. I bet she's out sick because she caught Ebola from her desk.

I neaten the heaps of magazines strewn all over and pluck all the dead leaves from her spider plant before moving on to sort her top drawer. I divide and stack each of the seventy-two packets of salt and soy sauce.[133] I realphabetize her files and line her pile of Payless' finest in neat little rows under the far side of her desk. I step back to admire my work and commend myself on my organizational prowess.[134]

Finished, I go to the bathroom to wash my hands and blot the sweat from my brow. Pat stops me on my way back, and I assure her that, no, I don't need help finding my desk again, silently adding, "Considering I USED TO BE A VICE PRESIDENT." However, I so transformed Kathy's work space that I actually do walk past it once. Satisfied at a job well-done, I glance at my watch to see how much time I've killed. Surely a few hours have passed by now.

---

[133]Kathy, wherever you are, we should discuss your sodium intake.

[134]Of course, I did a good job. I used to be a vice president, you know.

Nine twenty-seven a.m.

It's going to be a long week.

• •

"Have the temp file those."

"Ask the temp to make your copies."

"The temp will messenger them over."

"See if the temp will make us a lunch reservation."

"The temp isn't busy—let her do it."

My name is Jen, goddammit, not *the temp*. Jen. J-E-N. It's three freaking letters long and phonetically correct—how hard can it be to remember? And why do they need to speak to me so slowly and deliberately, like I'm a 'tard or a terrorist? Would a terrorist strap dynamite to her cashmere twinset? I think not. I am fighting the urge to go all Shannen Doherty on these people.

• •

I finally talk to Jerry my third day on the job. He walks out of his office and over to my desk.

"Hi. You're the temp, right?" He hands me a sheet of paper.

Yay! This is my chance to make a good impression. I'd heard Jerry was looking for another salesperson, and I know I'd be phenomenal. For the past two days, I've been studying old contracts and piecing together the way they conduct their sales process. I've reviewed a bunch of their PowerPoint presentations, and I've already begun to tweak the pitch to best suit my personality. I've heard him on the phone interviewing other candidates, and I've formulated well thought-out answers. Given half a chance, I would rock this job. "Yes, Jerry, my name is Jen Lancaster and I'm—"

"That's great. I need a copy of this please."

Ouch.

I walk over to Xerox machine, make a copy, and beat Jerry back to his desk. I realize that I'm here to support him, but wouldn't it have been more efficient if he'd done this himself? He walked right past the damn copier when he left his office. I hand him the papers before he sits down, trying to catch his attention so I can engage him in a conversation about my skills and experience. I've got to be subtle, though, because the temp agency has strict rules about temps trying to land full-time positions at their assigned company.[135]

"Here you go," I say, smiling my largest cheese-eating grin.

"Uh-huh." He picks up the phone and turns away from me.

Hmph. If I'm going to get this job, I'll have to prove I'm not invisible.

. . . .

"Hi, um . . . err . . . um . . ." Jerry stammers. He stands in front of me holding a box of mini candy canes and a giant stack of folded papers.

"It's Jen," I tell him helpfully. *Yes, you know, Jen? The well-dressed, impeccably groomed girl you've walked by for the past five days??* But I smile brightly, confident he'll ask me for a résumé as soon as he realizes how competent I am. "What can I do for you?"

"Kathy started this project before she left, and I need you to finish it. We're sending Christmas gifts to our advertisers. Tape one candy cane to each card and place each set in an individual FedEx box."

"But don't seal the boxes, right?" I ask. Aha! My opening! Obviously I am clever, because I *know* these boxes shouldn't be sealed.

---

[135]The agency doesn't place salespeople, though, so I figure it's OK. I just have to make Jerry think it was his idea.

Otherwise, I'd have to reopen them to include their gifts. If he were only sending cards, I'd use envelopes because it costs less. Look at the way I think strategically! Hire me this instant!

"Why wouldn't you seal them?" Jerry gives me a puzzled look.

"So we can include gifts later, of course."

He shakes his head. "There is no other gift. The candy cane and the card *is* their gift."

"Wait. I don't understand. Why would anyone spend $20 per box to ship a penny's worth of candy canes? That doesn't make any sense. Surely this isn't the only thing you're sending your clients by way of holiday greeting. This is some kind of test, right? There's got to be more, because . . . because . . ."

Jerry's face turns bright red. And, although I used to be a vice president, I realize I'm not going to be selling magazine advertising anytime soon.

Ring . . . ring . . . ring . . .

"So, Chuck, you're saying when you have another open temp position that matches my skill set, you'll call me and I don't have to keep calling you? All right . . . OK . . . Um, when do you think that will be? Hmm . . . Well, it's bound to snow in hell at some point, right? Talk to you then."

. . . .

Ring . . . ring . . . ring . . .

"Yes, I *know* my student loan payment is late. . . . No, I don't intend to be one of those deadbeats who gets an education and then dances off scot-free. Are you even allowed to say stuff like that to me? You have no idea what kind of rent burden I'm under. . . . Oh, I see. . . . Yes . . . And what will happen to my credit rating? Yikes . . . OK, when? I guess I can auction off a couple of my purses and make a payment when they sell . . . Yes, *thank you*, getting a job is an excellent suggestion—I'm not sure why I didn't think of it myself. *Good-bye!*"

. . . .

Ring . . . ring . . . ring . . .

"That's fantastic news! I'm so glad to hear it! When do you want me to start? Great . . . Outstanding . . . I'm really looking forward to getting back to work. Oh, I almost forgot. We never even talked about base salary. . . . Really . . . OK . . . You know, at some point during our three interviews, you might have *mentioned there was an initial investment.* . . . Um, no . . . Mr. Jackson, if I did have $5000 right now, I would shove it directly up your pyramid-scheming ass."

. . . .

I'm SO bored. It's the Christmas season, and I spent all my temp money on presents, so I can't do anything. I haven't gone to any holiday parties because we're on a tight rent-paying budget.[136]

For a while I played the Sims, the purpose of which is to build interesting lives for these simulated characters by having them interact nicely with other Sims. The better the interaction, the happier they are. All I want to do, though, is decorate their houses, and I laugh when they get into fights. I wonder if this says something about me.

Lately I've been haunting a Web site called OddTodd.com. Todd Rosenberg, a laid-off guy in New York, created a Flash cartoon about

●

---

[136]Box wine may be fine for my purposes, but I am not about to bring it to a party.

a day in the life of the unemployed. His blue bathrobe–clad character slogs through his day worrying about his bank balance (nonexistent), his 401(k) plan (a jar of pennies), and not having the means to go to a strip club. Substitute *strip club* for *Nordstrom's shoe department* and *this is my life!* Every time I get discouraged or worried about money, I log on to watch the cartoon again. (I must have seen it a hundred times so far.)

Todd's site includes his writing, and it sounds like having an outlet has really helped him with his job search frustration. Maybe I should do something similar?

Really, why not start a Web site? I mean, what else do I have to do? It's not like I've got anywhere to go. (If I didn't have to take the dogs out, I bet I could go DAYS without wearing shoes.) Now that I'm not in the position to refer business to them anymore, I never hear from any of my *friends* at the PR agencies. I still talk to old pals like Melissa and Shayla, but I'm tired of them offering to buy my lunch. I HATE being pitied, and if that means I interact less, so be it.

Maybe if I started a Web site, something good could come of it. That girl from SaveKaryn.com suckered hundreds of people into giving her money to pay for her $20,000 credit card debt, *and* she got a book deal out of her story. OddTodd has a virtual tip jar, and people voluntarily give him money all the time. Of course, he actually produces cool cartoons, whereas I have no discernable skill, but still . . . if I had something to do with my time, I might stop obsessing about money so much. And maybe if I kept my hands busy, I wouldn't be able to snack so much.

Anyway, I'll consider it.

• •

I just invented the Twinkwich—a sandwich made by wrapping a Hostess Twinkie around a Ding Dong hot dog–style. This insane, long-stretches-of-boredom-laced-with-short-bursts-of panic-attacks-induced eating has to stop.

Step One: Create Web site.

Step Two: (deep breath) Move.

. . . .

My Web site is up! I now I have my own corner of cyberspace. I put a picture of myself on the front page with the word UNEMPLOYED across my eyes, and I don't mention my last name, so it's kind of cryptic. Then I listed every company that's rejected me so far under the heading *Companies That Suck.* Each time I look at my home page, I laugh myself into an asthma attack. I'm going to send the link out to some of my friends and see what they think.

I already feel less stressed, so this was definitely a good idea.

. . . .

"Honey, it's almost noon. We've got to be at the broker's office in an hour." I gently shake Fletch to wake him. He's been extra tired lately, so I let him sleep when it's my morning to take out the dogs.

Fletch hasn't had one nibble on his résumé in the past month, and it's starting to get to him. Back in October, he was superconfident about his chances, but lately his enthusiasm has waned. The eruption of WorldCom has devastated the telecom industry, and there's a ton of people fighting for a handful of jobs. I try to build him up as much as I can, but some days he's just overwhelmed by sadness.

I think deciding not to renew our lease has hit him harder than it has me. I mean, I've loved living here and showing the place off, but he was the one who picked out the neighborhood and found this apartment and his salary allowed us to afford it. Deciding to move has to feel like admitting defeat.

"Tired. Very tired," he mumbles into his pillow.

"I know you're tired, but we've got an appointment. You have to get in the shower. Let's move it." I yank the comforter off him.

He wraps the sheet over his head. "Nooo. Too sleepy. Want to snooze."

I'm getting aggravated. I've been up for four hours looking for jobs, walking dogs, cleaning the house, and making breakfast. "Sweetie, come on. You *have* to get out of bed. You've snoozed about ten times already this morning. We have less than a month to find a place, and we need to be on time for this appointment, so please get up." I tear the sheet away, and he curls into a tight ball.

"Shh, sleepy. Go 'way."

Sometimes I need to be gentle with Fletch. And sometimes he needs a bit tougher love. "GET YOUR DEAD ASS OUT OF THIS BED RIGHT NOW!"

That seems to do the trick. He scrambles out of his flannel pajamas and into the bathroom.

While Fletch showers, I make him a fresh pot of coffee.[137] I print out some promising real estate listings from the brokers' Web site, find my Mont Blanc pen, and start to fill in the rental application.

Name. Easy enough. *Date of birth, social security number, current address . . .* done. *Current rent.* I fill in the dollar amount and stare at it for a minute. Wow, that's a lot of money. A LOT. How did I ever agree to pay this much a month to live in a place that I don't even own? I could have taken a year's rent and bought a brand-new, fully loaded Lexus. It seems sort of surreal that Fletch and I routinely shelled out this much cash without a second thought.

I run my hand over the smooth, cool granite countertop in my gourmet kitchen, wondering if it was worth it. Then I remember when Shayla and Chris came over for the first time. Although it was

---

[137]See? I'm not a total shrew.

winter, it was a particularly warm night, so we decided to use the roof deck. We set it up with comfy chairs and coffee drinks and put Sinatra on the stereo. Right as they stepped onto the deck to take in the incredible skyline vista for the first time, as if on cue, ol' Francis Albert began singing "My Kind of Town." It was like a scene from a Meg Ryan movie, and at that moment, I thought my heart would burst with pride.

I'm misty at the memory, so I continue with the application. *Length of residency.* Three years. *Landlord's name and phone number.* Another easy question . . . that's Pammie Kozul at 1-800-SHE-SUCKS. Nope, I'm not bitter about Pammie keeping $2000 out of our security deposit because I "destroyed that beautiful wallpaper in the bathroom," even though any judge in the world would consider its removal a mercy killing. But it would cost more to fight her than we'd recoup, so it's not worth it.[138]

And finally, I get to the employment section.

Uh-oh.

Landlords are going to expect one of us to have a job, aren't they? Shoot. What I am going to fill in for this part? Maybe if our credit were still perfect, I could be honest, but we no longer have that luxury. We *will* have rent money because we've held on to most of Fletch's severance, plus we have his unemployment checks, but we can't put that on the form. We'd be better off saying we're drug dealers—at least that's a growth industry.

I really hate to stretch the truth, but what other choice do I have? After much deliberation, I say that Fletch is a self-employed consultant. Technically, Chris *did* call last week with a question about a router, and to thank us, he took us out for drinks, so that's a form of

---

[138]Since she has such a twisted concept of beauty, I thought she'd appreciate the lovely mosaics of poop my dogs produce now that I take them to make big potty on her lawn every day.

compensation, right? And Fletch *has* talked about doing consulting—it's just that no one's hired him to do it yet. So it's not *really* lying when I provide large numbers in the *Salary* line—it's a prediction.

When I get to the part where I have to detail my own employment situation, I say that I'm a freelancer—*free* being the key word here. I mean, I *do* spend a lot of time posting my most trenchant thoughts on my Web site, and I already have a small fan base. At some point, it *could* turn into a moneymaking enterprise, although I presently have no idea how.

Besides, I've earned the right to call myself a writer because this rental application is a tremendous work of fiction.

. . . .

We meet our apartment broker, Brandon, in his office, which looks like the basement of a run-down fraternity house. The desks are of the plywood and sawhorse variety and the couches are circa 1962. I can practically feel my shoes sticking to what should be beer-soaked floors. Brandon matches his surroundings perfectly, from his three-day stubble to his filthy U of I sweatshirt. Melissa says she and her fiancé found a condo-quality apartment through these guys, but I'm a little wary. I'd expect this guy to slip a roofie in my cocktail, not to find me a cute but cheap living space.

Since the burden of maintaining our application's lies falls on me, I do the talking. "Brandon, it's been a few years since we've looked for a place, and we have no idea how far our money will go. Like anyone else, we want the most apartment for our dollar but there are some basic amenities we need."

"What specifically?" Brandon leans forward and cups his chin in both of his hands.

"We absolutely have to have a dishwasher and air-conditioning, or we'll get divorced," I reply.

"She doesn't deal well with hot or dirty," Fletch adds helpfully.

I whip out my typewritten list. "We need two bedrooms, if not three, and at least one and a half baths. Plus, it has to have a tub. Jacuzzi would be nice, but not absolutely necessary. We also like exposed brick walls, skylights, stainless appliances, granite counters, glass block windows, and hardwood floors. What else?" I flip to the next page. "Oh, yes, it's got to be safe to walk the dogs in the neighborhood—naturally we'll need a landlord who accepts pets—and we have to have a deck or a patio, preferably with a southern exposure. A duplex apartment would be nice, but we also like town houses, coach houses, and lofts. And if you could find all of this for a thousand dollars or less in a good neighborhood, that would be ideal."

"Lemme see if I've got this straight. You want amenities, safety, and affordability?"

"Exactly!" Maybe Melissa was right—this guy does know what he's doing.

"Easy enough. Pick two."

• •

"Well, that was a bust." I'm totally discouraged. All the apartments in good neighborhoods in our price range are either tiny or decrepit.

"I didn't think that one off of Western Avenue looked so bad. What was wrong with it?" Fletch asks. "It had a yard."

"Yeah, but it was right next to that business that stores all those gas canisters. If somehow we managed to not get exploded, we'd still hear those workmen loading up their trucks all day. Clang! Clang! Clang! No dice."

"I liked the artists' lofts on Paulina. What was the problem there?"

"Exactly what would we do with a twenty-five-foot-long, sloping concrete ramp in the middle of the apartment? You know we'd get a couple of beers in us and try to race our office chairs down it, and boom! Broken Wrist City. Considering neither of us has health insurance now, it seems like a bad idea. Plus the bathroom was grody."

"How about that one off of Fullerton? The one with no closets?"

"You can't seriously be considering it. IT HAD NO CLOSETS. How do you build an apartment without a closet? Where do you stow your vacuum? Where would your coats live?"

"Yes, I'm kidding. The *Silence of the Lambs* trapdoor in the pantry was a deal breaker for me."

"What did that door lead to? I was too scared to look."

"I don't know, but it was dark, dirty, and full of spiders."

I shudder. "No, thanks. But, really, what are we going to do? We have to be out of here by the end of the month, and we need to schedule movers. We should probably know where we're moving first."

"Well, it might make things a bit tight, but other than moving to the suburbs—"

"Perish the thought."

"I'm with you on that. We don't have a lot of options at the $1000 price point. Let's up our search to $1200 per month and see what Brandon can do for us in Bucktown," Fletch suggests.

· ·

Nothing.

Brandon could do nothing for us at that price, nor at $1400. Plus, he's lost his gas cap since the last time he drove us around and is now using a sock to plug the hole. He's turned his car into a giant Molotov cocktail. I'm sitting in the backseat, huffing gas fumes, while Fletch and Brandon figure out our next steps. In my gasoline-induced high, I hear myself agreeing to see apartments off the beaten path for $1600 a month. There's no way we can pay that much until one of us starts working, but everything's so pretty and floaty right now that I find myself saying yes. I inhale deeply and smile.

We pull up to a craptacular crumbling limestone building on the unfashionable end of Ohio. "Blech," I say. "Hate the 'hood, hate the building. Next."

"Jen," Brandon pleads, "just give it a shot. Sometimes these places are nicer on the inside than you'd think."

Fletch shoots me a warning look. We've seen about thirty apartments so far, and I've found something wrong with each of them. The problem is that none of them are the Dot-Com Palace. I want to stay in my home and I hate that we can't afford it anymore.

"Fine." I trudge along behind them, kicking up small sprays of snow with my boot. "But I guarantee you, I won't like it."

We climb the freshly painted staircase, and Brandon works the double locks. He opens the door to a spacious apartment with brand-new hardwood floors, a gourmet kitchen with granite counters, stainless steel appliances, and cherry cabinets. The kitchen is huge and modern with a gorgeous breakfast bar. Opposite the kitchen is a living room flanked with a marble fireplace, an ornate mantelpiece, and recessed, backlit shelving. The room has exposed brick walls and is at least three times the size of what we have now. "Is this the same place?" I ask, wondering if the gas fumes made me lose a chunk of time.

"It sure is." Brandon beams. This is the most positive reaction he's gotten out of me so far.

We check out the first bedroom, and it's spacious and bright with a walk-in closet. Nice. Attached is a spankin' new bath decked out in sandy limestone tiles and glass block. Correction, *very* nice. "And you're sure this is only $1600 and they take dogs?"

Neither Brandon nor Fletch hears me. They're in the back room, which is the master suite. I join them, and when I notice the south wall, my jaw drops. One-third of the room is covered in dreamy aquamarine marble with sparkly blue-gold veins. Centered against the wall is the biggest Jacuzzi bathtub I have ever seen. It has three steps leading up to it and could easily accommodate two people. It's not a tub—it's a bathing altar. If we lived here, my dream of sitting in the tub while watching TV could finally come true.

We all stand gawping at the bath's magnificence. The only other lavatory I've ever seen like this was in Vegas, when the Luxor upgraded me to a high-roller's suite.[139]

Next to the tub is a gigantic glassed-in shower, and beyond that is a double marble vanity with cherry cabinets, framed in adjustable lighting. On the other side, a cherry-shuttered door conceals the commode.

On the opposite wall, huge French doors lead out to a spacious balcony, and almost the entire wall is made of panes of glass. And to my left, there's an enormous walk-in closet, brilliantly outfitted with adjustable shelving and bars. This is truly one of the most lavish living spaces I have ever seen.

"So are we looking at your new master suite?" Brandon asks with a giant grin on his unshaved maw.

"No."

In unison, Fletch and Brandon shout, "WHAT?"

"I'm a very modest person, and this bathroom, although lovely, leaves no room to the imagination. If I wake up in the morning and see Fletch in that clear shower soaping up the crack of his ass, we'll get divorced. Next."

I think Brandon is going to cry.

• •

---

[139]When I flushed the toilet in the first room, it sprayed water up like Old Faithful. Let me just say this—no one likes seeing human waste, and it's particularly disturbing when it's hurtling at 100 miles per hour at your face.

"Jen, this is IT. If we don't find something today, we're going to have to live in a van down by the river because our lease is up in ten days," Fletch says sternly. We're in the parking lot outside the apartment brokerage, about to meet with Brandon to see another round of choices.

"Chris Farley was a tortured genius, and I won't have you using his words against me," I retort.

"Regardless, we have to make a decision. We've looked at a dozen different places that could have worked but you've nixed all of them for patently ridiculous reasons."

"That's not true."

"We didn't take the place on Ashland because the stove was electric. Why do you care? YOU DON'T COOK."

"I might cook if the stove were gas." I pull a tube out of my bag and apply a fresh coat of gloss. People? I can't stress this enough. When it's cold and raw outside, you MUST protect your lips or else they'll get all flaky and disgusting.

"OK, what about the place on Division with the roof deck?"

"The railings were too low. One of the dogs could have fallen over the side." I fluff out my hair. Since I'm not getting it colored as often, I have to wear it a bit bigger so my roots don't show. And, yes, I'd allow my ears to freeze and fall off before I covered my head with a hat.

"And the beautiful loft on Cortez?"

"The dark wood floors were fugly." I rim the inner part of my eyelids with BeneFit Eye Brightener and I instantly look refreshed.

"How about the duplex on Wabansia?"

"The hallway smelled like curry." A couple of quick blots to my chin, forehead, and nose with rice paper and I'm ready to go.[140]

"You *like* curry. You order it whenever we go for Thai."

"But I don't want to smell it in the hallway! Every time someone

---

[140]In a pinch, you can use a Starbucks napkin.

comes over, they'll ask, 'Are you cooking curry?' And I'll have to say no, and then they'll feel sorry for me for having to live in a place that smells like curry. I don't want to live anywhere that will engender sympathy."

"What was wrong with the town house on Erie with the yard and the skylights?"

"The corner supermercado was skeevy. Those people were standing out in front of it eating mangoes and throwing the pits on the ground. Yuck."

"You wouldn't have to shop there."

"Doesn't matter. I don't want to live within fifty yards of anything skeevy."

Fletch pounds his fist on the steering wheel. "That tears it! You've lost your vote. I know you don't want to leave our apartment and you're doing everything in your power to make it more difficult. I don't want to leave either, but we *do not have a choice.* The boom is *over.* It was nice while it lasted, but now we have to be adults, face our new economic reality, and make necessary changes. As it is, I'm not sure how we're going to come up with $1600 each month, but we'll worry about that *after* we've got a new roof over our heads. So right now, we are going to meet with Brandon, see all the places he has to show us, and we're going to choose one of them. Agreed?"

I contemplate his outburst. It's rare to see such an outpouring of emotion from him, so he must really mean business. Finally, I grunt, "Agreed."

"Thank you." We exit the car and Fletch zips up his parka.

I wrap my cashmere scarf around my neck and put on calfskin gloves before adding, "But if someone leaves mango pits on our lawn, *you're* picking them up."

Brandon takes us to ten different listings, and each is worse than the last. I'm frustrated, tired, and dreading living in any of them. As we pull into the brokerage office's parking lot, Brandon gets a call. He chats for a moment before addressing us.

"Hey, that was this guy Bill on the phone. He has a nice place on Superior that I've wanted to show you, but I didn't have the keys. He's over there now if you guys want to take a look. Sounds like a decent fit because it has all the amenities you want. I know it's pretty late, but do you want to swing by?"

"Bring it on," I say wearily.

"Can you try to be a little more positive?" Fletch asks.

"As you wish. Maybe this place will have empty crack vials on the porch, too!" I say brightly.

We drive to a west-side neighborhood I've never heard of before. It's dark and the streets are deserted, which, in my opinion, is a good sign. The last place we saw had thugs standing around in hooded sweatshirts, and they scared the pants off me. The cars on the street seem decent, and there's some new construction, which is also encouraging.

We're greeted at the door by Bill, who has big white teeth, an expensive coat, and stupid spiky hair. He's superenthusiastic and shakes my hand really hard while clapping me on the back.

I already hate him.

Bill leads us through the apartment and explains how he owns a mail-order cigar company but is starting to dabble in real estate development and this is one of the first buildings he's redone and he's really proud of the results and urban renewal and entrepreneur and blah blah blah. . . . *Uh-huh, whatever. I'm a lot more concerned about a washer and dryer than I am about your résumé, pal.*

After our tour, Fletch asks the men to excuse us for a moment. We go upstairs to discuss the apartment.

"This place has everything we want. It's all new, there's central AC, and there's plenty of space. We're taking it," Fletch says.

"Shouldn't we check out the neighborhood in the daylight before we decide?" I ask.

"Bill has five more showings tomorrow. If we wait, we'll lose it."

"The thing is, the apartment is fine, but I hate the landlord."

"He seems nice and professional. What's the problem now?"

"He crushed my hand when he shook it and he's reality-show handsome. He looks like he should be on *The Bachelor*. That bothers me."

Fletch rolls his eyes and hisses, "To think I believed your objections couldn't get more ludicrous." In a louder voice, he calls down the stairs, "OK, guys, let's talk lease."

9

Cannibal Birds

Weblog Entry 2/12/03

MSNB-YOU-SHOULDN'T-SEE

We recently disconnected our satellite dish
to prepare for our move, so we're back on the
building's basic cable. Because I haven't been able
to consume my usual banal menu of *A Wedding
Story* and *The Real World/Road Rules Challenge*,
I made the mistake of watching MSNBC.

Not smart.

Every single one of their reports has caused me
MUCH anxiety.

First of all, I'm highly concerned about Al
Jezeera reports of suicide attacks and possible

use of radiological devices. I'm also worried about nuclear proliferation in North Korea, France's rallying to weaken NATO, and the possibility of links between Al Qaeda and Iraq. And watching the Dow spiral down on the lower right-hand corner of my screen while these reports are read doesn't exactly help my stress level, either.

While the disastrous possibilities these stories propose put me on edge, the news that scares me the most is the segment I recently saw about college students and their increased consumption of club drugs such as Ecstasy.

When discussing usage statistics, the MSNBC reporter showed what now passes for a college party . . . it was a bunch of unkempt girls and dirty boys sprawled over all the flat surfaces in someone's dorm room while horrific house music thumped in the background. Since they were "trippin' on E" they took turns touching each other, as apparently tactile sensations are far stronger when chemically enhanced. They also took turns making out with each other—boys on girls, boys on boys, girls on girls, boys on dorm furniture, etc. until someone shouted "Switch!"

Excuse me, but this is NOT a college party.

I consider myself an expert on parties as my college career spanned from 1985 to 1996.[141] In this eleven year period, I probably attended at least one party a week. Doing the math, that makes me the veteran of at least 572 parties.[142] So consider me an expert when I say every party started with well-groomed

---

[141]Another long story starring boys, beer, and an errant Visa card.
[142]Which may explain most of my tenure.

attendees. Even if you weren't the prettiest debutant at the ball, you made the most of what you had. The men were gelled and pressed and each of the women sported their cutest clothes and a face-full of cosmetics. There was none of this shaved-headed, random-facial-haired, poorly outfitted foolishness. And no one forgot deodorant, either. If anything, the whiff of Polo Sport and Liz Claiborne perfume was practically overwhelming.

Second of all, parties never took place in anyone's DORM.

Ever.

I mean, how the heck could you sneak twenty kegs past the RA? Fraternity houses had entire floors devoted to party space. And even apartment party-throwers cleared out the community living area to make room for lethal trash can punch because having space to circulate was the key to throwing a good party.

Back then we had one drug and it was called ALCOHOL and that was just fine. There wasn't any crank or smack or crack or stank or what-ever else the kids do now.[143] If drugs had been more readily available, no one would have done them because we were all concerned about failing piss tests and losing our internships.

At our parties, if kids hooked up it was behind closed doors. Mostly we just drank and laughed and gossiped and smoked Marlboros, much as we do now as adults at work functions. This is because the purpose of

---

[143]Granted, there may have been people doing coke but they were way too cool for my cow college.

college parties is to prepare the youth of our nation to mainstream into corporate America.

So, please kids, pick yourselves up off the floor, take a shower, starch your khakis, crack a Pabst Blue Ribbon, and head over to the Delt house.

The future of American business is depending on you.

Although we're moving in two days, we still make time to meet my cousin's family for a delightful dinner at Carmine's. After hugs, kisses, and promises to do this more often, Fletch and I are on our way to catch a cab when we walk past Jilly's.

Jilly's . . . *sigh.*

Standing outside their door, I'm instantly transported back to 1999, where we're in the throes of the dot-com gold rush. Most weekends we put on all our finery and get together with the rest of the young turks for four-digit group dinners at the Signature Room, Tavern on Rush, Gibson's, etc. But no matter where we start, we always end up at the piano bar at Jilly's, hanging out with the rest of Chicago's young digital elite, drinking martinis, crooning along to Frank and Dino, and tripping across the dance floor while roving bands of photographers document our heyday on film.[144] Invincibility permeates our souls like the smell of expensive cigars infuses our Brooks Brothers suits and Burberry shifts.

Of course, those days over. The young turks have gone the way of our success, status, and jobs.

And yet Jilly's still stands, having been reclaimed by baby

---

[144]Which we can purchase for only $5 per Polaroid.

boomers. I LOATHE baby boomers. Boomers are the only people who emerged from the dot-bomb unscathed. I blame them for the economic crash. They're the ones who used people like me and Fletch to build their pretend companies and their wealth, and then they bailed out before everything came crashing down.

"Feel like nipping in for a quick one?" I ask Fletch. He looks as wistful as I feel.

"I do, but we're limited to one apiece. We need to tip the movers."

We wedge our way through the crowds and up to the bar, waiting for a stool to come open. As seating at Jilly's is as precious and fleeting as a bull market for tech stocks, I grab an empty chair and plant myself in front of a couple of half-full drinks covered with napkins. I shove the glasses out of my way to make room and then gesture to my favorite bartender, who immediately knows to pull out the Stoli and Spanish olives. Seconds later, we're presented with two swimming pool–sized cocktails.

Fletch holds his drink up in a toast. "To new beginnings."

"Whatever they may bring." We clink glasses. I sip the icy vodka, close my eyes, and I'm back in The Day again . . . *mmmm, stock options . . . ooh, venture capital . . . aahhh, the e-volution. . . .*

I'm jarred from my reverie when someone shoves my stool. I assume it's the crush of the crowd or Fletch on his way back from the men's room, but when I twist around, I come face to face with an angry boomer. He's the owner of the covered beverages and has returned after fifteen minutes of dancing to reclaim his spot at the bar.

Angry little eyes flash at me through tiny titanium bifocals and he accuses, "You took my seat."

"I most certainly did not. I sat down in an empty chair."

"Those are my drinks."

"And?" The LAST thing I'm going to do is hand my prized seat over to some boomer asshole without a fight. "Haven't you ever been in a restaurant? A napkin is the universal signal for 'I'm done.' The drinks were covered. This chair was empty. I sat down. End of story."

"This is my chair."

"You certainly present a compelling argument. I am simply floored by your powers of persuasion. Tell me, are you an attorney?"

He shoves my chair again. "Listen, little girl, I'm a regular here, and the bartenders know when I cover my drink, it means I'm coming back, so get your ass out of my seat right now."

I nod at the bartender. "Roger, you know this guy?"

"Never seen him before, Jen. Is there a problem?"

I smile. "No problem." And to the boomer: "Since I'm nice, you can have this seat in a couple of minutes because we're almost finished. Until then, piss off." I shoo him away. He glowers at me before skulking back to the dance floor. Dance now, old man. Because someday I will rule Jilly's again.

Roger leans across the bar so that I can hear him over the noise. "Hey, where you guys been? Haven't seen you in here for a long time."

"Roger, I wouldn't even know where to begin."

· ·

It feels like we've been packing for months now, but it's only been a week. We've already got seventy cartons stacked up in the dining room, and we haven't even boxed up our personal items yet.

As I pack, I'm struck by the sheer amount of junk that I own. I now understand I have no right to bitch about being broke because I was really foolish with the money I had when I had it.

I start to tabulate what I could have had instead of what I do have. In this cabinet, I have twenty-five half-full bottles of body lotion, and they aren't cheap, either. I've got the sublime—the sparkly designer tubes—and the ridiculous—the glycolic-acid-which-burns-off-several-layers-of-skin—and yet my legs are totally scaly. I never remember to use them until after I put on my pants, and by then, I'm too lazy to take them off again. Figuring that each bottle cost an average of $40, I would have $1000 now, which would pay for two months of COBRA for Fletch and me.

Moving on to the next shelf, I find my nail-care toolbox. I open it and see at least twenty shades of matte red[145] from OPI and Christian Dior, each of which cost an average of $10. I kept buying new bottles because I never got around to finding nail polish thinner to salvage the ones I already had. I have four identical bottles of Dutch Tulip and I'm embarrassed by my largesse. Did I mention that $200 would pay for a month of electricity? Add this to the seventeen trays of $30 eye shadow I own and never use,[146] and all of a sudden, I have the means to pay for six months' phone service.

The living room is a monument to my impulsive spending habits. I've got more than two hundred DVDs, including cinematic greats such as *Monkey Bone*, *Corky Romano*, and *A Night at the Roxbury*, leading me to believe not only do I have awful taste in films, but I also have a Chris Kattan fixation. What I don't have is $4000 earning interest in a money market account.

The DVDs reside on the same bookcase as all my hardbacked books. Instead of waiting for the paperback edition or, *God forbid*, going to the public library, I had to have hardcovers. Had I checked these books out instead, I could afford an entire year's worth of insurance on both vehicles.

But these expenditures are nothing compared to what's in my closet. My sweater compulsion could have easily afforded me a se-

---

[145]Shimmery polish is trashy.
[146]Electric blue? What was I thinking?

mester of grad school, and if I didn't have an affinity for fur-trimmed coats, I could fund an entire MBA, including a new laptop.

Now on to the mother lode—shoes. My stacked-heel loafer collection would have paid for two months' rent and my summer slide assortment a whole season's worth of groceries. My crocodile-skinned pumps alone might have funded a year of DSL service. And why the hell did I need so many pair of athletic shoes? It's not like I exercise. But if I did, my sneaker budget could finance a health club membership at one of the city's swankier gyms.

Eventually, I get around to packing my purses. Even minus the ones I've auctioned, I still need two giant boxes to hold them all. None of these babies were a bargain, either. Why, exactly, did I need a lavender-and-brown Kate Spade bag for $300? Do you know how hard it is to coordinate those colors with anything else? I've used the damn thing twice in two years. And while I dig my white floral Spade bag, I never carry it for fear of getting it dirty. It sits in my closet doing nothing. Why didn't I just give its $275 ticket price to a deserving charity instead?

Finally, I examine the cornerstone of my beloved but ridiculous collection—my giant chain-strap Prada bag. I loved this purse when I saw it, and damn the price, I HAD to have it. Yet now it's covered with dust, hasn't been touched in months, and has brought me nothing but bad luck. I examine every inch of it and sigh deeply. The silver links are starting to chip and the Prada-embossed lining is torn. The worst part is that the cost of this bag could have paid for professionals to box up all this stuff.

Fletch comes in to work on his side of the closet. "How's it going?"

"Depressing," I reply.

"I'm sad, too. But this is what we have to do."

"I'm talking about all this stuff. What was I thinking? Why did I buy so much? And why didn't you stop me?"

He snorts. "Because it would have been impossible."

I look over at his tidy row after row of Johnson & Murphy shoes, neatly hung Hickey-Freeman suits, stacks of cashmere sweaters, and rung of custom-made Thomas Pink shirts. "You're one to talk."

He sits down heavily on the edge of the bed. "Now we know better. We've learned an expensive lesson."

I join him. "I just hope we didn't learn it too late."

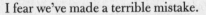

I fear we've made a terrible mistake.

We've moved to the frigging barrio. I knew we should have checked this place out in daylight. Yes, our apartment and landlord are decent, but that doesn't change the fact that except for my building's tenants, no one here speaks English.

NO ONE.

Which is probably why I've never heard of this neighborhood before. I don't speak any of the languages in which I may have heard it discussed. All the signs are written in Spanish or Polish, and there are six lavanderias within walking distance. Not Laundromats: LA-VANDERIAS. The shop around the corner sells *Pollo Vivo*, which translated means *live chickens*. I have no idea where I can buy a cup of coffee around here, but if I need access to an industrial-strength clothes dryer or want to kill my own dinner, I'm all set. The cashier at the local McDonald's even tried to take my order in Spanish. Excuse me, but am I not smack in the center of the United States of America? Unless I need to order a beer or tell someone I have a pencil, I'm screwed. Perhaps I should have paid more attention when Bill was discussing "urban renewal."

When we looked at this place, the new construction next door must have blinded me to the tenement two doors down. There are at least fifteen fresh-off-the-boat immigrant families squashed into a building made to hold four. I can't walk the dogs down the strip of grass bordering their property because of all the food they leave out, ostensibly for the birds. In the past two weeks, I've seen moldy tortillas, loaves of bread, cans of tuna, and a large sandwich with all the trimmings. Since when do sparrows eat beefsteak tomatoes? Yesterday the dogs almost yanked my arm off when we ran into a rat feasting on the tenement's offerings; the rat slipped into a big crack in the side of the building as soon as it saw the dogs. That place has to be totally infested.

Today was the kicker. We were taking our a.m. potty run, and I stumbled across a pile of pancakes. Who leaves an entire short stack out for the birds?? I imagine the people inside, throwing their hands up and crying in Slavic accents, "Vy ve haf so many rats?" I feel like shouting back at them, "Because you feed them Continental breakfasts!"

One of us has to find a well-paying job soon because we simply CANNOT stay here.

. . . .

Since our neighborhood doesn't have an official name, we've settled on "Sucktown." We've been in Sucktown three weeks and we've yet to meet any of the building's other tenants. I'm pretty sure I won't like them. Bill's going to have to paint lines in the parking lot because none of the residents can figure out how to park their cars on an angle without a guide, so half the time we're stuck leaving the Caddy on the street, which is SO not acceptable.

I'm particularly concerned about the people downstairs. They have tapestries on their windows and Grateful Dead stickers on their door, so I fear they may be hippies. Plus they crank up their music every time our dogs trot across the floor, so I wonder if their ceiling isn't properly soundproofed. What am I supposed to do, crate them like veal? Dogs run sometimes; deal with it. Ya lives on the first floor, ya takes your chances, you know?

The dogs and I are thundering down the stairs for our evening constitutional when I finally bump into Hippie #1. We introduce ourselves and make inane small talk, which has nothing to do with what we're both thinking.

"Hi, Bobby, I'm Jen. It's a pleasure finally to meet you!" *So you're the jackass who pays half the rent I do and yet still hogs up my parking space.*

Bobby gives me an insincere, fishy handshake. "Nice to meet you, too. How do you like living here?" *Jesus Christ, do you people keep a herd of water buffalo up there? What's with the noise?*

"It's great, thanks. Oh, this is Maisy and Loki. We've really been trying to keep them quiet. Hope they don't bother you!" *HA, HA, HA, MOTHERFUCKER! Keep parking in my space and SEE how much louder we can be.*

"Oh, no problem, we love dogs." *You enjoy that loooong walk back to the house from your parking space down the street? Why don't you bring the noise level down a couple of thousand decibels and maybe I'll move my car?*

"What do you do for a living?" *What kind of job allows you to smoke so much pot that I get a contact buzz every time I walk into my den?*[147]

"I'm a bartender and my girlfriend, Holly, is a poet." *Did I mention that we hate yuppie scum like you?*

I guess Holly's unemployed, too? While reining in the dogs to go outside, I say, "I guess they're ready to go. See you later!" *Hope you like show tunes 'cause I'm buying tap shoes.*

"Nice to finally meet you!" *Vengeance is mine, sayeth the down-*

---

[147]Good thing I'm not having children—with the amount they smoke, MY kids would come out with flippers.

stairs neighbor. When he opens his door, I catch a glimpse of the six-foot bong in his living room. Nice.

The dogs and I wend our way down the street and, because another dog is coming toward us, veer off to walk by the tenement. As we pass, a flock of birds scatters. I look down to inspect this evening's treat and see they were gathered around a pile of chicken bones, which means . . . *the birds in this neighborhood are cannibals!!*

Seriously, that's it. We can't stay here.

It's time for drastic measures.

To: Sandy Case
From: jen@jenlancaster.com
Date: March 8, 2003
Subject: Senior Account Manager

Sandy,

I see that Birchton & Co. is looking for a new Senior Account Manager. If you recall, I was set to interview for this exact job on 9/11/01. When weighing the events of the day, I chose to cancel our appointment rather than risk the unknown by going downtown.

Because of the cancellation, you decided against giving me another shot at an interview.

A year and a half later, I look back on that day and am confident I made the right choice. I took the most sensible, prudent action I could based on the information I had at the time. I stand behind my decision.

Now *you're* faced with a choice, Sandy. You can simply delete the email from the pushy girl, or you can interview the woman who'll make the same kind of discerning and savvy judgment calls when it comes to your clients.

Should you choose the latter, I can be reached at the contact information below.

Best,

Jennifer A. Lancaster
***

Holy shit, I got the interview.

. . . .

"How'd it go?" Fletch asks from his spot on the couch. Next to him are a pile of mini candy bar wrappers and half a glass of bourbon. I swear I don't know how Adult Protective Services has not yet intervened in our lives.

"Pretty well, I think. Sandy wants me to come back later in the week to talk to another one of the partners." I toss my briefcase onto the kitchen table and flop into the chair next to the television. "At one point, though, I knocked her socks off. Literally, I'm talking socks FLYING across the room."

"What was the question?"

"The usual 'Where do you see yourself in five years?' foolishness. What Sandy doesn't know is that I just finished reading an article by Peter Drucker in the *Harvard Business Review on Managing Your Career*.[148] Instead of giving the road map of career progression from point A to B to C like everyone else does, I totally took Drucker's words out of context and said, 'It's rarely possible to look ahead more than eighteen months and still be reasonably clear and realistic. Instead, I choose to focus on where and how I can achieve results that will make a difference in my present position within a year and a half time frame. After that, I'd be open to whatever change and growth these results presented.' I'm telling you, she sat there with her mouth hanging open before she finally said, 'That's the most articulate answer I've ever gotten to that question.' "

"She have any idea how full of shit you are?"

"Not yet. So what's been happening around here?" I eye his cocktail. "Are you celebrating something?"

"I am. I got a call from that ISP, and they want to fly me out to New York for a second interview."

"That's fantastic!! When?"

"Probably Friday."

"How great would that be if we both got offers in the next week? We could be out of Sucktown and back in a normal neighborhood before summer."

"Amen. I just hope we're gone before one of the members of the Russian Army dies on the job site."

Oy. The Russian Army. Not the real one, mind you. We're talking

[148]Peter Drucker is a BUSINESS GOD.

about the ones next door doing construction. Actually, I think they're Polish, but Fletch says he's heard them speaking Russian. We've taken to calling them the Russian Army for simplification purposes because we discuss them A LOT.

The Army is building an $800,000 home next door to us, which will be nice. This neighborhood needs to be gentrified, like, yesterday, and expensive real estate will help. However, I'm not sure we're going to survive the building process, as I'm concerned this may be their first job ever.

I've always lived in city neighborhoods on the rise[149] so I've seen an awful lot of construction in my time, but I've never witnessed a project like this one. First off, no one wears hard hats—unfortunate because they drop stuff ALL THE TIME. Bricks, beams, pallets, you name it, it comes crashing down with frightening regularity.

Last week I had to put my hood up when walking down the breezeway to my mailbox. Their welding created a virtual blizzard of falling sparks. And when I got to the front of the house I noticed my LAWN WAS ON FIRE. Later, I smelled singed hair and saw their foreman yelling and hopping around, clutching the back of his head. Call me a jerk, but when I spied his bald spot, I laughed out loud.

They aren't using a Dumpster, instead choosing to stuff construction debris in all the neighbors' garbage cans up and down the alley. Since the cans are full, the other residents are simply throwing their trash on the ground, and it's a virtual rodent fiesta!

"I think one of them lost a finger today," Fletch tells me. "I half expected to see a rat run off with it in his mouth."

"Serves them right. I'm still mad about the phone." Recently we lost phone service, coincidentally right after they bumped into the pole with their big machine with the shovel on the front of it. I heard the noise and went outside to inspect the damage and saw a ton of

[149]That's Chicago for you.

loose wires hanging from said pole. The one guy who can speak English on the crew swore they had nothing to do with it.

I, um, *politely disagreed.*

Let's just say after I mentioned the Department of Naturalization and Immigration, he suddenly remembered the accident and got it fixed. What's nice is I now know how to say *Bitchy Fat Girl* in Russian.

Or possibly Polish.

Weblog Entry 3/10/03 [150]

IT'S ALL GREEK TO ME

Did you know that Lifetime has a separate movie network now? I made this happy discovery when our satellite dish was installed at our new house. I'd always figured that Lifetime was a repository for Tori Spelling movies[151] but had no idea how many of today's most sought-after actresses got their start here. Presently they're running a Road to Fame series featuring B movies with A-list talent. Although I missed the Gwyneth Paltrow/Robert Urich opus, I caught *Dying to Belong*, starring Hilary Swank.

I was not disappointed!

In the movie, Hilary is a college freshman who goes through sorority rush with her nerdy, wannabe roommate Jenna Von Oy.[152] They pledge Pi

---

[150]It's a little surreal how many people log on to read my stupid opinions on stuff.
[151]Thou shalt not disrespect Tori Spelling!
[152]You may remember her as Blossom's buddy Six.
[152a]And yes, it scares me that I know this.

Gamma Beta and thus the drama began and anything resembling reality ended.

Seriously? I laughed my ass off.

I have rushed, pledged, and held leadership positions within a sorority, so I'm intimately familiar with collegiate Greek systems. It was painfully obvious to me that the writer/director/producer of this masterpiece couldn't say the same. They took every bit of negative, stereotypical anecdotal evidence and smushed it together to make this movie.[153] Anyway, the gist of the movie is that Six dies during a hazing incident and all the sisters clam up in the Pan-Hellenic version of *omerta* to protect Pi Gamma.

Yeah, right.

I pledged to protect my sorority's rituals to the grave, too. But I have to tell you the minute I had a couple of drinks in me, I was comparing handshakes and secret knocks with the rest of my Greek buddies. The stuff that seemed so solemn when whispered by candlelight was HILARIOUS after ten Miller Lites. So I guarantee these sorority girls would have thrown the guilty party under the bus the second the cops started to question them.

If you want a real picture of what life in the Greek system is like, check out MTV's *Sorority Life*. I watched this program over the summer and found the cattiness, the bullshit, and the liability discussions so much like my own experience that I sweated for a

---

[153]I doubt any of them have been near a Greek chapter, like, ever.

minute over whether I'd gotten all the signatures on my pledge paddle.

Point? The real "secret" of these secret societies is why we joined them. It wasn't for sisterhood or ritual or lifetime commitment or the privilege of sharing a bathroom with 87 other girls. The secret is . . .

. . . we joined them to meet boys.

"Good morning! Are you in?" Fletch greets me from his station on the couch. He's parked in front of *The Price Is Right.*

"I still don't know." I'm back from a breakfast meeting with Chris Birchton. I've had four more interviews with the company, bringing me to a total of six so far. I've met three vice presidents, two partners, and today, a founder. "I mean, yes, I'm dying to work for these guys. I know their client base, I love their approach to doing business, and I'm so impressed with their integrity. Every person I meet makes me want this job more. I'm just not sure how I did today."

"How come?"

"The founder was walleyed. I tried to maintain eye contact, but I didn't know which one to look at—they were kind of all over the place."

"They won't hold that against you."

"I guess. We talked about compensation today and he hinted about making an offer, so that's a good indicator. And how about you? Anything happen while I was gone?"

It's been two weeks since Fletch's trip to New York. While he was out there, he met the entire executive board of the company. They treated him to a swanky lunch at a private club and pretty much fawned all over him. With the battering his ego's taken lately, I'm glad an employer finally recognized what an asset he'd be.

After he made the rounds, the recruiter told Fletch they were going to hire him and to expect an offer letter any day now. Normally this would be cause for great celebration, but the whole situation strikes me as a little off. The recruiter didn't tell him any terms, like salary, benefits, or start date. If you're going to make an offer, you make the offer and *then* back it up with a letter, you know?

"I called them and they said everything was proceeding as planned. I definitely have the job, although they're still checking references." Fletch shrugs and returns his attention to Bob Barker.

"Wait a minute. It's been four days. What do they need to know that they can't find out in four days' time? You should have them talk to me; I can tell them whatever they want. Not only am I married to you, but I met you at work, so I know your work ethic. It's good."

"Thanks, but I don't think so."

"Why not? I'd be totally honest. I'd tell 'em your drawbacks, too. Your taste in music sucks, you have an obsession with keeping your car clean, and you still haven't unpacked the boxes in the den. On the upside, you're a snappy dresser, you're smart, and you always pick up the lunch tab. What's not to like?"

"When you put it like that, I'm a shoo-in. By the way, Courtney called. She and Brett are having dinner tonight and she wants us to join them for a drink afterward."

"Can we afford it?"

"We'll manage. After all, we're both about a week away from starting work, right?"

· ·

Wheeeee!!! Drunkieee like a Monkeees! Courtnneee and Bretttt are cuttttte. KISSY KISSY. And stoooopid, stoooopid Kathleen is beeeingg meeeeannn to Court!! I tolle you she's BAAAAADDD. I talllked and taaalked about Birchycompany and saidddd it was GGGGRRRRRReeat! Court saysss Brichtooom LURVES me and I haaaaavve a joooooobbb! Wooo hooo! Ricccchhh aaaagaiiin!!

· ·

"Hey, sweetie, guess what," I call, walking in the back door. "It must be Take Your Child to a Dangerous Construction Site Day! There's a ton of little kids crawling all over the haphazardly stacked pallets of bricks and Mount Garbage. I'm going to stand on the porch with the cordless phone so I can call nine one one when one of them gets flattened like Wile E. Coyote. Fletch, you've *got* to see this!" Silence. "Fletch? You here?" More silence. "Honey, where are you?"

I walk up the stairs and find Fletch sprawled facedown on the bed. "Fletch? What's up?"

Face in his pillow, he mumbles, "I didn't get the job."

"WHAT? How can that be? What happened? Did you get a bad reference?"

"No, the recruiter said my references were great. They said an internal candidate came up late last week, so they gave the job to him."

"No! They can't do that! They can't tell someone they have a job and then NOT GIVE IT TO HIM. They can't! I don't know if it's illegal, but it's totally unethical."

"They did it anyway."

"But why are you just lying there? Why aren't you up in arms? This is infuriating! Why aren't you mad?"

"I give up."

"You can't just give up. What does that mean, anyway? You give up?"

"I'm tired of fighting."

"But this is bullshit. Can't you sue them or something?"

"They never gave me anything in writing."

"Honey, if this is a joke, I'd sure appreciate it if you'd spring the punch line on me now. Really, you got a six-figure salary and an office, right? Right? Fletch? Right??"

Fletch looks at me like he's carrying the weight of the world on his shoulders. "It's no joke."

"What if you'd quit a job contingent on them making an offer? What if we planned to move because they said they were hiring you? They simply cannot do this."

"Jen, it's done. I don't want to talk about it anymore. Just leave me alone so I can take a nap."

"Those motherfucking weasels. I want revenge."

"Jen, let it go. It's over. It doesn't matter." He pulls the covers up to his ears and turns to face the wall. I try to hug him but he pulls away.

I head downstairs to pace and plot. After practically wearing a path across the floor, I realize there's nothing I can do to settle the score that isn't dangerous and illegal. I lie down on the couch, take off my glasses, and have a cathartic cry.

I'm not sure how much more stress I can take. My stomach is constantly in knots over our financial situation and I hate all this uncertainty. I'm filled with regret over my old lifestyle. Why did I make such bad choices? Why didn't I listen to my dad when he said the bubble was going to burst? Why didn't I acquiesce to my mother's pleas to sock away 15 percent of my paycheck each week? What, exactly, led me to believe I was invincible? Why didn't I follow my brother's advice to buy a cheaper place somewhere less fashionable instead of pissing an ocean of money away on a trendy rental?

How come I never realized that my compensation was a fluke and I had no right making the money I did with the experience I had? I used to base my self-worth on what I did and how I lived, but now that times are different, I've propped myself up by being proud of my abilities. But what if I'm really not as smart and competent as I thought? Then what? The tears come hard and fast.

Loki wedges his way in next to me, and Maisy positions herself next to the couch, munching on a bone. I bury my face in the ruff of Loki's neck and allow the self-pity to wash over me.

I hate feeling sorry for myself. In the scope of things, I've been pretty fortunate and this self-pity is weak and contemptible. I force myself to stop crying and decide to go to the gas station for a Dolly Madison fruit pie. There's almost nothing sweetened apples and frosty pie crust can't make better. I reach for my glasses and they're not where I left them. On my hands and knees, I look for them under the couch but they're gone.

Then I see that Maisy is not chewing one of her Brontosaurus bones. Rather, she's enjoying $600 worth of custom-made, Italian-framed tortoiseshell glasses, which I loved because they made me look exactly like Ashley Banfield on MSNBC.

And then the floodgates really open.

To: Sandy Case
From: jen@jenlancaster.com
Date: March 26, 2003
Subject: Senior Account Manager

Hi, Sandy,

I just saw that the position I'd interviewed for was re-posted on Monster.com, along with a different Birchton & Co. job. This leads me to wonder if Birchton is expanding the search to find the best candidate, which would make sense given all the talent currently available. If that's the case, could you please let me know if I'm still being considered? Another opportunity has come up for me,[154] but I don't want to pursue it until I know whether or not your organization is interested, as Birchton is absolutely my first choice.

Many thanks,

Jen Lancaster

---

[154] I'm totally bluffing.

To: Chris Birchton
From: jen@jenlancaster.com
Date: April 5, 2003
Subject: Senior Account Manager

Chris,

I haven't heard from anyone at Birchton for almost two weeks. After having six interviews, I'm more than a little curious about my status. I saw that the job listing was re-posted after my final round of interview, so I'm not sure what to think, especially as no one has taken me up on my offer to provide references.

Although I really liked the people I met and the job sounds like an interesting challenge at which I know I'd excel, it's not going to hurt my feelings if a more appropriate candidate is selected. I would, however, appreciate a head's up one way or another.

Thanks,

Jen Lancaster

"Birchton and Company, how may I direct your call?"

"Sandy Case, please." I am getting an answer TODAY about this job.

"May I ask who's calling?" If this receptionist were any more chipper, I'd find a way to worm through the phone cord so I could strangle her with it.

"Tell her it's Jen Lancaster."

"Sure thing. Hold, please." I listen to the Muzak version of "Summer of '69" while I wait. Yuck. I hate Bryan Adams almost as much as Dave Matthews.

"Um, Jen? Sandy's on another line. Can she call you back?"

"No. I'll hold."

"It could be a while."

"I said I'd wait." Sandy's dodged my calls all week.

I hear muffled conversation in the background and seconds later, Sandy answers. "Sandy Case speaking."

"Sandy, it's Jen Lancaster. I'm calling to check on the status of my application."

I can hear Sandy exhale on the other end of the line. "Jen, I'm sorry. I've been meaning to get back to you but it's just been so hectic around here that I haven't had a chance."

"Well, now's your chance. Can you please let me know what's happening? I ask because I have another opportunity,[155] and I'm hesitant to move forward with them until I know my status with Birchton."

"Jen, I'm going to be honest. We're not hiring you. We all met you and thought you'd be a great fit. We were ready to extend an offer. Then we saw your Web site, and we found its content to be inappropriate. You know, some of your 'Companies That Suck' are our clients, and we simply cannot have an employee denigrating them."

[155]Still a big, fat lie.

"Whoa, wait, stop. First of all, I'd planned to take the site down once I started working,because it was a joke, and second of all, how did you even find out about it? My picture is obscured and at no point do I ever mention my name or that of my former employer."

"How we found out is irrelevant. I'm sorry, but we're going to keep looking."

"I understand you have to do what you think is best for your business. However, the polite and professional thing to do would have been *to tell me two weeks ago so I could stop wasting my time*."

"For your own sake, I suggest you take down that awful Web site."

"You know what? My site is funny. And if you can't appreciate my sense of humor, then your not hiring me is for the best. Thanks, anyway." I hang up before she can say anything else.

We are in so much trouble.

* * *

Weblog Entry 4/10/03

A FAIRY TALE

One upon a time there was a beautiful Executive Princess named Jennifer. She worked for a wonderful company who treated her nicely and paid her even better! She was very, very happy.

Her product line was doing great, so her company decided they would buy one of their competitors so they'd be even stronger in the marketplace. Princess Jen was a little concerned, because she'd been through mergers with other companies. She went to each of her eleven bosses (yeah, you read that right) and said, "I am concerned. I've never been through a merger where there weren't job losses." Her eleven very nice bosses promised her that her position was secure because she did such a terrific job! Hooray!

Two days later she went to work and they gave her a box and showed her the door. She said, "What happened? You promised me that every thing was going well. And that my job was secure." They were real nice and super apologetic, and said she was let go as "a business decision." She never got a better explanation.

Jen was really happy because every potential employer simply accepts the explanation of her layoff as being a "business decision." Boy, they never question that! It certainly doesn't sound like she was selling confidential information or stealing office supplies! And these potential employers always believe that a person who was crushing her goals would be cut loose for no apparent reason. So her search to find a new job with a livable salary has been so easy!

Now she has to sell her Cadillac in order to keep paying for her apartment in the ghetto.

And she's really fucking bitter.

The end.

I can deal with the fact that I have to sell the car, even though I wasn't thrilled with the idea at first, to put it mildly. I kind of launched into Fletch when he brought it up,[156] until I realized that all

---

[156]An entire plate of mashed sweet potatoes may or may not have been thrown in protest.

we really have right now is each other. If we start attacking each other over what could have been, we'll fall apart. Plus, I'd rather have a couple of bucks in the bank. If a little extra money returns the smile to Fletch's face, then I'm all for it. As it is now, the car's just sitting on the street depreciating like mad, and the insurance on it in this 'hood is insane.[157]

What I can't deal with is what happened with Birchton. Granted, if they didn't think my site was funny, I probably wouldn't have meshed with their corporate culture. Maybe if I worked there, I'd feel constrained all the time and couldn't really be myself. Regardless, I'd have liked the chance to try.

I don't understand how they found out about my Web site. Yeah, it's been getting more and more hits lately, but it's almost totally anonymous. Even the domain registry is under Fletch's name, so there's no way to trace it back to me. I've tried to call Courtney to see if she has any scoop because Birchton's still her client and she talks to them all the time, but I haven't heard back from her. Come to think of it, neither has Brett. I hate bugging people at work, but this is making me crazy, so I'm going to call her.

I dial Courtney's direct line. "Good afternoon, thank you for calling Corp. Com.," answers a male voice.

"Mo? Is that you?" It sounds like my buddy Maurice, who's an administrative assistant at Corp. Com.

"Yes, it is. May I ask with whom I'm speaking?"

"Mo, you big nerd, it's Jen!"

"Jen girl! I miss you! Things aren't the same without you. When are we getting together for daiquiris?"

"Let's wait till it gets a little warmer so we can go somewhere outside. I'd say a couple of weeks."

"I'm going to hold you to it."

---

[157]More than once I wished someone would just steal it already.

"Good. It's been way too long." I'm just about to launch into gossip mode when I remember why I called in the first place. "Sweetie, why are you answering Courtney's phone? Is she out?"

"Girl, Courtney's gone."

"You know what? I can't say I'm surprised. Last time we got together, she was on a tear about how moody Kathleen's been and how much business has dropped off. I'm glad to hear she finally got out—that place was totally stressing her."

He drops his voice. "It's no fun anymore. Everyone here is boring and ugly. Remember Friday Fiestas and margaritas at lunch? Completely over now."

"Aw, sweetie, I'm sorry to hear it."

"The good news is that it's got me thinking of opening my own Birkenstock shop up in Boystown. If I do, will you help me with the marketing?"

"Anything for you, Mo."

"Uh-oh, I'm getting the fish eye from Kathleen. I'd better scoot."

"It was so nice to talk to you. Oh, wait, I almost forgot. I want to get ahold of Court. Do you know where I can find her?"

"She went to work for one of her clients. Um, it's um . . . gosh, what's their name again?"

No.

NO.

She wouldn't.

I squeeze my eyes shut and clench my fists. Please don't let this be true. "Birchton & Co., perhaps?"

"Yes! That's it! Birchton! I think I've got the number—do you want it?"

"No, no, I've got it. Thanks anyway, Mo. I'll talk to you later."

"Bye for now, Miss Thang."

So now I know how Birchton got my URL. *Et tu*, Courtney?

How could she do this to me? I would never screw someone like this, not even my worst enemy. I mean, how could she listen to me cry about being jobless and broke for all these months and then knowingly and deliberately swoop down and steal the one good opportunity from me?

Granted, I didn't necessarily handle her feelings with kid gloves, but I always tried to act in her best interests. I got bossy and officious with the Brad/Chad stuff not because I'm a bitch but because I wanted to protect her. I set her up with Brett because I thought he could make her happy. And this is how I'm rewarded for being a decent, honest, albeit somewhat pushy friend?

Shoot, I tried to talk her into applying at Birchton long before I ever did. With her P.R. background, I thought she'd be a great asset to their organization. And even while I was interviewing there, I kept asking, "Are you sure you don't want the job? It would get you away from Kathleen and you'd be great at it." I gave her every chance to claim this job honestly, and instead she tacitly denied any interest while sticking a knife in my back.

I will never forgive or forget this.

You are dead to me, Courtney. Dead.

· 10 ·

Randolph Street Starbucks

Weblog Entry 4/13/03

WHEN I GROW UP

Oddly enough, I'm flattered my website had the power to keep me from getting hired. Any company who doesn't get what this site is about probably isn't the place for me. Unfortunately, I still need to do something to pay bills, so the job search continues.

As my current efforts to procure work in my field have been wholly unsuccessful, I feel I may be best off starting a different career.

But doing what? I have no idea.

Kids seem to have the inside track on good adult jobs, so I decided to seek advice from my six year-old nephew Cam. He proved to be an excellent sounding board and told me that he's considering careers as, "A banker like Uncle Joe, a painter like Jackson Pollock, or the guy who helps you find stuff at the grocery store." Well, these ideas sound good in theory, but I'm bad with money, lack artistic skill, and recently spent 25 minutes searching for canned olives at the local Jewel, so these careers are out.

I then queried Max, Cam's four year-old brother, what his future plans might entail. Max would like to paint houses, drive a truck, or "punch you in the stupid head."[158] Sarah, their two year-old sister, had the least enlightening suggestions, because all she could tell me was, "I like 'nakes! I like 'nakes! I like 'nakes!" I *really* hate snakes, so a job in the Reptile House is not realistic.

Since these are the only kids I know, I decided to re-examine my various college majors in order to come up with a new career. I graduated with a degree in Political Science . . . but I've already been a waitress and I wasn't very good at it. Apparently I am "not friendly."[159]

I'd previously majored in Archeology until my father strongly advised me to switch. He believed I'd quit the minute I got to a desert and decided it was too hot to be digging around outside.[160] Interior Designer is also out because I only like one style. I suspect clients would quickly tire of pink walls and cabbage rose prints.

---

[158]It does sound like my brother can feel comfortable spending Max's college fund on a tropical vacation.

[159]When I was young, I competed in the occasional beauty pageant, and while I was often a shoo-in for Miss Photogenic, I was never once named Miss Congeniality.

[160]He was right.

My only other major was Journalism and even though I love to write, I transferred out of that school because I wanted to make more than $17K/year once I graduated. Plus, I think newspapers frown on you writing feature articles about yourself, and, unfortunately, I'm my favorite topic.

I've determined the ideal job for me is one where I can write clever essays about my life and my employer will give me enough money not only to live a comfortable existence, but also to buy many, many new pairs of shoes.

Please let me know where to send my application.

· ·

To: jen@jenlancaster.com
From: Adam
Date: April 15, 2003
Subject: Loser

Jen,

My name is Adam and I am currently working for *[MONOLITHIC AMERICAN AUTO MANUFACTURER]* in Michigan. I chose engineering because I liked it and there are a lot of jobs in this area for engineers. There are women engineers here, too. They are a minority in this field and they get paid more for doing the same job I do, yet they move up the corporate ladder at an alarming pace.

Why the hell would you get a political science degree and live in Chicago? You need to re-locate to the Baltimore/D.C. area to put that degree to use. A Master's Degree in that field is definitely required to make a decent living. You claim to be an intelligent person so go out and get any job, move back in with your parents, go back to school and get a real degree. Or, do like most women do; find a man and have him support you while you go back to school.

Adam

. . . .

To: Adam
From: jen@jenlancaster.com
Date: April 15, 2003
Subject: RE: Loser

Hi, Adam,

I've not had any hate mail for a while and I'd forgotten how invigorating it can be, so thank you for writing! Fortunately, you caught me on a good day, so you won't be subject to my usual evisceration with the speculation to the root cause of your issues with women. Nope, the words "latent homosexual" will not pass *my* lips.

I'll even begin by agreeing with you. I don't think anyone at MAAM should be promoted or paid better strictly based on gender. Or race, age, handicap, or sexual preference for that matter. (So you're totally safe.) Personally, I believe an employee should be compensated solely on his performance. But I don't work for MAAM and I can't say that this isn't the case. Perhaps it's your perceptions that are faulty and not the ass-kicking chicks who work around you.

What I find interesting is that according to my website tracking software, you only spent six minutes reading my website. Yet in these six minutes, you feel you've figured out a better way for me to live my life. Presumptuous, don't you think? But if you'd dug in my site just a bit further and had spent more than an average of eight seconds per page[161] you'd have all the answers to your questions and the reasons behind my decisions.

---

[161]I really do love my tracking software.

Bottom line, I'm alarmed that a person with no eye for detail or passion for investigation is designing cars. So I not only hold you personally responsible for designing the shitty cup holder in my old Cadillac, but also for engineering a car that lost $35,000 in value in the five years since it was manufactured. Perhaps if *you'd* made a better car, *I'd* have had more than $2500 to live off of when I was forced to sell it. (And in cherry condition no less!)

Seriously, even the Koreans are kicking MAAM's ass, so here's a suggestion . . . get the hell off the Internet and start designing a better cup holder RIGHT NOW.

Supersize me,

Jen

We were ten minutes into our Easter road trip to my parents' house when something important detached itself from something else important in Fletch's SUV, stranding us on the Kennedy Expressway. Later, the mechanic described the problem using words like *manifold*, *gasket*, and *cracked block*, but all I heard was *la, la, la, really expensive, la, la, la.* The repairs took a big chunk of the money we received from selling my precious Cadillac. Now instead of having enough rent money to last all summer, we have A HUGE PROBLEM.

Normally I look to Fletch to resolve our crises, but it's hard for him to address this one when he can't even get out of bed. No, scratch that. He *can* get up long enough to head to the local package store to pick up a twelve-pack. I should get on him for drinking too much, but right now, a Miller High Life temporary escape is the only thing that makes him happy. Otherwise, he mopes around the house, full of regret.

He's not the only one who's miserable right now. Seems like everywhere I look, I'm haunted by bad choices. I feel sick to my stomach each time I open the hall closet and see row after row of designer purchases. Why did I need an $800 bag to make myself feel important? How was my life enriched by a mink-lined raincoat?

I settle in front of the television in an attempt to get my mind off our situation. I'm flipping through the channels when the face of another one of my stupid choices appears. Brian Lamb, founder of C-SPAN, is on and I'm suddenly reminded of our *interview* when I was in college.

Brian was my friend Dee Dee's uncle and, from what I understood, a damn fine one at that. He doted on Dee, and if she asked him to interview one of her friends as a favor, often he would. Although getting the internship was contingent on the applicant's talents, he'd always give her friends a chance.

As a poli-sci major, I salivated at the thought of working for C-SPAN. So when Dee told me the date he'd be in town (and planned to have dinner at the restaurant where we worked), I knew I'd have the opportunity to meet him and would happily pimp myself for a job.

We didn't have a formal sit-down planned. Brian didn't know we'd be meeting. I was too chickenshit to ask for a proper interview because I thought I'd be more natural in a social setting, so Dee agreed to just spring me on him. When my shift ended and I waited for him to make an appearance, I had a quick cocktail to calm my nerves. I wanted to be confident and relaxed. If I met him in the state I was in, I'd seem like an anxiety-ridden basket case and no one gives internships to mental girls. I had one tiny Johnnie Walker Black Scotch and soda because I was too nervous to eat.

After my drink, I felt less tense, but thought that maybe one more drink would make me even more confident. I mean, really, this was my career we were talking about! I had an obligation to present myself in the best possible light, so yes, please, add another Johnnie Black to my tab. Imagine, then, how much better I felt after drinks three, four, and five! By the time Brian came in, I was *relaxed,* let me tell you.

Dee led me over for the big introduction. This was my chance! My whole postgraduate future loomed before me! If I played my cards right, I could turn a C-SPAN internship into an entry-level job with a lobbying firm, at which I'd excel. I'd quickly go from lackey to power broker, and all the most important folks in Washington would have me on speed dial. "Oh, yes," they'd say. "J. A. Lancaster's the person to call to get things done." I figured I'd go by my initials because they're gender neutral. And then? When I showed up in a fabulously short skirt and long jacket? I'd blow their minds, and all the rich men in the office would want to take me out to dinner, where I'd floor them with the one-two punch of beauty and brains, and they wouldn't bat an eye when I ordered both the pistachio crème brûlée AND the chocolate lava cake because I wanted "just a small taste" of both.

I'd be the toast of Washington and news shows would clamor to make me a special correspondent. I'd tool around the Beltway in a convertible and a pillbox hat, having single-handedly resurrected Jackie Kennedy's Camelot style. I'd live in a deluxe town house in

298 · *Jen Lancaster*

Georgetown, just like Murphy Brown, and I'd have two giant, slobbery bulldogs who I'd name Winston and Churchill. The *Washington Post* would name me "D.C.'s Most Eligible Bachelorette." Next thing you know I'd be Mrs. Senator So-and-so and my soirees would be so cool that *Us Weekly* would cover them. Then my husband would get an ambassadorship somewhere really awesome like Fiji, and I could live out my golden years tanning on the beach with lots of white-jacketed butlers bringing me drinks served in pineapples so I wouldn't dehydrate.

Envisioning my glorious sun-soaked future, and with a great deal of confidence, I looked Brian Lamb square in the eye and said the three little words that would seal my fate with C-SPAN.

"I likessshh Congresssshh!"

Brian shook my hand like a trooper and returned to his meal, surreptitiously dabbing my spittle from his brow with a napkin.

There would be no big house in Fiji for this Congress-liking political scientist.

And I learned that without doubt regret-based hangovers are the worst.

Without stopping to consider my actions, I grab an empty laundry basket and march straight to the closet. I toss a pile of expensive purses and outerwear into it, then immediately go to the computer to pull up my eBay account. Within half an hour, I've listed everything but my Prada bag for auction.

I'm keeping it as a living reminder never to be stupid again.

Today I managed to get Fletch out of bed before noon, so we're watching *The Price Is Right* together. I've become obsessed with this show and I'm not sure why. Maybe it's because watching *TPIR* reminds me of being a kid home for summer vacation when my only concern was which bathing suit I'd wear to our swim club later that day. Or maybe it's just nice to see happy people. I swear I tear up every time someone wins a car, especially if the person is elderly or in a military uniform.[162]

I'm so into the show that conversation is only allowed during the commercials. At the first break, I ask Fletch, "What did Bill say?"

I've called our landlord repeatedly for the past six weeks to complain about our air-conditioning. Or lack thereof. Each time I talk to him, he politely brushes me off, explaining that our AC unit is new and top of the line and couldn't possibly be malfunctioning. It finally occurred to me that Bill might be one of those men who prefer to discuss business with other men, so I had Fletch call him right before the show started.

"He said he'd send the contractor over right away."

"Ha! I told you he was a misogynist."

"Misogyny isn't the problem, Jen. I suspect your explanation may have been faulty."

"Pfft. I told him fifteen times the blowery thing worked fine but it never made the big whoosh full of cold, cold air so the pipes didn't get sweaty and the issue was a lack of the chilly-making juice. I said we probably just needed another box of neon like we did when our AC was out in Lincoln Park. I'm not sure how I could have expressed the problem more clearly."

Fletch rolls his eyes. "I stand corrected."

"Did I tell you my mom called first thing this morning?"

"No. What did she have to say?"

"I got the 'You have to do something' speech again. I told her about selling the car and my purses and coats, and then I read her the

---

[162]My ex-friend Lynn used to say if she ever got onstage, she'd slip Bob some tongue. Yet she wonders why I no longer return her calls.

list of all the places I'd applied, yet she still wasn't satisfied. She kept repeating, 'You have to do something,' and I pictured her clutching her knees, rocking back and forth, all hot-water-burn-baby-like. I finally hung up on her because she was giving me an anxiety attack."

"Sometimes I can't believe she's a licensed therapist."

I shrug. "She's really good in a professional setting. But with me it's like 'The cobbler's children have no shoes.' Remember when she didn't hear from me for a few days, and she wanted to send Todd up to Chicago to look for me?"

"Weren't you traveling on business that week?"

"Yes, and that would have been any normal person's natural assumption. Instead, she thought I'd run away from home." Bob reappears. "Shh—it's on."

The next contestant wins a trip onstage by bidding $2 when the person before her bid $1. "That's dirty pool, missy!" I shout at the television.

"What just happened?" Apparently Fletch did not spend his childhood stalking Bob Barker, which probably contributed to why it was such an unhappy one.

"When the first few contestants bid an amount that seems too high, another contestant can choose to bid $1. Which is fine. It's almost a guaranteed win, and it's a good strategy when competing with morons who have no idea how much stuff costs. What's not fine is when a $1 bid is followed by a $2 bid, which totally screws the $1 person."

"Doesn't the $2 person generally win with that maneuver?"

"Yes, and that's why it's wrong. Look . . . see? That jackass just won the washer and dryer. Hmph. I hope she gets the putting challenge. No one ever wins the putting challenge."

Fletch yawns deeply. "Explain to me again why it was so important that I get out of bed to see this."

Before I can answer, the dogs start to go wild Vegas-style. I peer out the window and see a guy wearing a tool belt bending over our air-conditioning unit with a giant screwdriver. Unfortunately, it's not the kind of wild you'd hope for when a total stranger appears unannounced on your deck, holding a blunt instrument. It's more of a tail-wagging, dance-in-your-pants, could-this-be-the-happiest-moment-in-all-of-canine-history? sort of wild. The dogs had this same exact reaction when the crackhead pulled a rubber knife on Fletch when we lived in Bucktown . . . utter and complete joy at the pleasure of making the vagrant's acquaintance.

"So much for their careers as guard dogs," I say.

Fletch goes outside to talk to the contractor while I watch the end of the show. The jackass makes it to the showdown and totally overbids on her showcase, which includes a new car *and* a boat. HA! Justice is served.

"You won't believe what the problem was."

"What?"

"No one hooked our unit up to an electric source after it was installed. Although we could get the fan to run because of the furnace, it wasn't connecting to the AC's compressor, which is chilled by freon, hence all the warm air. The contractor's putting in a fuse now so we should be up and running within the hour."

I mull over this information. "What you're telling me is the blowery thing worked fine but it never made the big whoosh full of cold, cold air so the pipes didn't get sweaty and the issue was a lack of access to the chilly-making juice. Which means I was right."

Fletch nods. "Too bad Bill doesn't speak gibberish, or this could have been resolved weeks ago."

· ·

I've feared this day for many months. But each time our savings dipped to the level where possibility turned to reality, some sort of miracle occurred such as the arrival of a long-lost commission check and I was able to stave off the inevitable. I consider myself lucky to have been able to hold out for a professional job as long as I have.

But the day has come.

It is time . . . to work retail.

I imagine the hiring process will be easier for a retail job. Instead of being asked about my five-year plan, I'll simply have to confirm I can work on Saturdays and can lift fifty pounds. To land the gig, there's a good chance I won't have to do a PowerPoint presentation about market segmentation because their potential customers will be the ones who walk through the door. Although I don't know that a retail job will be easy, I'm confident that the search parameters will be a lot less stringent.

I'm off. . . . Wish me luck.

• •

```
To: Michigan Avenue Pottery Barn
From: jen@jenlancaster.com
Date: May 3, 2003
Subject: Sales Associate


Hello,


Attached you'll find my resume sent in con-
sideration for open positions within Pottery
Barn.
```

I'm an ideal candidate for employment because I paid my way through college by working retail.[163] I have almost seven years of retail experience and became famous within my old company for creating the "Ten Commandments of Customer Service." I'm particularly proud of Commandment Seven—*If a customer tells you to dance, strap on your tap shoes and ask if they'd prefer show tunes.*

I seek retail work now because I've gotten off the corporate fast track. When I was laid off from an executive position back in 2001, I worked a variety of temporary assignments[164] while searching for a position commensurate with what I had. But in so doing, I discovered I had a passion for writing and now getting published is my priority.[165]

However, I can't write all the time, so I seek a part-time retail position. Pottery Barn is the natural choice for me as it's my favorite store, not only for the merchandise, but also because of the service provided by its team members.[166] And with my service background, I

---

[163]Semi-lie. This is only because Dad pulled the funding once I flunked out.
[164]Lie. I've had one assignment and no other temp agency even wants to talk to me.
[165]Lie. But, actually, that *would* be kind of cool.
[166]Sucking up never hurts.

```
could never work for a store that didn't treat
its customers well.¹⁶⁷


I'd be delighted to discuss my qualifications in
person, should any opportunities be available.


Best,


Jennifer A. Lancaster
```

I haven't heard a peep from any of the stores where I applied last week. I think I may have gone in smacking of anxiety with a bit of crazy about the eyes. Today I'm changing my tactics. Maybe if I look like I don't need a job, my indifference will drive them MAD to hire me.

I stack all my jeweled bracelets on my wrists, make my hair big, and exchange my very average-sized wedding ring for the one Lagos ring I haven't yet sold. It's a large white topaz, and everyone assumes it's a gigantic diamond. I put on a cute-but-casual khaki skirt and the new sweater my mother got me last month—the only truly stylish-right-this-second item I own at the moment—and squirt myself with my few remaining drops of J'Adore Dior. (I hope it's enough to cover up the stink of desperation.)

I sail out of a cab and into Barnes & Noble on State Street. I chat up the information booth guy and, in what's supposed to look like an

---

¹⁶⁷Lie, again. At this point, I DO NOT CARE. I just need a job, any job.

afterthought, ask for an application in my best bored-society-wife-looking-for-a-bit-of-a-diversion-and-if-this-doesn't-work-out-I'll-just-nail-the-gardener voice.

I turn in the application with a flourish, cursed Prada bag causally slung on my shoulder, an iced latte clutched in my freshly manicured (by me) hand. I assure the desk guy again what a jolly good lark this working thing would be for a restless, kept woman, before sauntering out the door.

Then I walk ten blocks to the bus stop so I won't have to pay an extra thirty cents for a transfer.

· ·

Faux casual didn't work either.

Now what?

· ·

"Why is someone calling us so late on a Wednesday? It must be after midnight." I glance at the caller ID.

"Who is it?" Fletch is half in the bag on a school night. I tolerate this solely because it's about the only time he smiles or laughs anymore.

"Dunno. We don't know anyone with a cell phone in the 630 area code, right?"

"Probably a wrong number. Let voice mail get it."

A minute after the phone rings, we hear the doorbell.

"What the hell?" I ask. I look out the back window and see a couple of unfamiliar cars idling in our parking lot. "Fletch, what's going on?"

"I don't know. I'll go down and answer the door."

"Here, take this." I thrust a rolling pin at him.

"Do you want me to bake them a pie? I'll be fine." He heads downstairs to the front door.

I stand by the phone, ready to call the police. I see Fletch walk out to his SUV and talk to the small group of people gathered around it. One of the guys appears to have a badge. Exactly what *is* going on here? Did these guys catch someone trying to steal our car? Uh-oh, I hope our insurance is up-to-date. Fletch handles all our bills but I'm starting to wonder what kind of job he's been doing. Lately we've gotten calls from bill collectors, although Fletch swears it's by mistake.

I watch as he begins to take items out of the car. He makes a small pile of CDs and his emergency road repair kit. Then I see him take his keys out of his pocket and hand them to the man with the badge. Mr. Badge gets into the car and starts it, slowly backing out of our parking space.

A couple of minutes later, Fletch returns.

"What is going on? Who were those people? Why did he have a badge? Where is he going with our car?"

Fletch silently goes to the fridge, gets out another beer, and lights the first cigarette I've ever seen him smoke inside the house. He sits down heavily on the couch and puts his face in his hands. I rush to his side.

"Fletch, what just happened to your car?"

Fletch puffs slowly and pensively on his cigarette, finally answering, "It was repossessed."

"I don't understand. We're current on the car payment."

"Jen, we're not current on anything."

"What do you mean?" I look at him, waiting for a reaction, but he sits motionless. "Wait. Are you saying the repossession wasn't a mistake? What do we have to do to get it back?"

"We have to pay off the loan in full."

"Which is how much?"

"$7000, which is approximately $6995 more than we have. The car is gone. We're not getting it back."

I sit quietly for a few minutes, absorbing the information. "But what are we going to do without a car? How are either of us going to get a job without a car?"

"I don't know."

"If you didn't pay the car note, then what about the rest of our bills? Are we still OK? You said we'd be OK on bills for a while."

"I lied. I haven't paid a lot of them in a couple of months. All the money we have has gone toward rent and utilities."

I walk into Fletch's office and find a stack of unopened letters marked *Delinquent*, *Past Due*, and *Third Request*. "Why didn't you open these?"

"I knew we couldn't pay them, so I didn't bother."

"Honey, why didn't you talk to me about any of this?"

"I didn't want to worry you." Fletch drops his cigarette in an empty beer bottle, where it fizzles for a couple of seconds.

"So what can I do now to help?"

"I don't know, Jen. I just don't know."

To: jen@jenlancaster.com
From: David
Date: June 12, 2003
Subject: Idiots with Jobs

A year ago my wife and I got laid off from two
different companies in the same week. Like you,
the money runs thin eventually. So I am driving

down Long Island wondering what I can do about it and I come upon a diner advertising for people. Well, shit, I thought, I will give that a go.

Apparently not.

Apparently you can't get a job in a diner until you've had a number of years experience, or so the toothless wonder who ran the place informed me. "Oh no, you don't wait tables in a 3 million dollar diner straight off." So it would appear that while I was out there running 50 million dollar computer operations in Europe and the US, I was actually wasting my time. I should have been in Mamma's Greasy Poke Shoppe paying my dues for my future career.

I didn't get the job and I still don't have a job, nor does my wife, but I solved a problem that I know has been getting to you, Jen. Now we know why the idiots have all the jobs!!

David

To: David
From: jen@jenlancaster.com
Date: June 13, 2003
Subject: RE: Idiots with Jobs

David,

I am infuriated for you, although I can't say
I'm surprised. I hear this kind of story a lot
lately. One of my doggie park buddies (ex-
consulting firm employee) had an interview at
Neiman Marcus and the interviewer didn't see
how her previous experience controlling work
flow, communicating with the client, supervising
employees, and managing time and budget had
properly prepared her to ring up scarves, key
rings, and pantyhose.

It's completely insane out there—try to stay
strong,

Jen

To: jen@jenlancaster.com
From: Ickey
Date: June 13, 2003
Subject: get off ur fat ass

Jen, seriously, do you put as much energy into looking for a gig as you do bitching about the whole world on your website and why they are not as cool as you? There is a good job waiting for you at Starbucks . . . I can feel it. BTW, stay away from the scones. It's obvious you've already had enough.

Ickey

. . . .

To: Ickey
From: jen@jenlancaster.com
Date: June 14, 2003
Subject: RE: get off ur fat ass

Ickey, this site is definitely not for you. And by 'you' I'm guessing you're the kind of 25 year-old Advertising/PR flack who was always too hungover to listen when I came to your agency to present you with the tools you needed to better serve your clients and do your job.

Now I may have your industry wrong, but I'm
sure you're employed as it's obvious to me
that you have NO FUCKING CLUE what it's like
to lose your job, your status, your lifestyle,
and subsequently, your whole sense of self.
You can't fathom the humiliation of having to
beg off visits to your parents' house because
you're too ashamed to tell them your car was
repossessed, nor can you understand what it's
like to live in the dark like a Pioneer for a
week until you can pay your electric bill. If
you could, you'd have never sent me this
email.

You're probably also in the dark about my job
search techniques and don't know that I spend
every morning reading every new job posting on
every single search portal. Or that I spend a
good hour each day making pitch calls to sales
directors alerting them to my availability. Or
that I've practically alienated all my friends
and ex-colleagues by pestering them to see if
they've heard of something . . . anything . . .

As for the coffee shop career you suggested,
don't think for a minute that I haven't tried
to get one. I'll work hard wherever I'm hired,
just like I did when I worked my way through
college. That's right, I paid for much of my
college education by waitressing and working

retail.[168] No one sent me off to school with a brand new Jetta and a credit card like I'm sure yours did. I've worked damn hard to earn every single thing that I have.

But I digress.

A while ago, I took the VP title off my resume and left off the part where I sold upwards of $10 million worth of goods and services for my employers. I figured if I dumbed-down my resume, maybe I wouldn't look so overqualified. Although I don't agree with the idea of censoring my accomplishments, I did it anyway. By so doing, it means that maybe, just maybe, I can secure a job serving coffee to slackers like you who squander their employers' resources cruising Internet bulletin boards instead of doing the job they're paid to do.

BTW, Ickey, if I do land that coveted job at Starbucks, I assure you, I WILL spit in your latte.

Best,
Jen

---

[168]If I mentioned to Ickey that I flunked out after my sophomore year, I'd sound less credible.

My friend Katerina e-mailed me about a stunt a job-seeking nurse pulled in Sweden. She posted an ad stating she was ill-tempered and mean and probably wasn't terribly compassionate, but she needed a job working as a home health aid anyway. After her ad ran, her phone wouldn't stop ringing.

Thusly inspired, I've taken out classified ads in both the *Chicago Tribune* and the *Chicago Reader*. The following hits Wednesday:

UNEMPLOYED AND BITTER

Sarcastic ex–sorority girl seeks high-paying job in an idiot-free environment. Must allow employees to wear cute shoes. Interested? Contact jen@jenlancaster.com.

I am cautiously optimistic that something good will come of it. Then again, I am usually wrong.

Who knew so many foot fetishists read the *Tribune*?

"Sweetie, wake up. It's after one o'clock." Fletch barely stirs. "Come up, wake up just for a minute. We need to talk about the dogs."

Fletch mumbles, "I'm listening."

"I already took them out this morning, and they should be fine for most of the day. Can you please walk them around four p.m.? They should be ready by then."

Fletch burrows deeper under the covers. "Where are you going?"

"Don't you remember? I've got another interview for the part-time receptionist position at that architecture firm." Again, thank God for Shayla. She temped at this firm last summer, and they tried to get her back this summer. Instead, she referred them to me. I went for my first interview a couple of days ago, and I found out they received more than six hundred applications for the job. And while I was waiting for my interview, five people walked in looking for applications. One of them was a girl with a Burberry purse—when we made eye contact, we exchanged wry smiles. Welcome to the age of doing what you have to do.

"Good luck."

"Thanks, hon. Don't forget—dogs go out at four o'clock."

Although I manage to snow the office manager, the managing partner at the firm believes I'll be bored by the job and tells me as much in the interview. I swear to him there's nothing boring about paying my rent, but he doesn't buy it. Deciding to make the most of my cute interview outfit, I hit up every retail outlet on Michigan Avenue for applications.

It's almost six forty-five when I get home, and the dogs greet me sheepishly at the door, tails tucked, ears pinned back. Someone pooped in the living room, and they're both terribly upset about it. When I walk into the kitchen to grab paper towels, I notice another pile.

"Guys, what happened? Didn't you go outside?" I ask. "Fletch? Where are you? What time did you take the dogs out?"

I walk up the stairs, and I find Fletch in the exact same spot I left him in. I shake him awake. "Fletch? Are you taking a nap?" I notice he's still in his pajamas. "Honey? Did you even get out of bed today?"

He lies there, staring at the wall. "No."

"Are you OK? Are you sick?"

"I just don't see any reason to get out of bed."

"Are you sad? Depressed? What are you feeling right now?"

"Nothing. I don't feel anything." Fletch got like this to a lesser extent when we first started dating. I quickly convinced him that depression was no big thing. I explained that if he had diabetes, he'd take insulin. Since depression's a disease, if he needed a drug to cure it, there'd be no stigma in taking it. I sent him off to the student health center for meds, and it was smooth sailing emotionally for years.

"Isn't your medicine working? Do you need a stronger dose?"

"We can't afford my pills and groceries. I made a choice and I chose to feed us."

"How long have you been off of them?"

"A couple of months. I didn't tell you because I didn't want you to worry."

Fletch sacrificed his mental health to provide for mine.

I do not deserve this man.

It's time I start shouldering some of the emotional burdens around here. I don't know how, but I'm going to find a way to fix everything.

· ·

"Hi, I'm calling to find out if your hospital offers mental health services on a sliding scale. . . ."

"Yes, I'm looking for a low- to no-cost depression management program for my husband. . . ."

"So you're not sure if your clinic is accepting pro bono patients? Can you check, please? It's really important. . . ."

"I read about your experimental treatment program, and I want to find out if my husband is eligible to enroll . . ."

"You guys are my last chance—can I get him into this program or not? Uh . . . OK, well, please don't think me rude for saying it this way—but FIND A WAY TO MAKE IT HAPPEN."

. . . .

OK, he's in.

Next up, find *anything* that will provide a paycheck. And until then, I'm practicing Microsoft Word tutorials.

. . . .

To: Staffing Manager
From: jen@jenlancaster.com
Date: June 17, 2003
Subject: Marketing Coordinator Posting on Monster.com

Dear Sir or Madam,

Attached you will find my resume sent in consideration for the open Marketing Coordinator position. And before you say it, please allow me . . .

"This person is overqualified for this position."

Now that we've gotten *that* out of the way, let me explain why I'm an ideal candidate for the job. Since I was laid off from an executive position back in 2001, I worked a variety of temp assignments while searching for a 'real' job.[169] I've built my office skills and I can answer phones, collate, and plan executive travel with the best of them. Taking these assignments[170] has instilled a sense of humility I'd previously been lacking and now I'm certainly not above fetching your lunch or dry cleaning. The added bonus for your organization is that in a pinch I can also manage your ad campaigns, write your press releases, and target new clients. But you're still probably thinking . . .

"She's going to split the second she finds something better. She already alluded to getting a 'real' job."

Not true. My priorities have changed since I was laid off. Now my goal is to get my writing published, not to pursue the kind of career I

---

[169]Yes, I'm lying again, but we're talking life or death at this point.
[170]Or, rather, begging for them.

used to have. I'm looking for a position that
will allow me to leave my job at the office at the
end of the day so that I can go home and write.

"We'll never be able to afford her."

Try me. You might be surprised to find out
exactly how cheap I am.

Best,

Jennifer A. Lancaster

"Gah, what am I supposed to wear to this thing?" I am rushing
frantically around our bedroom, trying to decide what to put on for
my interview. By the time the hiring manager received my note, she'd
already found a full-time person for the marketing job, but she liked
what I wrote so much that she wants to talk to me about a three-week
temp assignment. If I got it, I'd bring home about $1500 total, which
means we could cover July's rent!

Fletch sits on the end of the bed, watching me. He was actually
up and out of the house with the dogs by nine thirty a.m. His meds
have regulated and every day he seems a little more like himself. Last
night, stone sober, he actually laughed out loud at the scene on *The
Family Guy* where Peter Griffin turns his house into a huge puppet.
I've never heard a more beautiful sound.

"What's wrong with what you've got on right now?" he asks,
completely deadpan. I'm wearing a towel turban, a ratty old bra, and

a cutoff pair of sweatpants. I paw through my antiquated wardrobe and settle on a summer dress and lightweight cotton jacket.

I throw on my makeup and dry my hair. "Hey, Fletch, do you have any girly-smelling cologne?"

"Um, no. Why do you ask?"

"I'm completely out of perfume and this jacket reeks of mothballs. I need something to mask the scent." I throw open all the bathroom drawers and paw through my old accessory cases, hoping to stumble across one of those free miniperfume vials that clerks used to toss in my bag when I'd buy my J'Adore Dior. I've got none, and I mentally kick myself for throwing them all away in a fit of undying love for my signature scent. And I don't have any fashion magazines, so I can't even rub a scented sample page across myself.

In a flash of inspiration, I pull open the pantry door and begin searching. I remember reading once vanilla extract could double as perfume. Aha! Here it is! I splash it all over myself and for good measure, run a fingerful of Crisco across my lips to compensate for being out of gloss.[171]

"Well, how do I look?" I go back upstairs and twirl for Fletch.

"You look nice." After I hug him, he has a puzzled look on his face. "But why do you smell like cupcakes?"

• •

It's the first day of my temp assignment. Earlier, I found myself waiting at the bus stop, grinning like a Miss America contestant at the prospect of going to an actual JOB. (With my big, sun-bleached hair, savage tan, oily pink lips, and pastel outfit, I looked more like Barbie's older, fatter sister, but still, having a purpose made my smile large indeed.)

---

[171]Scarlett O'Hara and her old curtains have nothing on me.

Of course, when the bus didn't show up after two seconds, I freaked out and hailed a cab. Five minutes later, I was in front of my temporary office, which meant I had forty-five minutes to kill before I was due to start working. So I crossed the street to Starbucks.

Here I am with my half-caf latte, sitting at the faux-granite counter, taking in the scenery. It's strange, but if I look straight ahead, I can see the building where I'm about to temp. To the right of it is the insurance company where I worked when I was fresh out of college. And to the left, the building housing Midwest IR.[172]

Years ago, while at the HMO, I'd run over here for a sandwich and a hot tea before they closed because I knew I'd be working through dinner. Later in my career, my assistants would dash over to fetch my coffee. Yet today, it may be *me* who comes here on the coffee run. I sit and wonder how, no matter what my professional standing, I keep winding up at the same damn Starbucks.

. . . .

Weblog Entry 6/26/03

THE PROBLEM WITH HEATHER

I'm presently temping in the Customer Relationship Management department of a very nice multinational corporation.

I know the company is nice because they've apologized profusely about the major yawn of a task they have me doing. I'm cleaning up their customer database. My job is to go through approximately one zillion emails that have stacked up since they fired their last temp for sleeping

---

[172]Where I used to be a vice president, if I hadn't already mentioned it.

at her desk—when she wasn't busy surfing online dating sites—and make appropriate changes to their records.[173]

About 90% of what I deal with is bounced emails. If an email bounces, I go into the database and unsubscribe that customer. The bulk of my job is OPEN, COPY, DELETE, PASTE, QUERY, DESELECT, CLOSE, and then repeat approximately three times per minute.[174]

I live for the opportunity to read the 10% of the emails that are actual customer responses. Most of these are requests to be removed from the mailing list, and this is where the fun starts! People compose angry and profane notes to get off a mailing list that they signed up for voluntarily. One of my favorites was from a woman who sent a multi-paragraph missive about the nerve of the company sending her email to her work address when she was a busy professional that didn't have time for our foolishness and she could not understand why she had to make the effort to respond to us about something that blah, blah, blah. It must have taken her at least fifteen minutes to write this note on her company's time. Quelle dumb-ass.

The angry letters are fun, but best email I've seen so far was from a girl named Heather. Apparently Heather is looking for an internship with this company, so she made the very wise move to send an email to a generic customer service address and not, oh, say, Human Resources or perhaps a specific person.

I read her cover letter and I was appalled. Not only was it written in three different colors (fuchsia, turquoise, and black), it was also done in

---

[173]I'm thinking I should do well here.

[174]So I'm not a VP anymore and the money isn't huge. However, it will allow me to buy groceries and Fletch's antidepressants, so I'm pretty damn thankful.

three separate type-fonts, making it obvious that she had cut and pasted the "best parts" from other sources.

Oh, Heather, *bad form.*

And you know those formatted letters in Microsoft Word where you fill in your own information? You highlight the area that says "street" and you fill in your own street information? Well, apparently Heather doesn't, so her cover letter says that she lives on Street, City, State ZIP. (I should mention here that one of her selling points was that she was (sic) "detail orientated.")

Heather must be a busy girl because she sent this heinous cover letter/resume out in a blanket email. I know this because I could see all the other recipients in the "To" line. More than 20 organizations' email addresses were listed. Oy.

But no one knows more than me how tough it is to get a job now, so I felt empathetic. I figured that she was a high school girl with big ambitions but not much training on job-finding protocol and I honestly wanted to help her.

I opened her resume attachment to find her contact information with the intention of sending her a friendly and informative "here's how your communication can be more effective" letter.

I glanced at her address and saw that she lived on a street in one of Chicago's richest suburbs where the home prices start in the seven-figure range. This surprised me because even the public schools up there are of higher quality than most of this country's private institutions. Although she should have known better, I gave her the benefit of the doubt and decided that I would still be a Good Samaritan and help her in her quest.

And then I saw it.

Holy shit.

Heather is not in high school. Heather is in *college*. And not only does she have a BA in English from the University of Illinois, but she's also only a year away from having her MASTER'S degree in Education.

And she was sending out misspelled resumes in the laziest format possible.

From her parents' North Shore mansion.

While I slaved away for less than a hundred bucks a day in a grunt job in order to buy food and medication.

DELETE

· 11 ·

Evict _This_, Motherf*cker

Weblog Entry 7/1/03

AMBER ALERT

Missing: One sidewalk, approximately 30' in length and 3' in width. Color is industrial light gray. Last seen leaving Westside neighborhood with members of the Russian Army. May also be in the company of two light gray cement stairs.

Reward if found.

*I*f you get this job we're totally sending Mike a fruit basket."

Fletch is back from a second interview out in the suburbs, arranged by one of his old colleagues. "Overall, I feel good about it. I like the way the manager leads his team, plus the job's less technical than what I had before, so I'd have an advantage over the other sales engineers."

"What about getting out there?"

"The commuter train practically stops in front of their building, so it was no problem."

"And taking the bus to the station was fine?"

"Smooth sailing through calm seas."

What a relief! I was worried he'd somehow miss his connections and wouldn't get to his interview, and then he'd be all bummed out again. Although the meds and therapy are working wonders, I'm still cautious about potential setbacks, and I'm doing everything in my power to prevent them, like not keeping any liquor in the house (even though Fletch's doctor says the drinking is a symptom, and not the main problem). I'm dealing with all the bills and bill collectors, so he doesn't have to worry about them. I've even started cooking dinner. Each night we have a meat, a vegetable, and a starch lovingly prepared by my own hands.[175] And instead of spending the money I got from selling my coats on fresh highlights, I bought Fletch a couple of new dress shirts and ties to wear to his interviews, despite the fact that my hair is *really* scary at this point.

"I have a good idea. Since it's so beautiful out, let's take the guys for a walk and dissect your interview."

"Let me get out of this suit and change into play clothes."

While I wait, I watch the Russian Army. They've been working next door for months, yet they just got a Porta Pottie. I shudder to think of where they were going before. They've also procured a radio, and earlier today I heard a bunch of Slavic accents singing along to the Strokes. It was rather cute and made me hate them a bit less.

Fletch bounds down the stairs with the dogs. "Ready, Freddie."

---

[175] I try to keep the swearing to a minimum while I'm in the kitchen.

"Let's locomote."

"Wait. Grab the other set of keys because I want to go out the side door." We generally use our back door because we only have to work one set of locks. "The Army's got a huge pile of debris out there, and I don't want to have to maneuver the guys over it. The last thing we need is a trip to the emergency vet."[176]

I lock the first door while Fletch and the dogs bound off ahead of me. At the foot of the stairs, he stops to check our mail while I unlock the main door. I'm dying to know more about the interview because it's the first solid lead Fletch has had in months. I'm afraid to get my hopes up, yet this one feels so promising.

"If they offered you a job, when would they want you to— AHHH!" Air whooshes past me as I free-fall for what feels like ten minutes before hitting the ground with a resounding thud. The impact throws up a huge cloud of dust and rattles every bone in my body.

"Jen! Are you OK?" Fletch asks, coughing and wiping grit out of his eyes.

From my spot in the dirt, I look up at Fletch standing in the doorway as I try to figure out exactly what just happened. "What— why—how did I get down here?" I look in incomprehension at my skinned palms and filthy knees. "What happened to the stairs? Where's the walkway?"

"They're gone. I guess that's what's in the pile out back."

"But . . . why?"

"I don't know."

"Shouldn't someone have warned us?"

"You'd think so."

---

[176]Given Maisy's penchant for chewing, we go to the doggie ER a LOT. The vet techs have taken to greeting us with "What'd she eat today?"

I run tentative hands over myself, assessing the damage. "Fletch, do you see little cartoon stars and birds flying around my head, too?"

He bends down to look in my eyes and places a hand on my forehead. "Are you sure you're OK?"

"I'm kind of scraped and I got the wind knocked out of me, but I should be fine."

"Good. You scared me." The dogs want to comfort me but they're not willing to jump off the ledge to do so.[177]

Fletch leans down and gives me his hand. I right myself and brush all the dirt off my clothes. "That was like base jumping, except without a parachute."

"Yeah, one second you were right ahead of me, and the next you'd completely disappeared. Boom. Gone. Tiiiiimbeeeeeer!" I notice a twitch at the side of Fletch's mouth. Then he has a quick chest spasm. His eyes sparkle wetly and he coughs into his hand. How adorable is that? He's so concerned about my well-being that he's *crying*. He's more sensitive than I ever imagined. Bless him, he's trying to hide his tears.

I hug him as he silently quakes in my arms. "Honey, it's all right to feel your feelings. Let it out. I'm just a little dirty and dazed, no worse for the wear. It was only a couple of feet—I couldn't have been hurt very badly." I hear him suppress a snort. "Really, I'm OK. I won't be leaving you anytime soon."

This man is a *saint*.

He gasps and shakes harder. "Fletch, I'm perfectly *fine*. You don't have to be so—Wait a minute. ARE YOU LAUGHING AT ME?"

---

[177]Man's best friend, my *ass*.

My temp assignment is bumping along. The job is unbelievably boring, but I have no right to complain about doing data entry when others are busy fighting a WAR right now. I recently got an e-mail from an Army officer who bought a DVD from me. He and his troops are stationed in Iraq, and they're buying up movies and books like crazy because between brief episodes of terror, there are LONG stretches of boredom. The officer told me everyone wants comedies because they all need to laugh right now. When I shipped his DVD, I also included a bunch of other funny movies and books. I figure they deserve this stuff, considering they'd probably give their eyeteeth to work a lousy temp job rather than being shot at.

I'm trying hard to make a good impression here because I'd like to land a permanent job with the company. I'm working really diligently and am not ashamed to brownnose the manager. He now loves me, although I can't say the same for others in the department.

I'm in a bathroom stall when I hear two coworkers enter.

"Her tan is ridiculous. Melanoma is never pretty. And what's up with her hair? Ten inches of blond and two of black? It's so natural . . . NOT!" says the one named Stephie. Yesterday I heard her and her cohort Angie prattling on about their upcoming trip to Cancún for HOURS. Stephie gloated about being such a great negotiator because she finagled a discounted rate for their September stay. Yeah, like it's real tough to get a lower rate during hurricane season. I had to put on my headphones and crank up Henry Rollins to drown out their incessant self-congratulations.

Angie adds, "Did you see her bag? Nice Prada knockoff, sweetheart. Did the street vendor promise you it was real?"

The people at this company have been decent to me except for these two. Stephie and Angie resent me because we're all working on the same project and I'm showing them up. Of course, *I* don't spend half the day scheduling bikini waxes and shopping for swimsuits on-line, so I have a natural advantage.

I flush and exit my stall, positioning myself between them to wash my hands. I smile at each of their pale reflections in the mirror while I slowly line my lips and blot my nose. In the old days I'd have gone all Columbine on these girls. Now I'm finding it's kind of fun to take the high road.

I say, "Enjoy your vacation, ladies," as I exit the lavatory in the wake of their stammered apologies. Because, really? The idea of them cowering in their hotel's storm cellar during Hurricane What-ever is satisfaction enough.

However, when I get home, I *am* burning this bag.

· ·

Weblog Entry 7/6/03

'TIL IT HURTS

I just received a lovely thank you letter from the Army Warrant Officer listed on my home page. I want to share an excerpt from his note in hopes that it will sway you to send the brave men and women in Iraq a nice treat.

Thank you for your generous care package. The books and DVDs will keep the troops entertained for weeks. It's really hard on the soldiers here; no showers, no flush toilets, or hot food. These are great Americans, these Army kids. I'm proud to be with them.

We are in Balad, Iraq, about one hour north of Baghdad and have been in the country three months. We travel all over Iraq, visiting

Army medical units and repair medical equipment. It is getting very dangerous now. Hope I get my troops home safely.

Come on, don't you have a nice book or DVD that you'd like to donate, knowing the pleasure it would give these folks, especially when they're enduring these hardships in the name of the United States?[178]

. . . .

My temp assignment has ended, so I'm back to tanning compulsively, freaking out about money, and spying on the neighbors. The Russian Army is almost done with construction on the McMansion next door. Since they apologized profusely and replaced the sidewalk,[179] we've had no additional incidents.

I've not felt quite as much animosity toward them since I had a nice chat with the developer. He came to this country ten years ago with something like thirty-five cents in his pocket, and now he's building and selling million-dollar properties. He says he wants to write a book someday and tell his story because it will be an inspiration to the people back in his home country.[180] Despite my best efforts, I rather like this guy and am going to have to find a new outlet for all my residual bitterness.

The developer told me that people already bought the place for something like $875,000. He says they're in their twenties and it's just the two of them. That blows my mind. How can two KIDS buy a house worth almost a million dollars in this economy?

---

[178]No, I don't know what's gotten into me lately, either.

[179]Although they also erected a big fence approximately a foot over our property line. Now going out the side door is like shooting out the birth canal.

[180]Which is POLAND, not Russia, and likely why the Russian curses my friend Roadie taught me didn't produce the desired effect.

Now that I think about it, I imagine these two will fill my bitter bill nicely.

To: jen@jenlancaster.com
From: Kelly from Canada
Date: July 12, 2003
Subject: Unemployed and bored

Hey Jen;

I'm sitting in front of the Internet at home. I'm unemployed, bored and just spent my remaining credit on a TJ Max tube dress. I was wondering if you have any advice on how to keep active, fit and fun while at the same time juggling VISA, VISA and VISA bills. My brown hair is growing in over the blonde and I'm going nuts.

Help!

Kelly

To: Kelly from Canada
From: jen@jenlancaster.com
Date: July 12, 2003
Subject: RE: Unemployed and bored

Hi, Kelly,

Thanks for writing! The good news is that if you are still more worried about getting fat than getting evicted, you aren't yet at the hopeless stage. (The bad news is that it's coming.)

Kudos on getting the dress . . . utility bills can wait up to three months before they are shut off (don't ask how I acquired this knowledge) but there's NO WAY that dress would still be there the next day. Generate your own electricity by wearing the dress for an evening out! Work it and maybe you can even score free drinks or, better yet, a rich boyfriend that can pay for stuff. (Did that sound sexist? If so, I apologize. But surely women deserve some compensation for having to wear underwire bras.)

The highlights are a big deal. You must do what you can to get them fixed. I understand that some of the drug store boxed colors are pretty good. I think they go on best when a friend helps you. I was going to try this route, and then remembered some of the paint jobs my friends had done in their apartments. No, thanks. (I still love you guys, but seriously, this is my hair we're talking about.) Anyway, I think you're best off calling the better salons in your area to find out if they have workshops/seminars where you can have a good colorist attack your head for $15 in the name of learning.

As for VISA, I say screw 'em. If you have no job, they can't call you at work to harass you for not paying. In my opinion, the only reason to pay them is to keep this from happening. So if you can avoid them now, I don't see a problem! Of course, if you aren't free-spirited enough to want to savage your credit rating, pay the minimums, but only after you've made sure you've taken care of your basic needs: food, shelter, and style.

Ac-tive? Fit? I'm sorry but I am unfamiliar with these terms.

I have the perfect solution to cure your boredom! My Rx is free, fun, and four-worded . . .

. . . *The Price Is Right.*

Best,

Jen

....

"Guess what!" I exclaim, rushing in from the deck.

Fletch raises a beleaguered eyebrow at me.[181] "Is this going to take a while? If so, can it wait? I want to get this"—he holds up his application and consent for background check— "faxed back to HR by four-thirty." We are cautiously optimistic that Fletch will be getting this job. The hiring manager told Fletch they were going to make him an offer pending management approval, but it's been almost two weeks and, really? We've been down this road before.

He gets his last unemployment check this week and then we're officially screwed. If he doesn't land this job, we'll have to sublet our apartment and move in with my parents. My mother, who has zero faith in us, keeps telling me she's cleared out the drawers in the guest room. She's also saved the local paper's want ads because she feels it would be much easier to find a good job in a chiefly agricultural and industrial economy in a county of thirty-five thousand, rather than a metropolitan area of almost ten million. No delusions there.

"It can wait." I go back outside and hear voices coming from the deck below. I squint through the slats and spy the hippies downstairs having a barbecue. On their grill, I see corn, zucchini, eggplant, and what appears to be tofu. I'm completely flummoxed as I thought that all the pot they smoke would be giving them the kind of munchies only animal fat could satiate.[182]

A few minutes later, Fletch joins me. "What's up?"

---

[181]He hates my "guess what's" almost as much as my "we have to talk's."
[182]Once we were sitting at the counter at the Salt & Pepper Diner when a bunch of vegans walked in. They all ordered veggie burgers, and we watched the short order cook grill them in a big puddle of bacon grease. We died laughing when we heard them all exclaiming about how delicious the burgers were.

"I just saw the new people next door. The guy is approximately fourteen years old and looks just like Opie Taylor from Mayberry. I wonder if he's Ron Howard's kid? Anyway, at first I thought he was there to cut the lawn until I saw him yelling at the contractor."

"They've got to be behind schedule. I've only seen one guy working on the place for the past few weeks."

"His wife was with him, too. She appears to be a twelve-year-old Chinese gymnast."

"They look young. . . . This is breaking news how, exactly?"

"Because I can legitimately hate them now!"

"Why is that?"

"Even though they have their own two-car garage and driveway, they parked their Land Rover in OUR parking spot!"

"What's the big deal? We have no car—it's not like we need to use it right now."

"I don't care. It's the principle of the thing! They have a million-dollar home *and* a garage, yet they had to hog up *our* space. It's not right! What are we going to do about it?"

Fletch considers this heinous wrong. He looks from the new house to our parking space. I just know he's crafting the perfect plan to punish the neighbors for their avarice. What is he thinking? Lining the space with giant nails? Or broken glass? Surrounding their vehicle with breadcrumbs to encourage the cannibal birds to gather and, thus, pepper their shiny SUV with bird bombs?

"Perhaps we could use some of those leftover two-by-fours over there . . ." He points to the ever-growing pile of debris. See? I know we're totally on the same page about this. ". . . and erect you the cross you so richly deserve."

To: jen@jenlancaster.com
From: An Aussie Fan
Date: July 15, 2003
Subject: Can you help?

Dear Jen,

I work in a site office which is an obviously
male dominated workplace. I'm a 20 year old
blonde girl surrounded by mostly over 35
labourers, operators, and middle management who
seem to think they're funny. I'm subjected
daily to bad jokes about boring subjects that
have been recycled so much I can tell what
they're going to say before they say it. I will
often get the same "witty" comment from the same
person day in day out.

What do you think is the best course of action?
I usually smile politely and move the subject
along hoping the employee will get the point but
I'm obviously being too subtle for these
brutes. Any advice?

Asking in Australia

To: An Aussie Fan
From: jen@jenlancaster.com
Date: July 22, 2003
Subject: RE: Can you help?

Dear Asking Aussie,

I'm sorry it's taken a while to get back to you on your question but I had to consult an expert first. Sadly, although I think I am damn cute (as does my mother) I've never been the kind of looker to attract unwanted attention. To solve this dilemma, I had to query my pal, The Lovely Melissa.

Of course, I'm friends with Melissa because she's as mean as I am. She had me over for drinks this weekend, and after we discussed which ex-coworkers we'd like to hit with a sock full of quarters, I asked about your issue. Her advice was simple. You must insult them when they begin to annoy you. But the key here is that it must be a subtle insult, as it can't sting until they walk away from your desk, lest you get into an ugly confrontation. Your insult must be delivered with a big smile, so they are never quiiiiiite sure whether or not you're serious. For example, for the guy that thinks he's witty—let's call him Steve, for the sake of simplicity—you could say, "Gosh Steve, do you

know any funny jokes? Or is this the best you
can do?" Insert grin here, and you're off.

Although I encourage you to be pleasant at the
initial hello (no one wants to be known as the
office bitch), you should begin to deliver the in-
sults the second you'd like the fellas to move
along. Zing them often enough, and you'll be
greeted, but then left the fuck alone so that
you can work in peace.

And that's all you really want, right?

Best,

Jen

Woo-hoo, I got another temp job! It's only a short-term assignment, but I'll earn enough for a whole week of groceries. I'll be spending the next three days working as a receptionist. Everyone in the company will be gone on some corporate retreat, so I'm picturing myself running through the deserted halls in my jammies, à la Macaulay Culkin.

They told me to expect to be bored and to make sure I had something to occupy my time. They suggested I bring a book and said it was fine to use the Internet, although they did request I refrain from surfing porn sites.

I'm not sure if it was the twinset or loafers that led them to believe they needed to add that caveat.

Weblog Entry 7/22/03

HOME ALONE

I'm here at my temp job literally watching paint dry. A workman from the building came by earlier and said he was here to re-do the ceiling. In my most professional voice I said, "Um, OK?" at which point he hauled in all these brushes and buckets and ladders.

Wonder if I was allowed to authorize a paint crew?

As far as temp assignments go, this is kind of a dream. The phone barely rings enough for me to screw it up, although I've managed. I had to come in for training yesterday since I'd never used their phone system before. Out of the ten calls I answered, I messed up all but one, leading me to believe it's a good thing I didn't get the receptionist job at the architecture firm. Frankly, it's not quite as easy as I anticipated. Don't know why I thought it would come so naturally—back in the day, my sorority had to take me off of phone duty because I kept hanging up on everyone's boyfriend.

It's fun to tool around the web on the job.[183] However, I'm having trouble dealing with this freedom. I feel like a naughty child each time I get "caught" playing JT's Blocks when the delivery guys pass my desk. My first impulse is to hide my game, but again, I'm ALLOWED to do this, so I'm just being ridiculous.

---

[183]Getting a contact buzz on paint fumes is an added bonus.

Half the calls I've gotten today have been wrong numbers and my patience with them is running thin. They keep trying to dial a company a digit off from this one. I guess it's not as bad as when my brother's phone number was one away from the local Domino's. He finally had to change his number in order to get some sleep.

Actually, I pity *anyone* who gets Todd on the phone. This man considers unwanted phone calls a full-contact sport. When he moved to his new house he got a telephone number that hadn't been out of service long enough. Calls came in constantly from creditors, as the person with the number before had been a deadbeat. He got tired of trying to convince harassing callers that he wasn't "covering for" Donna Miller.

One day he received a call from her university's alumni association for the purpose of updating their yearly newsletter. My brother said he was Donna's husband and would be GLAD to provide answers. Among other outrageous fabrications, my brother told them that after Donna served a term in prison, she wrote the bestseller *Fear and Loathing in Lesbian Loveland.*

As the caller was a $5/hour phone-monkey, he had no clue that Todd was bullshitting him and he updated the directory accordingly.

You see, a $10/hour phone-monkey like me would have known better.

. . . .

"How was your day?" Fletch and the dogs are stationed on our deck, basking in the late-afternoon sun.

"Eh, it was all right," I reply.[184]

"What happened?"

"You know how nervous I am to temp in the Sears Tower, right? And how I'm always on edge because I think it's the next big terrorist target?"[185]

"Yeah, you've mentioned it a couple of thousand times."

"Well, I was relatively calm until this morning when I opened the coat closet to put my umbrella away and—"

"What you're really saying is that you were snooping."

Was he watching me on closed-circuit TV or something? "Yes, fine, I was having a look around. That's no crime. Anyway, I ran across all these little nylon packs. I opened one up and saw that they were filled with disaster-relief supplies like flashlights and masks and bottles of water. Do you know what this discovery means? It means that for once my paranoia isn't unfounded and that scared the pants off of me."

"What'd you do?"

"I spent the rest of the afternoon fighting a panic attack. Every time the phone rang, I practically soiled myself."

"That sucks."

"No kidding. By tomorrow, I'm going to need a defibrillator to revive myself after my four hundred thirty-first heart attack. Or possibly some dry pants."

· ·

[184]My day was nothing a fistful of Xanax couldn't cure, but I ran out of them ages ago, so I had an ice-cream bar instead. OK, two ice-cream bars. And some cookies. And a bag of Skittles.

[185]I have no proof of this, but I probably don't need to remind you that it is, in fact, generally all about me.

Weblog Entry 7/31/03

I SPY
. . . .

While trying to take my mind off the fact that rent is due tomorrow and we have NO POSSIBLE WAY TO PAY IT, I got an email asking for more neighbor gossip. I'm thrilled to oblige and temporarily escape worrying about more pressing matters.

A couple of days ago I heard the awful people downstairs *doing it* at 5:30 in the afternoon.[186] OK, when I'm in the middle of a finance-induced panic attack, the LAST thing I need is to hear a couple of dirty hippies going at it like guinea pigs. So you can't really blame me for shouting, "Maybe if you ate some meat you'd last longer!" when they'd finished, right?

Anyway, today I was rewarded with a beautiful clear blue sky and I spent the afternoon outdoors. I was on my lounge chair facing the alley when I observed the 12-year-old Chinese gymnast/millionaire pull up to the new house next door.[187] Her car was packed to the gills with possessions and it looked like she was ready to move stuff into her new mansion. But guess what . . . it still wasn't ready! I know this because her tiny lungs were surprisingly powerful and I heard her shouting at the contractor. The girl was FURIOUS.

Anyway, she sped off with the words "breach of contract," "attorney," and "tomorrow or else" hanging in the air. At this point, I

[186] At least in Bucktown our amorous neighbors had the decency to wait until sundown and turned on some music.

[187] I wonder if she was sitting on phone books to see over the dashboard. My guess is yes.

closed my book and stopped pretending to read, because real live drama trumps literature any day. I watched the contractor freak out while barking commands into his cell phone. In less than five minutes, a dozen of his relatives showed up at back door armed with cleaning supplies.

First off, I saw a handful of little kids with the gorgeous Slavic complexions and naturally highlighted hair for which I would kill. Next I saw an old Polish hippie trudge past with his trademark tie-dyed shirt, Birkenstocks, and salt-and-pepper ponytail.[188] He was joined by the guy we call Uncle One Shirt, due to his penchant for wearing the same top each day. I've seen him in a half-dozen different outfits, but for some reason he chooses to vary them by week and not on a daily basis. He's the only one I've seen doing any work on the house lately, and that's consisted of pushing an empty wheelbarrow back and forth across the alley. Very strange.

A few other relatives filed past, with Grandma bringing up the rear. She's in her 70's and generally sports a babushka which is why I almost busted a gut when I spied her wearing a t-shirt featuring Robert Smith of The Cure. I wondered if Grandma wasn't actually some very hip indie rocker, so I kept murmuring lines from "Boys Don't Cry" and "Head on the Door" and "Just Like Heaven" at her while she worked in the backyard. I'd hoped for a flash of recognition, and perhaps a thumbs-up, but since she ignored me, I'm pretty sure she didn't understand a damn word I said.

I spent the rest of the afternoon sipping a grape soda and covertly observing the action from my table with the umbrella bent down for

[188]He's there all the time. We call him Wavski Gravski.

maximum spy-ability. At one point, Cousin Simpleton thought it would be funny to hose the group down Gestapo-style with the power-washer and I had to go inside the house so they wouldn't hear me laughing. Ditto when I saw Grandma scrubbing the rough-hewn pine fence with Murphy's Oil Soap. Seriously, though, I thought it was pretty cool to watch the family pull together to get the job done. They kind of rock.

Although they annoyed the bejesus out of me, I'm a bit sad to see this particular chapter come to a close. However, my adventures in spying aren't over. A Mexican construction team just started working on a project one house over and those bastards stole one of our garbage cans from the parking lot . . .

. . . game on.

"Sorry, Jen. I'm not trying to be unsympathetic; I'm simply telling you the truth. The well is dry. I've done all I can. I can't spare anything else," my mother says.

"Are you absolutely sure? We'd be able to pay you back really soon. We're still waiting for Fletch's background check to clear, and as soon as it does, the company will give him a start date. It's going to happen any day now." I am begging—unsuccessfully—for a loan from my mother to cover our rent. Although we've been told that Fletch has the job, everyone is dubious, particularly my mother.

"As is, half my check each week goes to pay for your wedding, and I've already lent you everything in my savings account. I wish I could do more, but I can't. I suggest you start packing. You're welcome to live here until you get back on your feet. The guest room is all ready for you."

"What about Dad? Would he consider a short-term loan? With interest? Can you ask him? Please?" She sets down the phone and I hear a muffled conversation, punctuated by laughter. That can't be good.

"I guess you heard. If not, he gave a definitive no."

"I appreciate your trying. Thanks, and I'll keep you posted."

Asking my parents for a loan was my last hope. At this point, I've officially tried EVERYTHING to raise the money for rent. No one would buy my eggs at the donor place because I'm too old, despite the fact I told them it was a fire sale and they could have them ALL for five thousand dollars.

I even attempted to sell my engagement ring, but since I don't have a receipt for the diamond, no one will pay me its full value. I'm so frustrated because I know we only need about one thousand dollars to make it, but I've exhausted all my resources. The only other ways I could raise the cash are A) illegal, B) dangerous, and C) incredibly icky, and therefore are D) out of the question.

It's not that living in my parents' house again would be so bad, although I would miss my friends here in Chicago. But I feel like if we move home to Indiana, there's no chance we'll ever be able to get back to where we used to be. I don't mean materially; if we were given the chance again, I think we'd live our lives very differently. Our values have changed completely and our wants are now vastly different. I could care less about Dior's newest line of lip gloss. What I want is for my husband not to get those furrows in his brow every time the phone rings. I want to see him walk in the door, whistling after a pleasant day in the office. I want him to put his dirty travel coffee mug in the sink instead of the dishwasher, where he's supposed to leave it. I want to go to my parking space and get into my car—what kind it is doesn't matter anymore—and be able to drive somewhere. I want to get up in the morning and have a purpose, whether it's answering phones or writing the great American novel. We've learned

346 · *Jen Lancaster*

what is and isn't important, and all we need is one more chance to prove it.

I'm deep in thought when the phone rings again. Maybe it's my mom and she's had second thoughts about lending us the money! I knew she'd come around!

I swivel to look at the caller ID and the smile fades from my face.

It's our landlord's secretary.

Shit.

. . . .

```
To: jen@jenlancaster.com
From: Kelly from Canada
Date: August 5, 2003
Subject: More advice, please!


Dear Jen:


My boyfriend and are in our mid-twenties. We've
been living together for two years and he hasn't
proposed yet. We're happy, but still a bit
worried because I long for more of a commitment.
Was my mom right when she said, "Why buy the cow
when you can get the milk for free?"


Sincerely,


Kelly (aka Waiting for the Ring)
```

. . . .

To: Kelly from Canada
From: jen@jenlancaster.com
Date: August 5, 2003
Subject: RE: Advice, please!

Dear Waiting Kelly,

Ah, the old if-it-ain't-broke-should-I-still-try-to-fix-it question . . . I know it well. First off, I don't agree with your mom. The milk-for-free stuff was relevant to her generation, but no longer to ours, considering gratis milk abounds. One simply needs to go to a bar around closing time—it's a veritable dairy aisle out there.

I also don't agree with the experts who say you shouldn't live together first. Their theory is that this is less of a commitment, and couples that live together are more likely to break up. Um, yes, and I think that's a *good* thing. Better to have one skirmish over who gets the toaster upon move-out then to fight about the custody of your children every weekend for the next fourteen years.

As I'm a fan on interpreting Judeo-Christian ethics to my own benefit, I think it's a much bigger "sin" to marry and divorce on a whim than to just give it a trial run by cohabitating. (I made this determination while living with my own boyfriend for almost seven years, BTW.) More couples divorce over non-dramatic issues like money and communication, rather than affairs and abuse. Living together is an excellent proving ground where you can work this stuff out without worrying about having to return everyone's wedding presents if you can't.

I'm slightly concerned about your age and your need for more commitment. If you are presently worried about your boyfriend's level of involvement, then marriage isn't going to give you any guarantees. Conversely, please don't let the fact that he hasn't asked you yet cast aspersions on the depth of his feelings for you. Maybe he's waiting to be more established in his career, or perhaps he's not financially ready to make the commitment. Although it's not the answer you want to hear, my best advice is to give this more time.

Does this mean that I sat by patiently for seven years, waiting for my boyfriend to pop the question after proving that we were compatible? No. I badgered him relentlessly for the first few years. You see, I desperately wanted a big Michigan Avenue wedding with the Vera Wang dress and the Tiffany princess-cut rock and your

choice of prime rib or lobster tails. And I
wanted it all to happen before I was 30, as that
seemed like the old maid cut off date. When we
got married last year, we chose a simple ceremony
in Vegas.

Turns out that the big production stopped being
important to me; just being married was enough.
What's interesting is that after living together
for so long, nothing seems that different now,
except the addition of rings and a license to
harass single people.

Bottom line? It's far better to let the
commitment happen naturally than to force it
simply because someone else says you should. If
you're truly compatible, then when the time is
right, everything will fall into place.

Best,

Jen

LANDLORD'S FIVE DAYS' NOTICE

You are hereby notified that there is now due the undersigned Landlord the sum of One thousand six hundred
twenty-five dollars ($1625) being rent and late charges for
the premises situated in the Village of Chicago, County of
Cook, and State of Illinois, described as follows: 1513 West
Superior, 2R, Chicago, IL, 60622 together with all buildings, sheds, closets, out-buildings, garages and barns used in
connection with said premises.

And you are further notified that payment of said sum so
due has been and is hereby demanded of you, and that unless
payment thereof is made on or before the expiration of five
days after service of this notice, your lease for said premises
will be terminated. Keller, Macon, Goldberger, & Associates,
One IBM Plaza, Suite 46, Chicago, IL, 60611, are hereby authorized to receive said rent so due for the undersigned.

Only full payment of the rent demanded in this notice
will waive the Landlord's right to terminate possession of
said premises under this notice, unless the Landlord agrees
in writing to continue such possession in exchange for re-
ceiving partial payment.

. . . .

I'm on the bed hugging Maisy. I've been shaking ever since I found
the notice on the door when we went outside for our walk. I should be
packing right now, but I'm completely paralyzed. Yes, I'd like to live
elsewhere, but because I elected to do so, and not because I'm so
worthless that I can't even manage to keep a roof over our heads.

It's over.

We lost.

We're moving home.

••••••••••••••••••••••••••••••••

Fletch enters the bedroom and comes to sit beside me. "Jen?" He bends down to kiss my forehead. I ignore him. I know we're about to have the "what's next" conversation, and I just can't bear it. To avoid looking at him, I bury my face in the pillow I'm sharing with Maisy.[189] Maisy—the traitor—leaps on him and begins to lick his face. "Jen. You've been up here for hours. We need to talk. JEN. LOOK AT ME. This is important."

I sigh and my voice catches as I say, "I'll get started packing in a minute. If you want to work on the den, I'll do the bedroom."

"Why? We're not moving."

"Yes, we are. You saw the notice."

"I did. But we're not moving."

"I'd prefer to not go to court or get arrested for trespassing, thanks."

"Listen to me—*we're not moving*. When you went upstairs, I called the hiring manager and told him our situation. I said I needed an offer letter today. And . . ." Fletch pulls a sheet of fax paper from behind his back. I bolt upright, snatch it out of his hands, and begin to read. *We would like to cordially extend you an offer with a starting salary of . . .*

"Oh, Fletch, that's wonderful, but we still have the eviction issue and—"

"What issue? I explained to Bill's secretary that we were having a

---

[189]Even in my state, I can't help but notice that Maisy smells like Fritos. What's up with that?

cash-flow problem because I wasn't getting any consulting gigs. I told her that because of this, I got a traditional job so we'd never have an issue paying the rent again. I sent her a copy of my offer letter and arranged to pay rent and associated late fees when I get my first paycheck, so they rescinded the notice."

"We're going to be OK?"

"We are." We hug while Maisy tries to worm her way between us. I say a quick prayer of thanks and silently pledge never to allow us to get that close to the precipice again. "You know, I couldn't have gotten through all this without you."

"Really?"

"Yep, so now I want to do something for you. When I go to work on Monday, I want you to sit down at the computer and start writing."

"What do you mean?"

"You've talked about becoming a writer for the past six months. This is your chance. If you're really serious about this as your career, start writing and let's see where it goes."

"Really? But what about temping?"

"Don't worry about taking any assignments for the moment. Besides, I'll need your help getting out of here in the morning. If I'm going to be in the suburbs by eight a.m., I'll have to be up really early. I probably won't be home until seven o'clock every night, so the dogs will be depending on you, too."

This is it.

We got our "do-over."

I promise I'm going to be a different person—a better person—from now on.

"Thank you, honey." I smile contentedly with my head resting on his shoulder. "Hey, Fletch?"

"Yes?"

"When you get paid, do you think . . . would it be possible . . .

could I get some new shoes? Wait . . . wait . . . Fletch? I WAS KID-
DING!"

. . . .

Weblog Entry 8/11/03

AN OPEN LETTER TO EVERY COMPANY
THAT DIDN'T HIRE ME

If you hear the hoof beats of the Four Horsemen of the Apocalypse,
there's no need to worry. They're simply hanging around to herald the
fact that FLETCH STARTED HIS NEW JOB TODAY.

::cues the Halleluiah chorus::

The company that hired him took a couple of lifetimes to extend
him an offer, and then one more to wait for the offer to be official,
pending a background check. Don't know why I was nervous that
he wouldn't pass, as his resume was non-fiction and there aren't
a lot of skeletons in his closet.[190] Armed with a travel mug of
coffee, an anticipatory smile, and a kiss on the cheek, he was
off to the bus stop this morning, thus beginning a new chapter of
our lives.

And it's about damn time, as we have something like $5 left, most
of it in coins.

[190]I don't think he's Captain Honesty because of any great moral obligation.
Rather, his short-term memory stinks, so it's easier to just be truthful.

Now that I don't have to spend my days actively worrying about basic needs, I've decided to rearrange my career goals and focus on finding a way to get paid to write. But before I embark on my great writing career, I've got to get this out of my system.

Ahem.

Hey, all you companies that decided not to hire me in the past 685 days . . . remember me? No? Well, I'm the one who sent you all those resumes and clever cover letters. I'm the one who called your VPs of Sales relentlessly to alert them to my availability. It was me who went to every lame, horrific, and uncomfortable networking event just to try to meet some of you live. Those were my ads you saw in the *Chicago Tribune* and *Chicago Reader* just to show you I existed. (And if you recall, I was the gal who received nothing for my efforts except emails from perverts.)

To refresh your memory, I'm the lady who submitted to your pre-employment quizzes, allowed you to query my credit and education records, peed into your plastic cups, and was grilled by person after person at your company. Remember when you had me interview with six different people? And when you had me present a business plan that you eventually stole?

It was me who smiled through gritted teeth, nodded and said with my heart in my throat, "That sounds great!" when you told me about base salaries $40K less than I had just made doing the exact same job. And I'm the one who stood by the mailbox, cordless phone in hand, waiting for you to tell me something . . . anything. Seriously, you don't know that I'm the woman who moved to the 'hood, and sold her jewelry, her car, heck, most all of her stuff once her unemployment checks ran out so that I could pay rent while I kept trying to attract your attention?

You don't recall that I'm the one who cried and felt worthless and doubted my once highly sought-after abilities because I couldn't even get a receptionist job? It was me who spent 22 months having the same uncomfortable telephone conversation with my parents about my lack of progress. And you didn't know that between buying pantyhose and taking cabs, I spent a thousand dollars for the privilege of doing so, and yet have nothing to show for the effort?

Well, guess what . . . *I remember you.*

So, to all you companies that didn't hire me, I say, PISS OFF!

You had your chance to hire me, you bastards! So don't you come sniffing around here now. I wouldn't accept your lousy, thankless sales job on a double-dog dare! I'm taking every bit of competitive information I have to my grave! Ha! You will never benefit from my contacts or expertise or professionalism! Your copy machines and press releases and financial services are going to have to sell themselves because I refuse to ever do it for you again! I gave you every opportunity to bring me on board. You had your chance; you blew it.

You're on your own now, Corporate America . . .

. . . good fucking luck.

Fletch has been at his new job now for a couple of weeks. He gets up at five a.m. so that he can catch the bus by six in order to get the train at six twenty. I'm up with him, making breakfast, packing lunch, fixing coffee, and ironing shirts. I figure if he's going to be tired all day, I'll be tired with him. Plus, having the opportunity to pursue my dream of being a writer is a small price to pay.

Our first priority is getting another car, and we should be able to do so within the next couple of months, if we sock away all Fletch's commissions. As the downstairs neighbors have declared war on us since my little comment, I'd like to live elsewhere. However, it's not realistic right now. When we advertised for sub-leasers a couple of weeks ago, no one was interested, so unloading this place will probably be harder than I thought. Thankful as I am to have a Chicago roof over my head, I'm not going to stress about it.

I think maybe we've come out of this unscathed.

文

"Hello?" I reach the phone on the last ring before voice mail takes the call. I almost missed it because I was upstairs wrestling a towel into my overstuffed bag. Shayla and I are about to take advantage of the last nice day before school starts, so we're off to the beach.

My brother is on the line. "Jen, I've been trying to call you—where have you been?"

"Showering and taking the dogs out and stuff. I'm going somewhere, and I didn't want to get stuck having a boring conversation about Indiana basketball with you. Seriously, if I didn't care about high school sports when I was IN high school, why on earth would I care now?"

"Did you listen to any of my voice mails?"

"No, why would I? All you ever say is 'Pick up, pick up, pick up' because you refuse to accept it's VOICE MAIL and not an answering machine. Anyway, is this going to take long? I've got to get going."

"Dammit, Jennifer, stop talking. Our mother was in an accident this morning."

"*What?* What happened? I thought she was in Connecticut. Is she OK?"

"Auntie Virginia was driving Mom to the airport in Hartford, and they were hit by a truck. The car was totaled. Auntie Virginia is fine, but Mom's in the hospital with broken ribs and a punctured lung. They hit a guardrail on her side of the car. The doctor says she's going to be OK, but it was touch and go there for a little while."

So when I was busy watching *The Price Is Right* and playing fetch with Loki, my mother was bleeding on the side of a highway? I suddenly want to throw up.

"Oh, my God, how can I get a hold of her? How is she doing?"

"She's really shaken up and she's in a lot of pain. She's asking for you."

"What should I do?"

"Dad's going to drive to Connecticut, and he needs you to come with him. Because of the lung, she won't be able to fly for a while, so he's driving her back when she's released from the hospital. He expected you to be on the road already, so get moving."

But I can't get moving.

I never told my family about the repossession, so they don't know I have no way to get to Indiana. The last thing I want to do is burden them with this knowledge. Since Fletch hasn't been paid yet, I don't have enough money to take a train or fly, and my credit cards have been maxed out for months, so I can't rent a car.

My mom is scared and alone, and all she wants right now is me. But because of all the selfish, foolish mistakes I made in my past, I can't get to her.

This is just about the worst feeling in the world.

....

Weblog Entry 9/6/03

LEAVING THE DRIVING TO THEM

"Wait, Jen, I'm confused. How did you get to your parents' house? Did your dad pick you up?"

No.

"Did you fly?"

Nope.

"Did you take the train?"

Negative.

"Did you—heh, heh, heh, take the BUS?"

Yes. Yes, I did.

And no, I'm not kidding.

I was slightly terrified at the idea of riding Greyhound since I'd never done so before. But I also was a tiny bit exhilarated; it just seemed so *On The Road*, although having not actually read the whole thing, I wasn't sure if I would be more like Jack or Neal Cassady.

As I figured getting to see my mother would outweigh any risks, I booked my ticket. I caught a cab to the bus station and began to get nervous when the driver assumed that I was kidding about the whole Greyhound Station destination. When I assured him that I was serious, he apologized and said I just didn't look like a typical bus rider. I wasn't sure whether to be delighted or offended.

I entered the station and suddenly understood what my cab driver meant. I *didn't* look like any of these people. The people in the Greyhound terminal certainly didn't seem like the same people I'd bump into at O'Hare or Union Station. I'm so used to being around happy travelers . . . families excited to be on their way to Florida, young sales execs ready to fly out to Houston to "totally NAIL the Pennzoil account, boo-yah!" and amorous honeymoon couples about to jet to Hawaii for a week of never actually getting to see the beach.

But there's little joy of travel at the bus station. Everyone looked sad, weary, elaborately tattooed, and pointedly NOT excited to be there. Like on the verge of violently-not-excited-to-be-there. I imagine a lot of this had to do with the atmosphere. The bus station was not a cheery place, and it lacked the charm, warmth, and sanitation of, oh, say, a third world country's sewage treatment plant.

Actually, after having a good look around, I realized why the scene was vaguely familiar. It reminded me very much of HBO's prison show *Oz,* both in atmosphere and clientele. I broke out into a cold sweat when I noticed that some of the "inmates" were eyeing me. I wondered if I should immediately "take someone out" with a weapon I'd fashioned by whittling down a plastic spork. Then I figured they'd eventually realize I was no better than the rest of them since I was taking the bus, too, and would leave me alone. And even if I had been hassled, *nothing* was going to keep me from getting to my mother. So, I bought a cheeseburger, opened a book, and waited for my ride.

Now here's where I'd like to begin to detail *The Journey from Hell* . . .

. . . but I can't.

The bus was OK.

No, actually, it was very nice. It was clean, comfortable, and cool. No crying babies. No foul stinks. No erratic driving. As an added bonus, a Greyhound employee was deadheading to a different station, so he sat up by the driver and they quietly gossiped like sorority girls about stupid customers.

While the miles rolled away, I popped open my roasted almonds and closed my book. I noticed that I had an excellent vantage point; I never realized that from a bus you could see inside of every car! I amused myself for almost an hour by spying on other drivers. I was a bit disturbed to see how many people smoke pot while they're driving. I started to record their license plate numbers but then realized that I am not the Hall Monitor of the World. I had no idea what I'd actually do with the information. Maybe if I'd had a phone with me I could have called the police? But I'm thinking since these cars were going about 12 miles an hour on the expressway, there's a good likelihood of them being caught without my help. And if I called the police four hours later when I got to my house, they'd just think I was a kook.

Besides, Jack Kerouac would have *never* been a narc.

· 1 2 ·

Jennyslvania

```
To: jen@jenlancaster.com
From: Cal Canter
Date: September 12, 2003
Subject: Little Blaster


Jennifer — aka "Little Blaster,"[191]


Some time ago your brother told me
about your web site and being the
arrogant snob I am, (also very busy
and very impressed with myself), I
```

---

[191]My college nickname. My brother was Blaster. For almost a year, one of my best friends in the fraternity didn't know my real name.

never bothered to look it up. Hopelessly bored tonight, I found a scrap of paper with your web address on it (actually, didn't even remember that it was yours), so I dialed it up. Several quick observations, if I might—

1. Credit should be given to your character that being un-employed for almost 2 years has not made you bitter. Heh.

2. Perhaps you are setting your sites too high for a job in retail. There is always opportunity in fast food that can lead to management positions.

3. I didn't get a chance to read all of your web site (specifically the article about Peggy Noonan, and I might add that next to the bible on my nightstand is a copy of *Ronald Reagan, When Character Was King*), simply because I do work and could not possibly have to time to read the entire thing. (I will have my secretary read it tomorrow and summarize it in a memo for me.) Try to remember George Orwell's 6 rules to better writing—1. Never use a long word where a short word will do—2. If it is possible to leave a word out, leave a word out, etc. . . . . This might add a little brevity and make the reading go quicker.

4. Remember, if you go 5 years without meaningful employment, you live in Chicago, where panhandling is not only an option, it is an opportunity.

5. Your writing is both good and entertaining, however, Stephen King is the exception to the rule about financial success of writers (while they are living). If you become classified as a successful writer you will either starve to death or someone will turn up some dirt on you and you will go the way of Bob Greene, leaving the literary scene humiliated and divorced, faced with unavoidable litigation.

Jen, Al Gore invented the Internet. It is grossly overrated. If *Survivor* wasn't over, only one episode of *The Bachelor* left, *Joe Millionaire* all but forgotten, myself and the rest of the world would not be sitting at a computer tonight.

Volunteer at the Church, help the illiterate, do something.

Nice web site,

Calvin, a friend of your brother's.

```
P.S. I have recently started a management
company to manage my portfolio of commercial
real estate properties. We are looking for
several in-house maintenance people. Feel free
to forward your resume, or we can fax you an
application. GED or equivalent required.
```

"Are you going to dignify this with a response?" Fletch asks. We're in the den, and Fletch is standing over my shoulder, rereading Calvin's e-mail.

"Maybe. When I read this the first time, I thought it was funny. Nothing like a little ribbing between old friends, you know? But then I reread it, realized he was actually being mean, and got mad."

"Regardless of shared history, no one has the right to talk to you like that. If you reply, what are you going to say?"

"I'm thinking about it now. When I come up with a response, I'll run it past you." He heads out to walk the dogs.

I grab a Diet Dr Pepper and a tumbler of ice and settle in front of the computer to craft a snappy retort. As I try to string together the perfect response, I begin to reminisce.

Calvin was in the same fraternity as my brother. I haven't seen or talked to Cal since he was a groomsman in my brother's wedding almost ten years ago. Cal and Todd's other fraternity brothers behaved rather inappropriately during the ceremony. Fortunately, they were so drunk none of them made it to the reception.

Todd's wedding was important because it marked a turning point in my "relationship" with Calvin and the rest of that crew. You see, when I arrived at college, I was a naive young girl, and I was impressed by, well, almost everything. I desperately wanted to leave my bourgeois roots behind me.

When I met Calvin and the rest of his clique, I was blown away by how smart and witty and worldly they were.[192] They'd all grown up in wealthy towns like Newport and Greenwich and Alexandria. . . . Certainly no one had spent his teens in an Indiana farming community like me! And they'd all done things I'd previously only read about in *The Preppy Handbook* . . . attended prep schools, summered on various Capes, captained yachts. As for me, I spent summers straining leaves out of my parents' pool. Granted, there are worse fates than having an in-ground pool and needing to clean it, but I didn't know it at the time.

At that point in my life, I'd never met anyone who could slam a Little Kings beer AND quote Arthur Miller AND had a wardrobe full of Alexander Julian shirts. Naturally, I was enamored of Cal, as he represented everything that my seventeen-year-old mind considered "cool." But I didn't want to date him because at the time it didn't occur to me that I could even be worthy of his affection. (Ironic, because I was 125 pounds at the time and had done the local beauty pageant circuit in high school.) Instead, I foisted my adorable roommate, Joanna, on him and lived vicariously through their chaste flirting.

What I so desperately craved from him was his acceptance. He'd always been grudgingly nice to me out of respect for my brother and because he'd been raised well. Take these factors away, and I probably would not have even existed in his world. Yet I so wanted to be liked on my own merits. I tried everything within my power to gain his respect but didn't realize that the role I played was that of a doormat, thus ensuring we'd never be equals. For example, in return for being *allowed* to hang out in his room in the fraternity house, I

---

[192]Or at least appeared to be in my young mind.

would voluntarily run errands and do chores. *"Need a button sewn on your shirt? Let me handle it!" "Want cute freshman girls at your next party? I'll round them up for you!"*

My indentured servitude didn't last long. The more I made my own friends, the more I took back the power that I'd so freely given away. Don't get me wrong, I was still in awe of him. But I'd gained the tools to better mask it.[193] Anyway, Cal eventually graduated, and I didn't see him again until my brother's wedding, although I'd occasionally hear an update about his so-called fabulous life.

So, when Cal and the rest of his cohorts acted like drunken buffoons at Todd's wedding—IN THEIR THIRTIES—the scales fell from my eyes, and I questioned why on earth I'd ever worshipped him.

I mean, really, on what planet is a cute and eager-to-please seventeen-year-old girl considered a liability?

I believe the last words I spoke to Cal before I received his e-mail were "Calvin, would you please shut the fuck up so we can finish taking these pictures?"

The seventeen-year-old Jen would have been crushed if she'd received a condescending note from Cal the Magnificent, even if it was just meant to tease her.

But what about the thirty-five-year-old Jen? The one with the big butt? Who lives in the 'hood and has a pit bull and actually LIKES polo shirts from Target? Who doesn't have a job and is married to a regular guy from Indiana?

She just laughed and laughed.

---

[193] And shortly thereafter discovered the joys of overcompensation.

To: Cal Canter
From: jen@jenlancaster.com
Date: September 14, 2003
Subject: Re: Little Blaster

Hi Cal,

I saw your name as the return address and assumed that my brother was playing some sort of trick on me. But as I read, I realized that Todd doesn't have the skills needed to fake your level of arrogance and that this email was indeed the real thing.

Aren't I a lucky girl?

I remain aware of your existence as Todd still starts the occasional sentence with the phrase "Calvin says . . ." You'll be pleased—although probably not surprised—to know that this phrase precedes his lectures on things I'm doing wrong in my life, so I hear your name *a lot*.

Thank you for your sage guidance on my job search. Sadly, I can't get a fast food job because I'm not bilingual, necessary in my West Si-ee-de neighborhood. We also own a pit bull, so I DO meet all the qualifications to begin rollin' with the Latin Kings. However, I'm keeping my gang-joining options open for now as a gal needs to choose her homies carefully, you know.

I have to disagree with you on a couple of points on my potential writing career. As for financial gain, I currently make NO money, so any money earned would be considered a success. And I can't see that anyone could find dirt or embarrassing stories about me that I wouldn't first exploit myself, case in point, my *Big Lebowski* Night story on the web site. In it, I detail losing my shirt and vomiting on my neighbors.

Hey, doesn't it seem like just yesterday I was shouting at you to "shut the fuck up" at Todd's wedding?

By the way, have you completely morphed into Judge Smails from *Caddyshack* yet? You were well on your way the last time I saw you. Hope all is well at Bushwood.

Fecklessly yours,

Jen (Todd's sister)

I'm outside pouring water on the newly laid sod in front of my building. As I finish dumping my eighty-sixth bucketful on the fledgling lawn to make sure the roots take hold, I realize I'm being watched. I look up to see two shadowy figures, although I can't discern who they are because I'm temporarily blinded by the setting sun and the sweat pouring into my eyes. Then one of the figures barks, "HEY, JEN!" and I jump about four feet in the air, sending my bucket flying.

There's only one person I know who speaks with the kind of volume that makes people mentally construct storm shutters and tape up windows. "Joel! Fletch says you've been away for National Guard training. Did you just get back? And, Irene, how are you? What are you guys doing here? We haven't seen you guys for ages! Please come in!"

After hugs and a few more cheerful exclamations from all parties, I give them the tour. Fletch is equally delighted, and we gather on our deck. I'm so pleased to see them that I don't realize I'm clad in cutoff sweatpants and a ratty T-shirt until I notice the odd looks I'm getting from the child millionaires next door.

Before Joel arrived and I tossed my bucket, I caught a glimpse of the millionaires hosting their first dinner party alfresco. Their table was covered with an expensive spray of lilies so fragrant that I could smell them from our deck ten feet away. On their immaculately set Bloomingdale's for the Home outdoor dining suite, pricey red wine twinkled in their giant crystal goblets. Their purebred cocker spaniel sat patiently at their feet, confident in the knowledge that a delectable scrap of proscuitto had her name on it. And I'm pretty sure I noticed sorbet being served in frozen objets d'art between the pasta and grilled rainbow trout courses.

Their guests fit the scene perfectly, too. The women had glossy, swinging bobbed coiffures and Just the Right Amount of makeup, dressed like an Ann Taylor catalog brought to life, their small, tasteful gold-hoop earrings and blindingly large engagement rings flashed in the late-afternoon sun. The men were hale and hearty in their Brooks Brothers casual wear and Rockports. They tittered about their healthy portfolios while lame jazz lightly wafted through the air on the outdoor speakers. Small lanterns and little candles provided a warming glow while the sun set.

The scene is truly breathtaking.

Until we come outside to mess it all up.

Honestly, I try to keep Joel's voice a decibel or two below ear-splitting, but to no avail. Joel cannot be contained. That's why we went onto the deck in the first place. Had Joel been inside our house, the hippies downstairs would have blasted their *Sgt. Pepper* album over and over.[194] The evening continues and Joel's topics of conversation grow louder and more inappropriate.

"THE CALIBER OF STRIPPERS IN TIJUANA ARE . . ."

"YOU CAN FASHION ALMOST ANYTHING INTO A WEAPON. SPRAY STARCH CAN BE DEADLY WHEN YOU . . ."

"SINCE MOST FIREFIGHTS TAKE PLACE IN AN AREA OF LESS THAN FOUR HUNDRED YARDS, I FIND THE ASSAULT RIFLE . . ."

The glances from the other side of the fence are coming fast and furious now, and through narrowed eyes, they survey our soiree. *"Wait a minute. Do they have a PIT BULL? That spastic dog is gnawing on the big black wolf-looking mutt and they're both demanding sips of beer! And what IS that girl thinking, wearing sweaty gardening clothes and a ponytail to entertain? Are they drinking beer? That isn't IMPORTED? Oh, my God, they're drinking directly from the bottle! Don't those savages own any pilsner glasses, for Christ's*

---

[194]The dirty hippies have permanently ruined the Beatles for me. Thanks a lot, assholes.

sake? How come the fat one is sitting on the AC unit? Why don't they just BUY more chairs if they don't have proper seating? And what is the loud psychopath shouting about now? Gah! How much longer until THOSE PEOPLE leave this neighborhood and we can have some peace?"

I guess it's official now. *We're* the white trash neighbors.

Why am I oddly delighted by this fact?

··

```
To: jen@jenlancaster.com
From: NYHS Publisher
Date: September 16, 2003
Subject: Rat Pack


Jen,


I ran across the Do We Need a New Ratpack? rant
you posted on Craig's List and I went crazy for
it. Everyone here read it and they peed their
pants. With your permission, I'd like to reprint
it in the new magazine I'm starting. Please
contact me at the address or number below.


Thanks,


Loren
```

··

To: jen@jenlancaster.com
From: Kate, DeFiore Literary Agency
Date: September 18, 2003
Subject: Craig's List Postings

Hi, Jen,

I saw your *To Every Company* essay on Craig's
List and I followed the link to your website,
which I then perused for an hour or so. You have
a strong voice and a great way with words.

I think you have a story to tell, and, as a
literary agent, I may be able to help.

If you're interested, I've included my contact
information.

All the best,

Kate

....

"Hello?"

"Hi, this is Joe Thompson. May I speak with Jennifer Lancaster, please?"

Joe Thompson?

How do I know that name?

"This is Jen speaking."

"Jen, hey, how are you?"

"Fine, thanks. How are you?" And who *are* you?

"Doing well, thanks for asking. Listen, Jen, we haven't spoken in a while, but hung on to your résumé because I liked your moxie." Oh, my God—this is the guy from THE MOTHER SHIP! I called him once a month for an *entire year*. I only stopped phoning him when he told me that *he'd* call *me* when he had something. I assumed that was his polite way of telling me to piss off.

"Jen, I have the perfect position for you in our municipal bonds publishing division. I want to get you in here as soon as possible for a round of interviews." He lowers his voice in a conspiratorial tone. "I shouldn't be telling you this, but your reputation precedes you and you're my first choice. Provided your interviews go well and your references check out, this job is likely yours."

The Mother Ship is finally CALLING ME HOME!!

. . . .

"Yes, I'm really happy for you, but I thought you decided to try making a living as a writer," Fletch says. "Given the interest you've garnered lately, I'm surprised you'd even consider this. What do you know about municipal bonds?"

"Well, nothing, actually, but the job wouldn't be selling bonds— it would be selling a *publication* about bonds." Which would be cool . . . right?

"Let me rephrase the question: What do you know about selling bond publications? Wouldn't you have to deal with all the financial people you used to hate?"

"No, no, I hated the stupid PR girls. The financial people were OK."

"Really? Is that why you're always going out for drinks with

Ben? And exchanging pithy e-mails with the Joshes? And having your nails done with *Lawrence*?"

My skin crawls just a bit. "I kind of forgot about them."

"I'm all for you bringing home a paycheck, but if you have a job you hate, you won't be happy. You'll try to compensate by overindulging, and that's ultimately how we got in trouble in the first place."

I roll my eyes. "Do you think I've learned *nothing* in the past couple of years?"

"I'm just saying you should weigh your options."

"I will, I will. Oh, can you give me a lift that day?" Fletch is already doing so well at his new job that we were able to buy a car. Granted, it's a preowned Ford Taurus and our loan rate is one percentage point shy of usury, but it beats the hell out of the Ashland Avenue bus.

"What time?" Fletch pulls up his schedule on his PDA.

"Does twelve thirty work?"

"Can do."

"Cool. I'm going to go do some research on the municipal bond market now. Maybe it's more interesting than it sounds." I give Fletch a kiss and go to the den.

• •

There is NOTHING interesting about the municipal bond market.

• •

I'm clad in one of my old power suits and I look fantastic.[195] My shoes have been spit shined, courtesy of Fletch, and I'm still a lovely light brown from my summer bout with tanorexia.

---

[195]Thank God, our dry cleaner was able to let out the seams, or else I'd feel like a sausage.

"I'm going to grab the mail. I'll meet you outside by the car," Fletch calls up the stairs.

"OK, see you in a minute." I slick a coat of Bloom's Dolci gloss[196] across my lips and I'm ready to go.

I lock up and try to ignore the sad doggie faces watching me from the window. I can't even look at them. If I feel this guilty leaving them for a couple of hours, what's it going to be like when I have to go to work every day and they're all alone?

When I get to the car, I notice a package on my seat.

"What's this?" I ask.

"It came for you in the mail."

"Really?" I tear it open and a variety of presents spill into my lap. I examine all sorts of treats, such as pretty nail polishes, a mixed CD, and bags of my favorite candy. "This is lovely!" I dig through the box searching for a note.

Jen,

I wanted to send you a token of my appreciation. I know it seems weird to send you presents, especially seeing how we've never met, but your advice has been invaluable to me. It's because of your input that I didn't dump my boyfriend . . . or should I say my FIANCEE!

Although I wish you the best of luck with your interview, the selfish part of me hopes you'll decide to keep writing instead. Whatever you choose, thanks for inspiring me on a daily basis!

Kelly in Canada

---

[196]Which totally smells like Dreamsicles.

Fletch glances at my lap as he navigates the car out of the alley. "Who's it from?"

Lost in thought, I finally reply, "A fan."

. . . .

The interviews go tremendously well, and as a company, the Mother Ship is everything I ever dreamed it would be. They make me a generous offer and I *should* be turning cartwheels. And yet, I'm just not sure. They gave me until Monday to make a decision, which is good because I have no idea what to do right now.

On the one hand, this job is almost everything I've ever wanted in an employment situation. The benefits are great, there's a tremendous opportunity for growth, and the money is spectacular. On the other, what if I actually have the chance to start a career as a writer? The literary agency wants to me to sign with them. Although being under contract is no guarantee of success, it's definitely a leg up. My mother asked why I couldn't take the job *and* write, but that's not how I operate. I can only do one thing at a time, and with what I need to learn about the bond market, I can't see doing both.

Fletch has been no guidepost whatsoever. He keeps telling me to do what I think is best, and he'll support whatever decision I make. What kind of bullshit is that?

I'm all stressed out and the fact that I just started Atkins isn't helping. I bet I could make sense of everything if I could just think about it over a plate of jelly donuts. While I'm busy crafting a decision matrix on a spreadsheet, my phone rings. "Hello?"

"Jennifer, it's your brother! What's up, Peeg?"

"Todd, this is exactly why I almost never answer the phone when you call."

"Hey, I need you to come down here this weekend."

"Calling me Peeg is the best way to ensure I won't help you with whatever it is you need."

"Get over yourself, Peeg. We need you to babysit this weekend."

Todd has never asked me to watch his children before. For some reason, I'd been painted with the "irresponsible" brush after that time I accidentally gave the kids a book of matches.[197] "I'm your last resort, aren't I?"

"Pretty much. Jean's sisters are all busy and her parents will be out of town. Mom was going to sit this weekend, but the doctor says she can't lift anything and she isn't well enough yet to drive herself down here."[198]

"Why doesn't Dad drive her?"

"The play-offs are on and he doesn't want to go anywhere."

I made an exception to my children-hating rule for Todd's kids. They're actually kind of fun, plus if I spoil them rotten now, I can eventually use them against my brother.[199] Still, they are a handful and because they're human petri dishes, they always contaminate me. I generally spend the week after seeing them in bed surrounded by Kleenex, a vaporizer, and empty mugs sticky from hot lemonades. "Yeah, I don't think it's going to work. Sorry."

"Why not?"

"I don't like you enough to help you."

"It's not for me, it's for Jean. I've got to cover a game that night,

---

[197]I still say it was a mistake anyone could have made. They were in a pretty box from a Las Vegas hotel! What kid wouldn't like them?

[198]She is on the mend and can go twelve hours without her pain meds, thus proving that she's far tougher than I will ever be. Case in point, Fletch once had to confiscate the pills I got when I injured my back. Apparently when he heard me singing the "I-Like-O-Din Vicodin" song, he determined that my usage had become more recreational than medicinal.

[199]As soon as the youngest one turns ten, I'm teaching them all to smoke and swear.

but Jean's going away for a sorority reunion. If you don't come, she'll miss it."

Damm it, he had to go and throw the Jean card. She's the best thing that ever happened to our family. If we were the Munsters, she'd be our Marilyn. Never once has Jean pretended to shoot other Stone Mountain tourists with her golf umbrella while singing "The Sound of Music,"[200] described in loving detail the corned beef she once had in Dubuque, Iowa, in 1984, while having no recollection of her child's middle name,[201] or walked out of the house without remembering to put on pants.[202] Wearily, I consent. "OK, fine. When should I be there?"

"Tomorrow night around five. Thanks, Peeg."

"Bite me."

"One more thing: The kids are afraid of bees, wasps, and hornets. See you tomorrow."

Huh?

• •

You know what? Driving down to Todd's is actually a good idea. I'll have five hours each way to figure out what to do about the job. Plus I'll get to listen to all the cheesy music I like so much but am too embarrassed to play in front of other people.[203]

I stop for gas and snacks, and in a heroic moment of self-control, I decide against the Hostess cupcakes. The Atkins diet has been working, and I rather like not having my pants hurt anymore. I go low carb and opt for a Diet Dr Pepper and some sunflower seeds. I snicker to

---

[200]Mom.
[201]Dad.
[202]Todd.
[203]Vanilla Ice WAS groundbreaking—so there.

myself because I bet Fletch just felt a chill go down his spine. I've been banned from eating them in the car since the Sunflower Seed-Stravaganza (and subsequent Car Vacuuming-Stravaganza) in 1996. What can I say? I have lousy aim.

When I get to Todd's house, the children hurl themselves at me. Max, being the middle child, feels like a cannonball when he crashes into my stomach. With Cam, the eldest, it's more like being hit with a side of beef or perhaps a small freight train.

My brother stands in the doorway laden with photography equipment and a laptop case. "Bye, kids. I'm going now." He steps outside and then ducks his head back in. "Jen, I almost forgot. The kids have already had dinner, so they should be all set. Also, try not to let Max see you eating."

"Why not?" I'm puzzled by such an odd request.

"If he sees you eat any food he doesn't like, he'll throw up."

"Gross! But I'm hungry, so tell me what he does like."

"Chicken fingers, candy, and surprisingly, clams."

As soon as Todd leaves, Cam begins his eighteen-hour monolog about the benefits of owning Yu-Gi-Oh trading cards, and I have a strange premonition of him someday trying to sell me a time-share. Little Sarah reminds me that she is pretty.

I set the kids in front of the DVD player while I clean up their dinner dishes. I'm determined to have Todd and Jean return to a sparkling house because I want it to look like I can handle things (and to convince them they would NOT have been better letting the neighbor's rottweiler watch the kids). I start to Girl Scout up the joint, leaving it in even better condition than I'd found it.

· ·

"Hey, Jen, can I have a glass of water?"
"Me, too."

"No, I don't like that glass. Can I have another?"

"Why did you put ice in here? Ice makes my tongue ouchy."

"Can I have a Mountain Dew instead?"

"I pretty!"

"Where's my straw?"

"Max spilled his again."

"TELL CAM NOT TO TOUCH ME."

"I berry pretty!"

"Can we have some popcorn?"

"No, we like the kind with butter."

"This doesn't taste right. Can you put some sugar in it?"

"WHEN IS MOM COMING HOME?"

"I like 'nakes!"

"Jen, can I change my shirt?"

"Hey, the DVD is skipping!"

"Can we watch Like Mike *again?"*

"I have to use the potty."

"I have to use the potty, too."

"I make potty in my pants!"

． ．

Todd and Jean have an unusual home. It's built into a hill, and the architecture is such that there are five different levels of living areas. So the fifteen minutes it should have taken me to clean up took more like two hours, what with the constant trips up and down two flights of stairs.

After the first movie ends and all the kids' demands had been met, my old babysitting training kicks in. I can't allow anything to be messy. I decide to be helpful and clean the boys' bathroom. Although they are housebroken, Cam and Max need a bit of work on their aim. I liken it to a bunch of monkeys trying to operate a firehose.

The bathroom takes longer than expected, and since it's three levels away from where the children are, I can't hear the orgy of destruction. Cam, the brains of the operation, found a large bag of candy hidden in the kitchen. Being a generous soul, he shared his findings with his siblings, and they all stuffed themselves as fast as their little hands could hurl the empty wrappers. After accidentally stepping on a kernel, Max decided to have a popcorn-smashing party with Sarah on the new carpet, and what better way to inspect one's Yu-Gi-Oh cards than to stick them all to the walls with chewed pieces of gum?

When I walk in the room, it looks like a pipe bomb exploded in a 7-Eleven. I consider placing a call to the National Guard to help me with the devastation, but I figure they might squeal on me and my true ineptitude will be revealed. I cannot let that happen.

The kids help[204] me clean up the room, thus making themselves very dirty and sticky in the process. I decide to bathe them because I don't want Todd to come home to find his progeny looking like they live in a coal mine.

The kids, however, have other ideas.

They flatly refuse to bathe or shower despite how much I to beg, cajole, and as a last resort, attempt to bribe with a handful of singles from my wallet. And although someday they'll place me in a cheap nursing home because of it, I break out the big guns.

"Hey, Sarah and Max? Wasps like to sting dirty children. And, look, there's one now!"

Tell me those little bastards didn't fly into the tub.

Because I don't want to see myself on the news, I only wash them above their belly buttons. Whatever is dirty below the equator is their business, not mine. In some respects, washing their hair is easier than I thought. The lather-rinse-repeat stuff isn't so taxing,

---

[204] I use the term *help* very loosely.

but getting them to decide which shampoo they'd like certainly is.[205] Artfully arranging the floating toys so Max can "have his privacy" is no damn picnic either.

With a debate over what style of underwear and pajamas they will wear to bed that would put Paris and Nicky Hilton to shame, I finally wrestle a super-sugar-charged Paris and Nicky into some cotton sleepers while Cam showers. This is also a lot less easy than you'd think. Cam likes a variety of water temperatures and refuses to touch the taps himself. I careen up and down the stairs again for the next half hour.

Finally, everyone is in bed. I read them a story and it's lights out. Aww, how sweet is that? They look like little pink angels, all clean and shiny, nestled together.

As soon as the last one closes his eyes, I tiptoe down the stairs to call Fletch. "Hey, it's me."

"How's it going?"

"Pretty well. I'm surprised at how comfortable the kids are around me finally."

"That's because they see you a lot now. Back when you were working, you saw them, what, like once every six months? They finally know you since you're able to spend time with them."

"Yeah, I guess I didn't think about that." I'm suddenly overwhelmed with guilt over missing crucial bits of Cam's and Max's early years. "Anyway, I'd expected more of a struggle getting these guys into bed. But you know what? It was kind of easy. My brother must be exaggerating how difficult this parenting stuff is. Sure, it took some doing, but I managed nicely."

"Glad to hear it."

"Parts of the evening were trying, but it's such a great payoff to see the kids all happy and snug in their beds. Maybe . . . maybe you

---

[205]Whoever said, "Children need choices," deserves a swift kick in the ass.

and I should reconsider our decision to be child-free, especially now that we're not completely broke. After all, I got everything done! Seriously, I must be some kind of superwoman because I was able to keep the house orderly and the kids clean and it's only . . . only . . . Fletch, I'm not wearing my watch. What time is it?"

"Not sure. Let me put on my glasses." Fletch sets down the phone and I hear fumbling in the background. "Jen, do you realize it's one thirty-three in the morning?"

"Oh. Perhaps I'm not quite the domestic goddess I'd imagined."

"Maybe not. Would you mind if I went back to sleep now?"

"Um, no, I guess not. 'Night, Fletch. Love you."

"Love you back. Have a safe trip home."

I find myself driving out of town this morning with a wrecked manicure and dirty hair, sure of two things. One, I'm not taking the job. And two, I'm getting every organ even vaguely related to reproduction cauterized immediately.

. . . .

"What do you think this is? We've been all paid up for a while now. Do you think it's a complaint about the dogs?" I hold a certified letter from our landlord in my hand. Although it was delivered an hour ago, we were too preoccupied to open it. When the postman rang our doorbell to get us to sign for it, Maisy and Loki went crazy. To retaliate, the dirty hippies cranked the soundtrack to *The Great Escape* up to ten and drove off. We first tried to call our landlord to complain but his voice mail said he'd be out of the country for the next month.[206] So we called the police. In the excitement of spying

---

[206]Yeah, sure. Who leaves the country for a whole month? He probably got some cheesy reality show gig.

on the neighbors being lectured by a burly Chicago cop, I'd forgotten about the letter.

"Open it."

I tear the envelope and experience a brief spasm of terror when I see it's from our landlord's attorney. But as I read the pages, I let out a whoop of joy.

"What does it say??" Fletch dashes behind me to read over my shoulders. He scans the page. "You're happy that our landlord is converting our apartment to a condo?"

"Honey, look at this line. Bill wants to switch us over to a month-to-month lease."

Fletch looks confused. "That means if he sells this place, he has the option of giving us thirty days' notice to vacate the premises. Why is that good?"

"Don't you get it? If he has a thirty-day option to end our lease, *so do we.* That's how it works.[207] We won't have to honor our eighteen-month lease and won't have to live above these fucks"—I hop up and down a couple of times for good measure, rattling the entire building—"for the next year."

"That's an unbelievable coincidence. I got an e-mail from my friend Mike yesterday. He has a nice town house in River West he's looking to lease and wanted to see if I knew anyone who'd be interested. It's got a small yard, it's only a couple hundred a month more than this place, and it's in a great neighborhood. I felt jealous of whoever was going to live there when I saw the attached photos because it's really nice. I had no idea yesterday that it could be *us.*"

"Call him! Let's go see it!"

---

[207]You'd be surprised at the amount of lease law a gal can learn when researching loopholes in eviction proceedings.

"Before we go running off half-cocked, let's think about this for a minute. Moving will be expensive, and we aren't even close to being out of debt yet. Are you sure it's a good idea?"

From the floorboards, I hear "*Twenty years ago today, Sgt. Pepper taught his band to play. . . .*"

"Positive."

Weblog Entry 10/31/03

MY BIG, FAT PRETEND WEDDING

The bad news is that The Lovely Melissa's wedding began exactly 48 hours ago and I have yet to recover from it. The good news is that I don't have to worry about being hung over at work tomorrow.

In the cab on the way to the church, I decided to pretend that this was MY wedding, since so many of the same guests would be at Melissa's. This way I could spend lots of time with people I barely got to speak with on my own Big Day, what with the everlasting dinner of multiple courses and the 400,000 pictures that our photographer, Ansel Adams, insisted upon taking.

I got teary-eyed watching Melissa walk down the aisle, ironic because I didn't shed a tear during my ceremony. At one point during the benediction, the minister spoke about heavenly grace pouring down on the couple and right at that moment, the skies opened up in a brief but powerful shower. God is all about good timing.

We got to the reception and immediately headed for the bar. Not surprisingly, it's where we found all our friends. And this is when things begin to get a bit hazy . . . they were pouring top shelf Martinis, I'd had a long, dry summer, and hey, it was MY day. It was really wonderful to reconnect with so many of my favorite people. I'd not been in close touch with most friends, having had such a rough year. Their years weren't much better than ours, so it was particularly satisfying to be together now that things have begun to turn around for all of us.

By the time dinner was served, I was well into my fifth Martini, and I also had glasses of champagne and white wine in front of me. I noticed Fletch was on his third drink and I got all officious, leaning over and instructing him that he needed to "schloooow doooown." I believe he rolled his eyes in response. Then there were some speeches and toasts and for a minute I couldn't figure out why they were all gesturing at the pretty girl in the white dress and not me, as it was MY day. Curious.

After dinner, we headed back to the bar where I promptly dropped a Martini (including the glass) on a ring bearer. I felt badly about it, although the first thing I did was laugh, thus not winning any favor from the child's mother. But really, when you cut through the bar to take your kid to the bathroom, you take your chances. At this point, Fletch revoked my Martini privileges and switched me to beer.

Things became very blurry, but I know it was a good time because I engaged in each of The Stupid Things I Do Only When Totally And Completely Sauced . . . I danced, smoked, and played with matches. The smoking was really more of me dropping lit cigarettes, and the dancing was downright dangerous. Fletch and I were the fattest people there and our "dancing" was a mosh, as it involved us hurling each other around the parquet and ramming our flailing limbs into walls, relatives, DJ tables, etc.[208]

Then, sadly, MY wedding came to an end. The rest of our pals knew when they'd had enough, so they all went home. So, we quickly made new best friends and headed to a pub in Lincoln Park that I'd normally avoid with a vengeance. Instead, I took the opportunity to dance[209] and to scarf popcorn off the counter anteater-style.

Somehow we made it into a taxi and got home. Fletch fell asleep in the cab, and upon exiting, I completely fell onto the street. I would have just passed out once we got home, but, unfortunately, I had a couple of chores to take care of first. The dogs needed to go to the bathroom, so I headed out in the rain with them. At some point I must have decided to re-dry my wet hair, because I found a decent sized clump of it I'd singed off, although I have no recollection of this and have yet to find the bald spot.

I was supposed to meet Carol and her family at the aquarium the next morning, and somehow had the presence of mind to leave them a voicemail apologizing in advance for not being able to make it. I was pleased at myself for being so responsible and considerate. After I left the message, I blissfully headed off to bed, wearing a face full of makeup, all my grown up jewelry, and a relatively restrictive girdle.

Suffice it to say, yesterday was rough, what with my apartment spinning and all.

---

[208]Dear God, I can only hope the ring bearer stayed out of our way.
[209]Yes, I was the only person dancing.

But today I felt better. That is, until Carol played me the voice mail I left for her at 1:03 AM. Somehow I thought I had been able to hold it together on the phone. Following is a transcript of the message I left:

30 seconds of heavy breathing, giggling, and intermittent hiccups (At first Carol thought it was a 911 call.)

"Oh, heeheehee, I waassshh wayyyting for a beep. But noooooo beeeeeeep. Why don't you hash a beep on your, your, ummmmmm . . . celery phone? Noooooo beeeeeeeep, hic, heeheeeheee.

Um, hiiiiii, itsch JEENNNNNNNNN!! It's thirteen o'clock in the peeeeeee eeeemmmmmmm. Heeeeeeeellllllllllllooooooooo! I went to my wedding tonight and it wash sooooo niiiiiiiiiice. Hic."

More giggling and the sound of a phone being dropped and retrieved

"Nannyway, I am calling to telllll you nooooooooooo fishies tomorry . . . no fishies for meeee! I hic, heeeee, can't smake it to the quariyummm. Maybeeee you can call me so I can say HIIIIIIIIIIIIII later hic in the day hee hee hee. Call me at, um, 312, ummmmmmm, 312, uummmmm, hee hee hee I can't member my phone, Hic. Do you know my number? Can you call me and tell me what it isssch? I LIKESH TURKEY SAMMICHES!"

10 seconds of chewing, giggling, and what may be gobbling sounds

"Okay, GGGGGGGGGooooooodniiiiiiiiiiggggggggggggg hhhhhhhhhhhhhtttttt! No fish! Um, how do I turn this tthing off? Shhhhh, calllls' over. Beeee quiiiiiietttt, hee hee hee."

15 more seconds of giggles, hiccups, shushing, and a great deal of banging

·

Perhaps this is why most people only have one wedding?

· ·

In the 1997 thriller *The Saint*, Elizabeth Shue plays the character Emma Russell. Emma is an Oxford-based scientist who's created the recipe for cold fusion. Naturally, dark forces want to take this formula for themselves, and the easiest way to do this is to kill her.

In one scene Emma is wet and running for her life through the snowy streets of Moscow, being chased in a balls-out pursuit by the Russkies who want her dead. In the distance she spots the American embassy and dashes toward it, knowing her life is on the line, and yet hoping that the hypothermia and exertion from the escape don't trigger her heart condition first. They show her hurtling toward her goal with the hot breath of the assassins virtually on her neck.

Just when you see that she's slowed to the point of the chasers being able to reach the hem of her coat, she gets to the gate, holds up her passport, and with her last breath screams, "I'm an American!" A couple of stern-looking soldiers allow her entry, slamming the door in the face of the evildoers. Emma is able to collapse in the arms of a sturdy Marine, knowing that FINALLY she is safe.

Point?

That's the exact same feeling of bittersweet relief that I experience when I enter the Molto Bene salon for the first time in six months and see the smiling countenance of the best colorist in the city, waiting to make me pretty again.

"Jen! I thought you'd left me!" Rory picks at a half-black, half-gold strand. "But, um, I guess you've been too busy to come in."

I smile. *Busy.* I guess that's one way to describe the past two years. "Something like that."

"The front desk idiots give you any trouble?"

"Trouble? No, not at all." You know what? Manning a reception desk and answering the phone concurrently isn't quite as easy as it looks. Granted, I couldn't concentrate because I was afraid a 747 was about to crash into the lobby, while the brain trusts here were aflutter about Justin Timberlake's solo album, but still, the concept's the same.

"What are we doing today? Full highlights and a lift?" I glance at the other patrons in the salon, and I see row after row of girls with ash blond highlights and the modified Jennifer Aniston *Friends* cut. They're wearing sweater sets and expensive shoes and flashy engagement rings. Half of them are attached to their cell phones and all are surrounded by shopping bags. They look like Generic Chicago Businesswomen and any one of them could substitute for another. For months I've dreamed of joining their ranks again, but suddenly, I'm hesitant.

"Let's do something different. I feel like going dark again."

"Ooh, bold! But do you want me to highlight a few pieces around your face for emphasis?"

"Um . . . . OK. But just a couple," I acquiesce. Hey, Rome wasn't built in a day.

"What other services are you having this afternoon? We have a new hot-stone reflexology massage that's to die for. I got it done after work a couple of days ago, and I thought I'd melt right into the table." Rory mixes a group of concoctions in black plastic bowls at the stand behind me.

"Just the color."

"Really? I thought you always got the rose petal manicure."

"Nah, my nails are in good shape today. See? I did 'em myself." I splay my hands out, displaying the fresh coat of Tropical Punch Pink. By manicuring them at home, I'm ahead of the game almost forty dollars.[210]

"Wow, I'm impressed." She drapes a plastic poncho around me and fastens the snaps at the back of my neck. In the mirror I can see her shaking her head while inspecting the damage. "Where's all your stuff?"

"I've got my purse on my lap under the cape. Why do you ask?"

Rory starts to expertly section off my hair with the end of a rat-tail comb. "No, silly, your shopping bags. I practically didn't recognize you in the lobby without being loaded down with a mass of glossy, cord-handled carriers. I even picked all the magazines off the chair next to you so you'd have some place to put them." She paints the hair from my crown with peroxide and wraps each section with a small piece of foil.

"Oh. I'm not really shopping anymore."

Rory pauses midstroke to gawp at me. "Are you kidding? Jen, Queen of Michigan Avenue? How come?"

"I'm trying to save some money."

"Yeah? Well, I admire your willpower." She brushes a coppery-colored toner on the strands in between each foil packet. I'm quiet while she parts and paints. "Look down for me, please. I need to get the back of your head. Anyway, I bet everyone at Nordstrom's shoe department misses you."

"Totally. Their kids are probably going to have to go to college in state now that I'm on a spending hiatus." We laugh.

---

[210]$40 × 26 times a year = Merry Christmas!

"Are you saving up for vacation? Or maybe something exciting?"

I think about this question for a minute.

"Actually, I am."

"Yeah, like what?"

Our future.

· E P I L O G U E ·

Weblog Entry, 12/14/03

WANNA BE LIKE SADDAM

So they captured Saddam Hussein today. Frankly, I can't blame him for hiding. I'm sure if I were a dictator, I wouldn't want to give up all the palaces and my likeness on every wall if some foreign country demanded it. Really, I suspect that living like Saddam would involve some sweet perks.

When Saddam was in power, he had all that lovely state-mandated control. I know that if I were a dictator, I'd also be a big fan of having unlimited power, especially as my own personal quest for domination came at a very young age. When I was three and tried to steal my brother's new Christmas toys, he told my mother, "First she was a seed, and now she's trouble." Another telling incident occurred in third grade, when I declared, "I can make Stacey Coopersmith do anything I want." (Fortunately for

Stacey, her family moved to Arizona in fourth grade. Although I did not believe I was the impetus for this move, I could never be sure.)

My policy of usurping control and violating borders followed me to college. Although my freshman roommate Joanna fought valiantly to hold on to her half of the dorm room, I eventually emerged victorious on my pursuit of additional sweater space. Upon move-out, I possessed approximately 75% of all available square footage.

So, if I were to become dictator of America, now known as Jennsylvania, I believe my first conquest would be Canada. Seems like a nice place, so I'd like to bring it under The Umbrella That Is Jen. My army would invade clad entirely in pink, green, and khaki items from Ralph Lauren and Lacoste. (And who says you can't march in Bass Weejuns? They are quite comfortable.) I wouldn't hurt the Canadians—soon to be called Jenizens—as I would not embrace Saddam's policies of violence. Rather, I'd wear them down until they were ready to surrender—much like Joanna—by constant verbal badgering.[211]

Although I like America a whole lot now, some things would have to change in order to morph into Jennsylvania. The White House would be painted pink, Kate Spade would re-make the flag in florals and plaids, and the national bird would become duck with orange sauce.

As the dictator, although formally addressed as Her Honor, The Governor, I would grab control of the media. Although I would still allow professional sports to exist, they could only be broadcast at times when I was asleep and could not be discussed in my presence. (Professional figure skating would be the exception to this rule, as it would become our national pastime.) Prime time would be filled with now-nightly episodes of

[211]Canada can keep Bryan Adams.

Trading Spaces, and Fox's program *24* would be changed to *24/365*. I would allow cloning so that another Kiefer Sutherland could film while the real Kiefer accompanied me to state affairs. The only exception to my policy of non-violence would be that anyone involved in the making or playing of the Feelin' Groovy Gap commercials would be put to death without trial.

I feel that I would be a benevolent and beloved leader, as Jenizens would receive many perks. First, my government would subsidize pedicures and highlights, paid for by a 50% surcharge on health club memberships. Every corner would have a Borders or Barnes & Noble, where my people could get free coffee, paperbacks, and pistachio ice cream. Of course, obesity would be lauded and not shamed, because over-consumption would help spur our economy. Fashion magazines would boast articles such as "The Fat Ass Is The New Black!" and "More Is More!" I would also introduce a Flat Abs tax. And if I didn't mention it, everyone would be entitled to three complimentary angioplasties.

Jennsylvania would be a paradise, full of tulips and dessert carts and beautiful handbags, all set to a perpetual and pervasive soundtrack of New Wave music. In short, it would be Utopia.

It just occurred to me that when a new regime is installed in Iraq, it will need a leader.

So, I'd like to humbly nominate . . .

. . . myself.

To: Landlord Bill
From: jen@jenlancaster.com
Date: April 16, 2004
Subject: Good for you!

Bill,

Congrats on your new job! I'm sure you'll be great, but I do have one bit of advice as you embark on the largest construction project in the country:

MAKE SURE THE CONTRACTORS CONNECT THE AIR CONDITIONING TO AN ELECTRICAL SOURCE.

Best,

Jen

To: Kathleen@Corp.Com.biz
From: jen@jenlancaster.com
Date: January 26, 2005
Subject: Open Position

Kathleen,

I saw on Monster.com that you guys are hiring a
Strategic Account Manager to build your public
policy vertical market. With my Political
Science degree and successful track record
within Corp Com, I'd be the ideal fit for this
job.

Too bad I can't apply for it because I'll be
busy finishing the layoff memoir the Penguin
Group just bought from me.

Bitter Is the New Black, available March, 2006.

Best,
Jen[212]

∠

---

[212]I think it's obvious at this point that I haven't learned a damn thing.

· ACKNOWLEDGMENTS ·

Gah, where to begin? Because I certainly didn't get here alone. OK, first the big guns—a million thanks to Kate Garrick, Brian DeFiore and the rest of team DeFiore & Co. You guys have no idea how much you rock. (Kate, I still don't understand how you could remain professional during even my most aggression-laced panic attacks.) (I mean, really, how?) (Perhaps you know I suck, but my innate charm makes up for it, yes?)

I also have boatloads of gratitude for everyone at Penguin/NAL. From the book's impeccable style and gorgeous cover (thanks, Art Dept. and Jaya Micelli!) to the fabulous promotion (yay, Sales and Publicity especially Mary Ann Zissimos, who has totally earned BFF bragging rights!) to my free rein over the content, your hard work made the process way too easy. I'd like to particularly acknowledge Rose Hilliard for her competence and my outstanding editor, Kara Cesare. Kara, from our very first conversation about *The Bachelor,* I knew you'd "get it"—thanks for far exceeding my expectations! I owe you a bathtub full of dirty martinis.

I want to send major hugs and kisses (who am I kidding—I want to send Fendi bags) to Mary Pachnos at Gillon Aitken in the UK and Lisa Highton of Hachette Livre Australia for making *Bitter* bihemispheric. (Is that a real word?) Thank you big, screaming bunches!

In addition, thanks to my parents, who with raised eyebrows continued to write me checks, never once breathing the words "bad debt" or "We can expect repayment when?" Love you guys and promise not to stick you in a discount nursing home when the time comes. Todd and the kids—thanks for the gentle (ha!) reminder that it's not all about me and to Jean for being one hell of a sister-in-law.

To my friends who continue to want to be around me despite the fact you're obligated neither by blood nor business—you guys are the best. Particular thanks to Melissa Lovitt, Shayla Thiel, Carol Kohrs, Jen Draffen, Nick Dorado, Mark Salyers, Angie Felton, Amy Lamare, Martha Kimes, Joellen Meitl, Don Brockette, Bill "Hackman" Medley, Mike "Roadancer" Shoupe, Debby Dong, Jolene Siana, and Katerina Paulic. Drinks are on me.

Finally, I'm incredibly grateful to everyone who visited and linked to my Web site over the past few years. (Bless you, Todd "Odd Todd" Rosenberg.) I'm perpetually delighted to hear from you guys, and your words of encouragement were a driving factor in bringing this book to fruition. Most of all, this book is for you. (And for the ass hats who sent me hate mail? Ditto.)

Oh, wait. . . . Fletch? I'd marry you again even if my mother weren't paying. . . .

Photo by Todd Lancaster

ABOUT THE AUTHOR

Jen Lancaster, a former associate vice president at an investment research firm, is now the proprietor of the popular blog www.jennsylvania.com. She lives in Chicago.

Bitter Is the New Black, Jen Lancaster's debut memoir about "why you should never carry a Prada bag to the unemployment office," launched Jen's career. As the *Chicago Sun-Times* wrote, "she's bitchy and sometimes plain old mean, but she's absolutely hilarious."

Bright Lights, Big Ass, "yet another memoir" from Jen Lancaster, taught readers why it actually often sucks living in the big city, and earned her more praise:

"Lessons we've learned from Jen Lancaster: Bitter is the new black; Target is the new Neiman's; pit bulls and surly neighbors are the new Samanthas, Charlottes, and Mirandas; and midday whiskey is always a good idea. *Bright Lights, Big Ass* is a bittersweet treat for anyone who's ever survived the big city." —Jennifer Weiner

"Jen Lancaster is like David Sedaris with pearls and a supercute handbag."
—Jennifer Coburn

"Wickedly funny, refreshingly honest, and totally unapologetic." —Caprice Crane

**Now Jen Lancaster returns with a third memoir
sure to please her growing fan base:**

Such a Pretty Fat

**One Narcissist's Quest to Discover If Her Life
Makes Her Ass Look Big, or Why Pie is Not the Answer**

In her previous bestselling books, Jen Lancaster peeled back the veil on upward mobility and big-city living. Now she's sumo-wrestling the biggest, stickiest topic of them all: her own fat ass. On the eve of her fortieth birthday, Jen decides she needs to make some changes in her life so she doesn't, you know, die. So she embarks on a six-month weight-loss program, kicking, screaming, and swearing all the way to the gym. The question is, can our heroine lose her ass without ditching the qualities that make her who she is—which, coincidentally, *is* an ass?

Look for SUCH A PRETTY FAT in May 2008.